Angels of Mercy

Angels of Mercy

White Women and the History of New York's Colored Orphan Asylum

William Seraile

Empire State Editions
An imprint of Fordham University Press
New York   2011

Fordham University Press has no responsibility for the persistence or accuracy of URLs for external or third-party Internet websites referred to in this publication and does not guarantee that any content on such websites is, or will remain, accurate or appropriate.

Fordham University Press also publishes its books in a variety of electronic formats. Some content that appears in print may not be available in electronic books.

Library of Congress Cataloging-in-Publication Data

Seraile, William, 1941–
    Angels of mercy : white women and the history of New York's Colored Orphan
Asylum / William Seraile.—1st ed.
        p.   cm.
    Includes bibliographical references and index.
    ISBN 978-0-8232-3419-6 (cloth : alk. paper)
      1. Colored Orphan Asylum and Association for the Benefit of Colored Orphans (New
York, N.Y.)—History.   2. Women philanthropists—New York (State)—New York—
History.   3. Women, White—New York (State)—New York—History.   I. Title.
HV995.N52C657   2011
362.73'2—dc22

                                                                        2011006835

Printed in the United States of America
13 12 11   5 4 3 2 1
First edition

Contents

Preface

The Colored Orphan Asylum, founded in New York City in 1836, is a remarkable institution that is still in the forefront aiding children. Although no longer an orphanage, its successor, the Harlem Dowling–West Side Center for Children and Family Services, maintains the principles of the women who organized nearly two hundred years ago the first orphanage for children of African descent in the United States.

Remarkably, the twenty-five founders fought against gender discrimination, financial difficulties, and initial black resistance to house children who were either neglected, mistreated, or orphaned. Many of the women were the daughters, wives, or siblings of influential New Yorkers who made their reputation and wealth as businessmen, bankers, merchants, or entrepreneurs. Some were ardently antislavery, if not abolitionists.

This study has several major themes that will be explored in its eight chapters. First, I will describe the efforts of the white women managers to procure a home for the children despite intense racial hostility and general civic disinterest. Although they would eventually receive financial backing from some of Manhattan's wealthiest citizens, including John Jacob Astor, Rufus Lord, Gerrit Smith, Gulian C. Verplanck, John Horsburg, Anson G. Phelps, Ann Jay, and Elizabeth and Sarah DeMilt, to name a few, the early years of the orphanage represented a financial nightmare.

Second, while the white female managers and their male advisers were dedicated to uplifting the black child, they harbored extreme paternalistic views that did not seek guidance from the African American community. The exception, of course, was the hiring of James McCune

Smith as the institution's physician, a position he held for twenty years. The orphanage accepted material aid in the form of nonperishable goods, volunteer labor, and small financial contributions from the black community, but it did not seek their advice and only grudgingly accepted it when it was given.

Third, the evangelical and mainly Quaker founding managers sought to save the souls of their charges. Later, in the nineteenth century, their successors adopted a harsher, moralistic tone as they (and other similar institutions) became more bureaucratic and professional. Their objective was to uplift the poor in their care and, in a sense, to "rescue" their charges not only from the evils of the street but also from the perception that they, and not the black community, could best raise the children into responsible adulthood.

Fourth, it was frank criticism in 1913 from W. E. B. Du Bois, editor of *The Crisis*, that highlighted the conflict between the orphanage and the community it served. It was not until 1939 that the white leadership decided that it was not enough simply to employ African Americans in menial positions; they also had to reach out and include them in the leadership of the institution. The orphanage's first black female trustee was elected in that year and was soon followed by others, including Jewish women and African American men.

Fifth, it had become clear in the first few decades of the twentieth century that the institution was an orphanage primarily in name, as most of the children under care were "half-orphans," that is, neglected or delinquent children. It was during this period that the trustees introduced the cottage system as a means to accommodate children in a less-institutionalized manner. Boarding the children out led to a greater interaction with black churches and families. An antidiscrimination law in New York State pressured the reluctant trustees to accept white children in the late 1940s. It was at this time that it was decided to close the "orphanage" in the Riverdale section of the Bronx and find boarding homes for all the children.

The Colored Orphan Asylum survived several fires, the nation's financial panics, wars, the Great Depression, and racial hostility so virulent that it led to the destruction of its Fifth Avenue building by a mob during New York's July 1863 draft riots. Over fifteen thousand children were raised in the orphanage during the period under study, and throughout its history, letters and visits have revealed that hundreds if not thousands of "old boys and girls" have looked back with admiration and respect for the home that nurtured them throughout their formative years.

Acknowledgments

In August 2002, the historian Gerald Horne was in New York researching a book. I was between research projects, and it was his suggestion that I check out the voluminous files on the Colored Orphan Asylum housed at the New-York Historical Society.

I am indebted to many who helped to make this research possible. I want to thank the librarians of the National Archives; the Schomburg Center for Research in Black Culture, New York Public Library; The New-York Historical Society; and the Rare Book and Manuscript Library of the University of Pennsylvania for their assistance. I thank the University of Pennsylvania for permission to cite from the Theodore Dreiser Papers and for the permission of the New-York Historical Society to quote from the records of the Manumission Society, the Association for the Benefit of Colored Orphan Records, Children's Aid Society Records, the "Riots, 1834" section of the American Historical Manuscript Collection, and the papers of Charles Chapin and Philip Hone. The New York Public Library, the Harlem Dowling–West Side Center for Children and Family Services, and the New-York Historical Society graciously allowed me to use photographs or illustrations in their possession. George Conliffe provided me with a photograph of himself as a member of the orphanage's glee club. Mr. Victor Remer of the Children's Aid Society provided me with assistance as he retrieved old volumes that delineated the names of children from the orphanage that were sent to the West. Janet Munch, the special collections librarian at Lehman College of the City University of New York, was extremely helpful with numerous leads that improved my level of research. I wish also to thank Arica Easely, a graduate student in history, and her cousin Fanny Crawford for permission to quote from the unpublished recollections of Thomas Henry Barnes. Barnes, a former "inmate" of the orphanage, put a face to some of the events described in the annual reports or minutes. This study has been greatly improved by the frank criticisms of anonymous readers and the insightful suggestions of Timothy Hacsi and Janet Munch. Karen Franklin, the former director of the Judaica Museum of the Hebrew Home for the Aged at Riverdale, in the Bronx, which occupies the former site of the Colored Orphan Asylum, showed enthusiastic interest in the project. Melba Butler, the former executive director of Harlem Dowling–West Side Center for Children and Family Services, the successor to the Colored Orphan Asylum, was very supportive of this project, and I thank her for putting me in contact with some of the institution's alumni. I spent a pleasant June afternoon in 2003 dining and conversing with several alumni of the Colored Orphan Asylum/ Riverdale Children's Association. Thanks to Madeline Davis Marshall, Gloria Torrence, Fitz Harvey, George Conliffe, Louis Eaddy, and Addison Eaddy for sharing their reminiscences of life at Riverdale during the early 1940s. I gained more insights into life at Riverdale when several of the alumni spoke eloquently about their experiences at an April 14, 2005, symposium at Lehman College. Louretta Smallwood De Haney, a nurse in the institution from 1940 to 1944, provided information about the institutional health care provided by the staff.

Finally, I offer blessed thanks and deep appreciation for the ladies who confronted racial prejudice in their efforts to provide a safe and comfortable home for thousands of children of color who otherwise would have been subjected to the fate of life on the streets. I would like to thank my wife, Janette, for her love and support, and Aden Seraile, Garnet Seraile McKenzie, and Kristen Rich for their assistance with my still-evolving computer skills.

Angels of Mercy

Introduction

Despite the 1827 abolition of slavery in New York State, African Americans in Manhattan and elsewhere were treated with contempt and, at times, with cruelty by much of the state's white population. Blacks in white churches were assigned to sit in separate pews or in high balconies crudely referred to as "nigger heaven." They had to stand on the omnibuses or ride in separate cars. Public schools were segregated by race. Persons of color were not permitted in cabins on the Hudson River steamers but were relegated to the decks, regardless of weather conditions. African Americans, along with their few but vocal white supporters, were victims of violence. The first half of 1834 in New York City was a troubled period of fraudulent elections, labor trouble, and bias against immigrants. Into this mix was added a virulent Negrophobia. Animosity against the small population of color broke out in three days of rioting in 1834. This riot would set the stage for the nineteenth century's greatest racial outrage: the 1863 Irish draft riot. The instigators in 1834 were zealous in their efforts to kill or maim innocent African Americans and their abolitionist friends and to prevent racial progress through alliances with white progressives. Raising the taboo of interracial sex, James Watson Webb, the racist editor of the *Courier and Enquirer,* accused abolitionists of supporting race mixing, a charge later vehemently denied by David Ruggles, a prominent black abolitionist.

The riot began on July 4, when hecklers interrupted an integrated celebration, which was rescheduled for July 7. On that date, Chapel's Sacred Music Society declared that the Chatham Street Chapel, which the music society had leased two nights a week, was reserved for them.

Angry that blacks were in "their stalls" (even though on that date the chapel was free for any taker), the riot began, according to the *Courier and Enquirer,* which alleged that Negroes had physically harmed a peaceful gathering of whites. Afterward, vengeful whites sacked the home of the abolitionist Arthur Tappan, burning his furniture and damaging his silk store. Arthur Tappan's brother Lewis suffered a similar fate when the mob broke into his home and burned his furniture in the street. The former mayor Philip Hone noted that the mob, encouraged that neither the police nor the military could fire upon them unless ordered to do so by the governor, grew larger. The enraged mob attacked the home and church of Dr. Samuel H. Cox and invaded and destroyed furniture and the organ at St. Philip's Episcopal Church, fueled by a rumor that the black priest, Peter Williams, had officiated at an interracial marriage. Eyewitnesses provided chilling accounts of the rioters' behavior. Fifty-five communications were sent to Mayor Cornelius W. Lawrence. An undated note from Miles Osborne indicated that he had mingled with the rioters and believed that their actions were motivated by the anti-American remarks of the Englishman William Farren, the stage manager at the Bowery Theater. Osborne warned that the mob intended to attack the police and release prisoners. Other notes warned of attacks against the African Methodist Episcopal Zion Church, at the corner of Leonard and Church Streets, and the African Free School No. 4, at Jefferson Street and East Broadway. Individuals who were married to white women were targeted for attacks, as were black merchants. Philip Hone recorded in his diary that the riot ended when the police and several thousand uniformed militia and private citizens worked to preserve the peace on the evening of July 12.[1]

The outrageous behavior of the mob against blacks, with their homes and institutions as targets, caused much consternation among people of color. Antiblack riots in Philadelphia, Rochester, New York, and in several communities in New Jersey and Pennsylvania prompted the delegates to the Fifth Annual Convention for the Improvement of the Free People of Color in the United States to adopt a resolution affirming "that the Christian forbearance practiced by [blacks] during their persecution . . . merits the praise and respect of the whole Christian world; and is a most successful refutation of the proslavery argument advanced in this country." The resolution concluded that colored Americans had displayed by "their peace, quietude and humility" that they were better persons than their agitators.[2]

The riot added more fuel to the simmering fire of Negrophobia in New York City. The *Castigator and New-York Anti-Abolitionist* newspaper continued to accuse abolitionists of race mixing. Equating an integrated society with amalgamation, the rabid editor lamented, "is it possible that we can ever be willing to see our daughters promenading our streets, arm in arm with a *thick lipped* negro . . . or see our sons . . . sauntering . . . arm in arm with one of those *kitchen* appendages, a negro wench, because Arthur Tappan has said they were as *good as white women.*" The editor bluntly condemned the unspeakable horror of sexual relations between a "strapping *buck nigger* . . . with the delicate and refined *white* female."[3] The antiabolitionist feeling was so strong that many whites actively hunted fugitive slaves who escaped to New York. In their eagerness to capture runaways, they were not above kidnapping free men and women to send to work in Southern cotton, tobacco, and rice plantations. Progressive New Yorkers responded in 1835 by forming the New York Committee on Vigilance. Organizers included William Johnston, David Ruggles, Robert Brown, George Barker, and James W. Higgins. Their diligence prevented the kidnapping of 335 persons in 1837.[4]

It was in this context of racial hostilities that the Colored Orphan Asylum (COA) was established by white women in New York City. Blacks in Manhattan, with their small population and limited resources, tried diligently to advance through self-reliance. They had, since 1800, organized mutual relief and benevolent societies, churches, schools, and newspapers, but the paucity of educated individuals and the lack of individual and collective wealth made difficult the task of speaking for themselves in matters of civil and political rights. Mutual relief and benevolent societies provided temporary relief to the ills suffered by the poor, but their lack of sufficient resources prompted benevolent whites to establish an orphanage on their behalf. A large building, a matron, staff members, and financial supporters were needed to run an orphanage. These could be provided by white women who were culturally programmed to be nurturers. Their control of an institution that served the needs of black youth met the day's societal standards of white paternalism. Without the involvement of black leadership in the day-to-day operations of the orphanage, the women avoided scandalous talk of social equality—or worse, amalgamation.

This study is an examination of the effort of a group of white women who, aided sporadically by limited financial support from African Americans, labored for over a century to maintain a home for black youth, first orphans and then also half-orphans and neglected, dependent, and delinquent children. The COA, the first in the nation for African American youth, was similar to other orphanages in the nation. Some orphanages cared for only Protestant, Catholic, or Jewish youth. In contrast, the COA housed blacks and occasionally American Indians until 1944, when a state law required them also to accept white applicants. Timothy Hasci describes nineteenth-century orphanages' missions as "to clothe, house and educate children; provide them with specific moral and religious code; and otherwise care for children until they could be indentured; placed in a family, or returned to their homes." The COA did not deviate from this pattern, although very few children were indentured to African American homes, and it was not until the early twentieth century when efforts were made to place them in the homes of black foster or adoptive parents.[5] Hasci notes that orphanages were either protective, isolating, or integrative asylums. "Protective and integrative [asylums] hoped to act as temporary replacement for children's own parents with what they considered superior parenting and socialization tactics," he noted.[6] For much of its history, the COA acted as an isolating institution. It kept the children inside the building, provided educational and religious studies, made it difficult for families to visit, and indentured the children to white families in the hopes of making them more "American"—meaning Anglo-Saxon—in culture and values. The managers viewed most of their charges as coming from a primitive culture rife with superstition, vice, and immorality. Despite this patronizing attitude, the African American community allowed them to care for their children, as the alternative—the almshouse—was not an option, with its depraved, mentally disturbed, and abusive inhabitants. Later, like other orphanages, the COA became an integrative facility, sending its children out to school, church, parks, and playgrounds. Like other early orphanage managers, the women who started the COA were elite benevolent women and evangelical perfectionists who wanted to "eradicate rather than ameliorate social ills." The earlier founders of the COA came from upper-class families and were the wives and daughters of prominent New Yorkers such as Chief Justice John Jay.[7]

Middle- and upper-class nineteenth-century women found establishing asylums to be a practical outlet for their desire to be part of a broader world. They were able to leave the home, where they were nurturers, to go into an asylum, which also was a home, without facing condemnation for "desexing" or "unsexing" themselves. Many of the earlier founders of the COA came from homes where the heads of the household were members of the New York Manumission Society. These families had an interest—albeit a paternalistic one—in assisting blacks. This interest certainly made it easier for the women to work to save black youth. The twenty-five women who founded the COA came from predominantly upper-class homes. Anne M. Boylan's research indicates that 34.9 percent of the founders came from homes headed by merchants or manufacturers. The others came from homes where the head of the household was a clergyman, artisan, lawyer, judge, shopkeeper, or physician.[8]

It is not surprising that 67.7 percent of the founders were members of the Society of Friends, or Quakers, as they were commonly known. Presbyterians, Protestant Episcopalians, and Methodist Episcopalians accounted for 10.7 percent each. None of the original twenty-five founders belonged to the Baptist, Reformed Dutch, Unitarian, Congregationalist, or Roman Catholic church. The Quakers' strong antislavery beliefs explain their high number. A majority, 55.8 percent, of the original members were married. Unlike single women, they had their husbands as a source of economic security. The founding managers of the COA were mature women, with a median age of forty at time of joining. Boylan's research shows that 30 percent were in the 30–39 age range, 23.3 percent in the 40–49 age group, 26.65 percent in the 50–59 age category, 13.3 percent in the 20–29 age range, and 3.3 percent were teenagers or sixty years or older. Working on behalf of black children made easier the transition of leaving the home (if only for periods of the day), because social evolution deemed them superior to the black children in their charge. Their asylum work provided them with a sense of authority and legitimacy that allowed them to escape societal roles that defined true women as those "who embraced piety, purity, submissiveness and domesticity."[9]

The women managers of the COA were able to acquire corporate status, thanks to the successful effort of the Society for the Relief of Poor Widows and Small Children, who acquired it in 1802. Incorporation permitted the managers, as an organization, to have legal rights that none of them could claim individually, "including the right to own property, bring legal suits, indenture minor children, invest funds, and control wages." The married officers "received concrete and often surprisingly broad powers that were theoretically restricted to male or unmarried female citizens." Despite these gains, the women did not abuse these rights nor deny masculine involvement. Male advisers counseled them on financial matters, offering suggestions to invest in stocks and bonds as well as in real estate. These men were involved in banking or Wall Street brokerage houses. This dependence on male financial advice allowed for "masculine authority into feminine realms devaluing women's money management skills; and separating women leaders' vocational work more fully from home duties." As finances were a "man's business," women's dependence upon his advice kept them from desexing themselves.[10]

This study is an examination of the Colored Orphan Asylum from its founding in 1836 until 1946, when it closed its building in Riverdale (the Bronx), New York. During that period, it was aided by prominent New Yorkers such as John Jacob Astor; John Jay and his daughters, Anna and Maria; Cornelius V. S. Roosevelt; Theodore Roosevelt Sr.; Frederick Douglass; James McCune Smith; Eleanor Roosevelt; Lena Horne; Bill "Bojangles" Robinson; and others. Their generosity helped to care for fifteen thousand children before the Colored Orphan Asylum, later known as the Riverdale Children's Association, closed its doors and began to operate as a foster care agency.

During its first century of operation, the COA maintained a paternalistic relationship with black New York, accepting their financial support but not permitting them to advise them on how best to serve the African American community. It was not until 1939 that the management deemed it essential to add an African American woman as a trustee and to work more closely with Harlem's religious and civic leaders.

1

Alas! I am an orphan Boy,
With naught on earth to cheer my heart;
No father's love, no mother's joy
No kin nor kind to take my part.
My lodging is the cold, cold ground,
I eat the bread of charity;
and when the kiss of love goes round,
there is no kiss, alas.

As the New York Orphan Asylum, founded in 1809, admitted only Caucasian children, it came as no surprise when Quaker women established the nation's first orphanage for children of color.[1] Originally slaveholders, in 1774 New York Quakers placed sanctions on members who bought and sold slaves. In 1778, they removed slaveholders from their congregations.[2]

The origin of the Colored Orphan Asylum has several versions, influenced by the passage of time, boastful pride, and marketing objectives. An original version noted that in 1834 two Quaker women, Anna H. Shotwell and her niece, Mary Murray, chanced upon two dirty and unkempt children at play under the watchful eye of a black woman. Upon learning that they had been abandoned by fugitive slave parents, the two gave the woman a few dollars to care for the children. Several days later, they found that the kind woman had four additional children under her care, having received enough funds to tend to their needs. This led the two Quakers to consider opening a home for homeless children of color. Later, Leslie Skiddy Parker noted that "a white woman . . . had taken [the two children] out of jail and not knowing what to do with them," turned them over to the Quaker women, who took them home. This version places the kindness on the part of a sympathetic white woman instead of crediting a black woman for her generosity. Anna Shotwell and Mary Murray were both extraordinary women. Twenty-eight-year-old Anna, the daughter of William Shot-well, a member of the New York Manumission Society, was a staunch opponent of slavery. Anna had decided at age twelve never to have an African American servant or laborer as long as slavery existed. Eigh-teen-year-old Mary Murray, the granddaughter of John Murray Jr., the long-time treasurer of the Manumission Society, "was a person of a strong and dominant will [who possessed] a good deal of executive ability united with a great persistence of purpose."[3]

The Colored Orphan Asylum was formed on November 26, 1836, in the home of William Shotwell. The founders decided upon the name "colored" in deference to the community's sensibilities. Many promi-nent men of color resented the white-led American Colonization Soci-ety's assertion that the black person's destiny was in Africa. These men, who had been born in the United States and had a mixed African-European ancestry, preferred the nomenclature "colored" over "Afri-can," which they believed better identified them as Americans and not Africans in exile. The founders of the COA, pioneers in child welfare for youth of color, included Anna Shotwell, Mary Murray, Eunice Mit-chel, Sarah C. Hawxhurst, Sarah Shotwell, Hanna L. Murray, Mary Shotwell, Eleanor Shotwell, Phebe Mott, Elizabeth Little, Abby Ann Cook, Stella Tracy, Ernestine Lord, Jane U. Ferris, Sarah Underhill, Margaretta Cock, and Sarah Hall. A board of twenty-five female man-agers and five male advisers was quickly organized. The Association for the Benefit of Colored Orphans in the City of New York immedi-ately received the assistance of prominent New Yorkers including Rob-ert C. Cornell, Charles King, William F. Mott, Robert J. Murray, Dr. James Proudfit, Mahlon Day, Israel Corse, Walter Underhill, Robert I. Murray, John Murray Jr., John Jay, and John Jacob Astor. Throughout the nineteenth century, a who's who of New York philanthropists, mer-chants, artisans, and bankers would befriend the institution. But it

HEROINES OF A CENTURY AGO

A trio of the founders of the Colored Orphan Asylum

Center—Anna H. Shotwell

Left—Hannah Shotwell   *Right—Mary Murray*

Anna Shotwell, Hannah Shotwell, and Mary Murray. (Collection of The New-York Historical Society.)

would be years before the Colored Orphan Asylum would have financial security, and even then it would be sporadic, as increased enrollment would lead to deficits. The fledging organization provided women with an opportunity to display leadership. As married women in the early nineteenth century were not allowed to own property in their own right, the managers noted in their constitution that "the husbands of any married woman who is or may be a member . . . shall not be liable for any loss occasioned by the neglect or malfeasance of his wife" but would be accountable if he received money from his wife, a member of the corporation. Thus, the women were able to "buy, sell, and invest property and to sign binding contracts." In time, they would learn how to lobby legislators for municipal or state funds.[4]

In early 1837, after no one would rent them space to care for black children, the managers decided to purchase a home. After receiving one thousand dollars from the Lindley Murray Estate, the managers made a three-thousand-dollar down payment with a six-thousand-dollar mortgage on the late Dr. Alexander Murray's two-story white cottage, located on Twelfth Street between Fifth and Sixth Avenues in lower Manhattan. In June, eleven children rescued from the cellar of an almshouse were placed in the home. Children who resided in almshouses, as noted by the commissioner of almshouses, lived in conditions of "neglect and filth and putrefaction, and vermin," with "bedding [that] was alternately used by the sick, dying and the healthy." The children had to walk or be carried to their new home, because no carriage drivers would take them. The managers also started a school for black youth, as there was none in their vicinity. Staffing the house with a black matron, a teacher, and an assistant, the women depended upon the kindness of family, friends, and strangers to survive. Donations of blankets, utensils, beans, potatoes, turnips, cabbages, wheat flour, cloth, andirons, and shovel tongs aided them in the beginning.[5]

The founders faced the arduous task of caring for orphans with considerable determination. As noted by Christine Stansell, they engaged in "corrective domesticity," employing rules and regulations to teach cleanliness, religiosity, and morality—lessons they believed that the parents had failed to impart. Unfortunately, they did not deem it necessary to consult with the black community. By not seeking their advice in matters relating to cultural differences between the races, this negligence led to a fractious relationship between the managers and the African American community of New York City.[6]

The first year of operation was nearly a fiscal disaster. The financial panic of 1837 led to widespread destitution, hampering the efforts of private and public relief agencies to alleviate the problems of the poor. The COA desperately needed funds to purchase winter coal and meat and to make payments on the mortgage. Treasurer Mary Murray faced the financial situation with distress. One day, she walked the streets unsuccessful in her solicitation for funds. She feared to return home without cash or pledges. But upon her return, a package was delivered that contained the exact amount needed for expenses.[7]

Believing that theirs was the work of Providence, the managers continued in their mission to house an oppressed group of children. Different circumstances could have easily ended the nascent organization's effort to serve children, as the financial burden would have overwhelmed the ladies. Instead, the work continued with hopes and prayers that further financial assistance was forthcoming.

Their highly anticipated financial break came in 1837, but at a price that caused friction with the city's African American leadership. William Turpin's will had provided that two hundred shares of the capital stock of the Mechanics Bank, valued at $1,175.00, be given to a society or institution to "promote the education and welfare of the descendants of Africa."[8] The trustees of the William Turpin legacy were divided over whom should receive the funds. Israel Corse, a supporter of the Colored Orphan Asylum, controlled the distribution of the funds, but the trustees Arthur Tappan and Simeon S. Jocelyn favored the Phoenix Society as the worthy recipient. The Phoenix Society, established in 1833 for the purpose of establishing a manual labor school, had been led to believe by one of the legatees that they would receive the money. Expecting funds, they overspent and were forced to give up their school room, lacking three hundred dollars for the rent. To complicate matters, they argued that Turpin had been an officer of their society and would have wished to have his funds support a black school. The *Colored American* newspaper castigated both the trustees of the Turpin legacy and the ladies of the Colored Orphan Asylum. Its editor, Samuel Cornish, criticized the appointment of white trustees "of every fund left to, or for the benefit of colored people." He accused them of dallying so long that they died before the funds got disbursed, which led to missing funds. Cornish lamented that six to eight thousand dollars was going to the Colored Orphan Asylum, which was not "an institution of learning, but rather a branch of the almshouse." The money belonged to the Phoenix Society, he concluded, because "we have five or six young men of established piety and talent, seeking a preparation for usefulness, and who are by sheer necessity driven from the seminary of learning." Cornish bitterly added that "the ladies knew when they applied for the funds that the Phoenix Society [had claims on it], and of the *strong probability* that it was intended solely for that society." A compromise was suggested in July 1838, when Cornish and Simeon S. Jocelyn met with the COA's advisers William F. Mott, Robert Murray, and Dr. James Proudfit and requested eight hundred dollars from the Turpin legacy. An agreement was reached the following month, whereby the Colored Orphan Asylum gave four hundred dollars to the Phoenix Society in exchange for the latter relinquishing all further claims upon the orphanage and trustees of the Turpin legacy. The ladies indicated that the funds represented their empathy for the disappointment experienced by the Phoenix Society.[9]

The ladies wanted to avoid a confrontation with Samuel Cornish and the *Colored American*. As the only African American newspaper in New York City (and the third in the nation), it wielded significant influence among its readership, an audience that the Colored Orphan Asylum coveted for support. In April 1837, the managers informed Cornish of their need to have the colored community assist with "donations of . . . furniture, clothing or bedding." Even before the Turpin controversy, the *Colored American* had objections to the orphanage. Cornish opposed "separate institutions for colored youth, as being contrary to the principles of the Bible, and at war with the best interest of our colored population." He concluded that God would deny His blessings to those who maintained separate race institutions which reflected "the spirit of slavery [and] contributed more largely to the persecution, and neglect of our colored population, than all the politics of the land."

This view was consistent with an earlier editorial's denunciation of prejudice. He vowed to use the press to speak against the evils of racism "IN THUNDER TONES, until the nation repent and render to every man that which is just and equal."[10]

Despite this sentiment and his anger over the Turpin controversy, Cornish made a remarkable turnaround that helped to smooth the way for the Colored Orphan Asylum to better communicate with the African American community, perhaps preventing it from further alienation from the community it sought to serve. In late October 1837, Cornish visited the orphanage, which led to a description of the roomy yard as "suited to the innocent gambols of the DEAR PARENTLESS CHILDREN." Cornish declared that the blessings of "the fatherless and the widow abide upon [the founders]," for the asylum "claims our prayers, its founders claim our little contributions in clothing and provisions." The impressed editor requested that the managers establish a monthly visiting day for the black community to bring money, clothing, and provisions or to mend or make clothes for the children. A year later, Cornish enthusiastically wrote that the female managers were worthy of the name Christian and that prejudice would be eliminated if more emulated them. They deserved immortality for acting in the image of Jesus by feeding hungry children, clothing them, and caring for them in sickness. "Go on good ladies, the Benefactor of the universe will be with you," he concluded.[11]

The officers of the Colored Orphan Asylum had much to achieve during that first year. Led by First Directress Martha Codwise, who had over twenty years experience managing charitable organizations; Second Directress Sarah C. Hawxhurst; Secretary Anna Shotwell; and Treasurer Mary Murray, they sought, in addition to fundraising, to stabilize the home. Staff turnover was common in the early years, because of low salaries or incompetence. They needed a matron and a teacher for the growing school, which had forty day students, until two schools for colored children opened in the area. They also had to consider the request of the community to accept half-orphans into the institution, a decision they decided in the affirmative. (Early nineteenth-century orphanages all were faced with the decision to accept more than full orphans, as contagious diseases and wretched living conditions for the poor left many families without both parents. The Boston Female Asylum, founded in 1800, accepted both half-orphans and full orphans, but the New York Orphan Asylum, founded six years later, sent inmates who had a living parent to the almshouse. The Roman Catholic orphanage in Manhattan initially accepted only full orphans.) Caring for more children demanded increased funding, but the almshouse commissioners turned down the managers' request for funds, because the commissioners did not feel obligated to finance the education of black children who were not "inmates" of the almshouse. The city's Common Council also refused to render funds to the managers, a decision that Leslie Harris argues stemmed from their reluctance to encourage an alliance between blacks and progressive whites in the aftermath of the 1834 riots. The Common Council made this decision even though the orphanage relieved the city of providing for children removed from the almshouse.[12]

Admission

The decision to admit half-orphans led the managers to formulate criteria for admission. Children came from the almshouse, were brought to the orphanage by relatives or kind strangers who took pity on helpless children, or came on their own in desperate search for food and lodging. The managers decided not to turn away those children who were abandoned or neglected. In November 1837, the managers revised their constitution to give preference to orphans while reserving the right to admit half-orphans at their discretion. Six half-orphans were admitted that year after the surviving parent agreed to pay a monthly fee of two dollars. Over the years, some children would be admitted from the Colored Home (which was founded in 1839 by Anna Jay, Mary Shotwell, and Anne Mott as a home for both the aged and abandoned children).[13]

By October 1837, the small asylum on Twelfth Street housed fifteen children. Five-year-old Benjamin Matthews came from the almshouse, but, like many others, he died of consumption. Jacob Beckett Lee, born in the South in about 1829, was brought to the asylum in October by

Maria Welk. His mother, Marie Lee, had died of cholera four years earlier. His father, whose name was unknown, was apprehended trying to escape from slavery. Jacob was apprenticed on April 19, 1839, as a house servant, but he absconded a year later. The fate of the approximate ten-year-old is unknown. His case was typical of many of the children admitted into the institution. Friends or even strangers cared for orphans or abandoned children until dire circumstances forced them to turn to the almshouse, the Colored Home, or the COA for relief. Not all half-orphans were accepted. Children who led a vagrant life and acquired evil influences were denied admission, out of the fear that they would be undesirable associates of other children.[14]

In November 1837, the managers admitted the Rawle children— the siblings Jeremiah and Adeline and their cousin Willy—all former slaves, even though they were not orphans. Minerva Rawle, the mother of Jeremiah and Adeline, was freed in Virginia by her owner. They and about forty other freed persons arrived destitute in New York City. The father was still held in bondage. Minerva, who was described by the managers as "vicious and ignorant [with] an ungovernable temper," consented to their admission. The siblings were eventually indentured, but Willy died on February 19, 1841, of "disease of the bowels."[15] Soon after, the managers decided not to make the admission of freed slave children a precedent, but circumstances did not allow them to honor this pledge. On October 15, 1838, John Tomata, who was born in about 1830 in Cuba, entered the United States with Ann Bridget Dulcie, who turned him over to the Committee of Vigilance of the Anti-Slavery Society. They brought him to the orphan asylum, where he soon contracted consumption. Knowing very little English, he uttered in his dying moments, "no father, no mother," before death claimed him on January 13, 1839. Like others, he was buried in the Presbyterian burial ground at the corner of Houston and Chrystie Streets. Another foreign-born admission was Henry Bushman, whose parents were killed in the Sixth Kaffir War, 1834–1835, against the Xhosa people of Cape Colony in South Africa. A trader brought the boy to a Mr. Chase, the American consul, who delivered him to the orphanage on June 13, 1848, with an agreement to pay his board. The ten-year-old, afflicted with cholera, cried about his inability to pray as he knew only "our Father" and feared that his ignorance would deny him salvation. A moved Anna Shotwell wrote that "he was a remarkably innocent and guileless boy, yet such was his humility, with the sense of innate depravity." Several interesting admissions occurred in 1858. On November 21, the off-spring of a relationship between a slave woman and her owner was admitted to the orphanage by her guardian, Elvira Bowden. The managers gave the Kentucky-born girl the name Harriett Beecher Stowe, in honor of the author of *Uncle Tom's Cabin.* Another slave child, Mary Davis, was born in Nashville, Tennessee. The mother was paying for the freedom of her two daughters, Mary and Harriett, but was two hundred dollars in arrears when the owner died, which led her to fear that the heirs would demand the children to cover the payment. It is not known how the children escaped bondage, but they ended up in Buffalo, where Maria Marshal of that city brought them to the asylum. Mary was indentured in Connecticut but ended up in Nebraska. The record's last notice of Mary was an 1860 notation: "last account of Mary was a sad one, gone to destruction."[16]

George Lewis lived with some degraded people who forced him to beg. The orphan was admitted on January 24, 1838, without the permission of his "family." George was so delighted with his new surroundings that he requested a new name. Since the managers did not believe that George Lewis was his true name, they called him Mott Cornell, after two of their advisers, William F. Mott and Robert C. Cornell. It was not uncommon for the managers to give admitted children unusual or humorous names. An illiterate and abused child whose parents were unknown was brought to the orphanage by a manager, a Mrs. North, after the girl came to her home begging. Mrs. North named her Mary Ann Topsy, because she was "lively [and] communicative" and resembled the character "Topsy" in *Uncle Tom's Cabin.*[17]

The COA's mission was the admission of children of color, but while they admitted biracial children, they were perplexed by the admission of Jane Guise, who was placed in the institution at age three by her mother. By age five, the child's complexion was indistinguishable from that of a white person. Since she possessed no visible African features "which could prevent her enjoying the privileges afforded to the white population," the managers wanted to send her to a white orphanage. The mother refused and continued to pay weekly board until Jane was indentured. The managers, in their understandable haste to improve the life of a child who could pass for white, thoroughly misunderstood the racial pride that some African Americans possessed, regardless of hue.[18]

Not all admissions were neglected or abused children. Benjamin Africanus, who was "quite forward in his studies," came from a middle-class family. His father, the Rev. Edward Africanus, was a schoolteacher and community activist in Flushing, New York. His parents died of consumption, which resulted in Benjamin's admission, but his unhappiness in the asylum led to a discharge to his uncle just a few weeks before the boy died of fever. The admission of Catharine Louise Smith was one that was replicated over the years. Her father died of fever, and her mother Julia, a Boston resident, agreed to pay a boarding fee. The admission records noted that Julia (no maiden name was provided, but she was either Julia Murray, Julia Jackson, or Julia Moore) was "one of our first children belonging to the institution." One of the asylum's most unique admissions was that of nine-year-old Charles Carter, whose father had deserted the family in 1867. Charles's mother, Mary, was the great granddaughter of Elizabeth Freeman, who had successfully sued her owner for freedom in 1781 in Massachusetts, helping to set the movement to abolish slavery in that state two years later. (A great-grandson, Willie, was better known as W. E. B. Du Bois.)[19]

Despite admitting children of former slaves, the managers decided, so as not to antagonize potential supporters, to remain "entirely independent of the exciting questions that have lately agitated the public mind, in relation to the colored race." Twenty-three children were in the home at the end of 1837.[20]

The increased requests for admissions resulted in the admissions committee requesting applicants to provide the name, age, place of birth, parents' names, and other relevant information of prospective inmates. Relevant information was necessary, because some offered false information. John Philip Bennet was admitted as an orphan on February 23, 1838. Shortly afterward, a man arrived claiming to be John's father, which led to the child running away from the asylum.

The man, whom the admission record described as having "depraved character," was his biological father and intended to place him in the House of Refuge. The young boy's character was also "depraved." When John was found, he was bound out to the Rev. Dr. William W. Phillips, the pastor of the First Presbyterian Church, located at 5 Wall Street. The Bennet fiasco made it clear that the managers had to develop controls not only for admission but for interactions between the matron and parents or guardians. It was decided in May 1838 that "at least one of the committee of admission to be present at the asylum when a child is received or provide another manager to supply her place." It was further decided that a manager be present to inform parents or guardians that the matron had the support of the institution and that the use of abusive language would be grounds to deny visiting privileges. Visiting was limited to the fifth day of each summer month, from 3 to 6 P.M., and from 7 A.M. to 2 P.M. in the winter. Children were not permitted to go past the building's front door without the matron's permission. While it appeared on the surface that the managers simply wanted to manage visitations to a bustling building where different forces competed for time and space, the controls actually represented a deeper power struggle. The white reformers were dedicated to imposing their moral standards on children who, they believed, falsely or not, had been corrupted by undesirable elements in the black community. The managers judged that fewer contacts with this community prevented the children's return to a vicious life, even if it meant that contact with relatives or guardians was kept to a minimum. Of course, some of the "abusive" language from family or guardians was a result of the white women's interference with relatives or friends who were unwilling to put up with the scheduled visiting hours or days. Although many institutions limited parental visits or sought to isolate children from depraved members of the community, the white-black dynamics of the COA exacerbated the situation. Not all parents or guardians were depraved in character, and resentment developed over the blanket charge.[21] The managers' desire to assist as many children as possible and concerns about maintaining a healthy home certainly played a major role in restricting visitors.

Disease and Death

The admission of sickly children and the widespread distribution of viruses and bacteria in a society that was unaware of the germ theory led to outbreaks of cholera, consumption, and scrofulous diseases. The asylum would not be spared the ravages of disease and early deaths throughout its early history. Five-year-old Robert Atkinson died April 2, 1839, of consumption. His death was the first of a child who was not an orphan or one who was deserted by a parent and suffered from neglect. His father, Noel, was a respectable free man who had purchased the freedom of his wife and son for two hundred and fifty dollars. His wife's death led him to bring his two sons, Robert and William to the asylum. Childhood death was common, as reflected in the last stanza of a poem.

The Dying Boy

Oh! Tis their songs [angels] so sweet and clear—
I think I hear them softly say
dear children stay no longer here;
come, come with us, we'll lead the way.
It must be heaven where they dwell—[22]

Annual reports provided narrative and statistical descriptions of diseases that kept the physician and nursing staff busy, often to the point of exhaustion and risk to their own health. The thirteenth annual report (November 15, 1849) was the first one to list all diseases and deaths by type and gender. The eighty-three diseases resulted in twenty deaths.[23]

The managers' motivation to care for as many children as space permitted led to the admission of some who were sickly. Elizabeth Johnson was found on the street but died of dropsy of the brain on May 29, 1838. Her mother, a former slave in the Empire State, had died a few years earlier. The fate of the father was unknown. Her grandmother, an ineffective guardian, was, according to the admissions records, one who "belonged to the most ignorant and degraded

Disease	Boys	Girls
Fever	3	3
Intermittent fever	1	1
Phthisis pulmonalis	2	3
Bronchitis	2	0
Pneumonia	2	0
Congestion of lungs	1	0
Scrofulous irritation of glands	0	3
Scrofulous caries	1	1
Scrofulous rheumatism	0	1
Conjunctivitis	6	2
Diarrhea	9	7
Tubercular peritonitis	1	1
Indigestion	8	0
Anemia	1	0
Enteritis	1	0
Cholera	7	10
Hypertrophy of heart	1	0
Pericarditis	0	1
Strangury (painful urination)	1	0
Congestion of brain	0	1
Onychia maligna	1	0
Dentition	1	0
Total	49	34

Deaths	Boys	Girls
Phthesis pulmonalis	2	3
Enteritis	1	0
Diarrhea	1	0
Pericarditis	1	0
Anemia	1	0
Cholera	6	3
Congestion of brain	0	1
Tuberculous peritonitis	0	1
Total	12	8

class of our coloured population." The poorly clad Elizabeth had to be outfitted before she could be admitted on February 13, 1838. Some children, such as Gustavas Thompson, a sickly child whose mother wanted him with her in his last days, were released to parental care. Soon after, it was decided that five managers had to agree to return a child, provided that three were members of the admissions committee. While many succumbed to sickness, not all deaths were attributed to deadly diseases. A nine-year-old orphan, Ann Williams, died after eating buds of stramonium, a poisonous weed from a nearby lot. She approached death calmly expressing a hope to "go to the good place."[24]

The health of children was connected to the managers' need for additional space. In less than two years after moving in, the small home on Twelfth Street was woefully inadequate. There were by September 1838 forty-five children in the asylum, and the fear of endangering the children's health (some had died of scrofulous diseases) limited the occupancy to fifty children. Several locations were considered for a new home, including a former state prison and the Leak and Watts Asylum, located seven miles away in Harlem. Neither was appropriate for their needs. During the summer of 1838, they asked Dr. James Milnor "for a donation from some property left by [Mary Thompson], a colored woman to his disposal." Milnor and the co-executor agreed to donate three hundred dollars. The managers sought additional building funds by taking children to neighborhood churches to ask ministers to solicit donations from their parishioners.[25]

Nepotism played a major role in the managers' efforts to find larger quarters. On October 8, 1839, the New York Manumission Society (some members were either advisers to or supporters of the orphanage) voted to give the women five thousand dollars with interest, provided that they purchase land to accommodate at least one hundred children and erect a building within three years. Soon after, in 1839 and the following year, two anonymous contributions totaling five thousand dollars were donated to the building fund. (It was revealed, after her death, that the donor was Anna Jay, a manager and daughter of Chief Justice John Jay.)[26]

Space was needed. By the end of 1838, nineteen months after opening their doors, the Colored Orphan Asylum had admitted sixty-four orphaned and neglected or abused children. Of the sixty-four, thirty-three were orphans; the remaining twenty-nine had one parent. Three had been returned to a surviving parent or parents. One child had absconded, another one had been sent to the House of Refuge, and nine, sadly, had died. Most of the deaths had been attributed to the children previously having lived in squalid conditions in damp rooms, which caused their feeble bodies to be susceptible to scrofulous diseases. The fourth annual report, in 1840, concluded with news of improved health. The death of only one child in the past eighteen months was attributed to boarding out sick children in the country or isolating them from the healthy ones. This reinforced the managers' desire to remove the institution "from the atmosphere of the city," with its filth and disease caused by poor sewage and questionable drinking water. This last point, often the crucial appeal for public support, was not hyperbole. The city's black population resided in the notorious Five Points area of lower Manhattan (today, the courthouse area), where vicious crime, disease, violence, and helplessness were constant reminders of poverty. In 1845, John H. Griscom's sanitary report described the black alley neighborhood of Elizabeth Street, near the Five Points. There "ranged next [to] the fence were a number of pig styes and stables which surrounded a yard on three sides from the quantity of filth, liquid and otherwise, [which rendered] the ground . . . almost impassable." The COA had to turn many applicants away, even though it meant further exposing them to filth, ignorance, and possible lives on the street, with its implications for dangerous and criminal activity. Even nonmalicious children sometimes had a negative effect upon the house. Elizabeth Brown became deaf after a summer illness but remained in the orphanage until June 18, 1839, when she was sent to the almshouse. It was not cruelty but pragmatism that caused the managers to remove her: her deafness and other infirmities had "rendered her a disagreeable as well an unwholesome inmate of the house."[27]

Death and Religious Belief

The Quaker managers did not seek to convert the children but were mindful of the need to teach them morality and a belief in God. They sought to have their charges "esteem moral and religious culture as the object to which all others should be made subordinate." In this regard, they were aided by Methodist ministers who preached on Sundays, and it pleased the managers whenever children, especially "bad" ones, readily accepted Jesus Christ as their savior. Death was common in the asylum's early years, and, as many died in the home, it was acceptable for all the children to witness the dying child's last breath. Death was not something to hide from the living, as would become the custom for later generations, and the managers believed it important for children to hear exclamations of faith from dying children. A dying girl "asked only to depart and be with Christ, and He, whose love assigned to her here, a brief and obscure existence, heard that prayer, and took her to mercy in Himself," noted the 1842 annual report. Many dying children passed away unnamed, but some whose brief lives and spirituality moved the managers were named in the minutes or annual reports. The impending death of eleven-year-old Adeline Hicks on September 13, 1842, was recorded as a tribute to her religious faith. Dying of consumption, Adeline said, "I have no fear of death. I know it is only *my body* that will be laid in the cold grave, my soul will go to Jesus, who died for me." A visibly moved teacher wrote "Lines on the Death of Adeline Hicks," hoping that children who read it would seek, like Adeline, to "have their souls washed and made white in the blood of the lamb." Children in the orphanage would gather around the bed of a dying child and express their farewells. It was difficult to reconcile the death of a young person who had not had time to live, to experience life and know physical love. "The only reassurance [people had was] that the child is now with an angel."[28]

The fear of death without salvation even affected those who entered the institution with vicious or profane habits. Some, such as William M. Jackson, an orphan who was admitted as an eight-year-old, became more prayerful. William was found in the streets in a deplorable neglected condition by Andrew McGoron, a Harlem resident, who brought him home, cleaned him, and provided him with clothes. William was a boy preacher. On March 18, 1849, the matron, Susan Benedict, and a teacher listened outside a closed door as he proclaimed, "oh, children suppose you were to die tonight unprepared, where, oh!

where would you go?" William asked God to bless the children and reach them before they died. "Oh, I do feel happy. I feel that Jesus smiles upon my soul. O that I may not be one of those who die unprepared," he exclaimed. William was indentured to Nathaniel Clark in Ulster County, New York. William wrote the institution on May 1, 1850, "I have given my heart to Jesus Christ, and intend to serve Him forever." Clark found William to be "a curious boy" who held prayer meetings. Either curiosity about the outer world or teenage hormones eventually got the better of William, for Nathaniel Clark wrote in an undated note that William had "left his place." Another pious boy told the doubting Thomas in the asylum that you had to choose either the road to heaven or hell. A laughing boy was told "you may laugh, but when you come to die, you will be sorry for it." The chastened boy replied, "children, I am sorry that I laughed; but I hope God will forgive me, and [use] the hammer of His word, and break my heart in pieces and take away this heart of stone, and give me a heart of flesh." Some girls held a prayer meeting, singing and praying for over an hour. They asked the matron for forgiveness for their bad behavior. Eight-year-old Hannah Ann Franklin wanted to learn to read. Her dying request was that the nurse read the Bible or a good book to her, particularly one that "described the death of pious children." Henry Johnson was devoted to prayer. He criticized the other children for their misbehavior, and he told the nurse, "I long to go to Jesus." He exclaimed that earthly music could never compare to its heavenly counterpart awaiting him. "And in this blessed hope, with a simple reliance on the saviour's love, was this humbled child of poverty and degradation redeemed from a world of injustice and oppression," wrote Anna Shotwell.[29]

Good behavior was a character trait cherished by the managers, who struggled in the early years both to teach and to properly discipline children who came to them lacking in common courtesy.

Education in the Asylum

Initially, the members of the education committee handled the teaching assignments, but, wanting a regular teacher, the managers hired

Ann Ray in 1837. Despite good recommendations, Miss Ray's youth and inexperience made it difficult "for her to maintain a strict discipline and order in the school." Unable to replace Miss Ray, the managers decided to retain her for three additional months, until illness forced her to leave her position. Increased attendance necessitated the hiring of Mrs. Sarah P. Melvin, the widow of James A. Melvin and Ann Ray's sister, as principal. Progress in the children's achievements was reported in early 1838, but the managers were dissatisfied with the principal. In April, they hired a Miss White to teach, and she was given an assistant who aided her for three hours daily in addition to her duties as a nurse and seamstress. It soon became clear that the assistant was incapable of adequately serving the school. Later, the managers decided that the assistant teacher needed to live in the asylum and care for children out of school hours. The challenge of finding women capable of providing quality teaching and good discipline would remain a problem for several years.[30]

The managers were torn between bestowing upon the charges caring understanding or harsh discipline. They debated the use of corporal punishment, an issue that they would revisit for decades. The managers were loath to whip the children, but they also understood that solitary confinement was a counterproductive measure in the case of children who became "noisy and violent, thumping against the doors, breaking the locks, etc." They would in the coming decades alternate between periods of limited corporal punishment and forms of psychological control.[31]

Needed funds for education came in the form of $425.93 from the commissioners of the public school fund. The managers also appealed to the New York Manumission Society for funds to keep the school functioning. For several years, the Manumission Society forwarded to the orphanage small but crucial funds. Additional funding was sought from John Jacob Astor, Rufus Lord, and Jonathan Goodhue, prominent New Yorkers all, who over the years became donors. In 1839, white Protestant churches contributed $315.71. An additional $61.29 came from St. Philip's Episcopal Church, a black church. Financial problems continued to plague the institution in early 1840. James McCune

Smith, who would soon become the institution's physician, aided the cause with $201.50, from the profits from the publication of his lecture on the Haitian Revolution. Smith praised the managers for seeking to educate black children when public funds were not distributed for that purpose and at a time when eight hundred children of European immigrants were educated and taught trades at public expense.[32]

The rudimentary lessons taught to the children employed the Lancasterian system, where older children provided instruction for younger ones while the teacher provided instruction to others. However, in early 1847 the managers decided to maintain it only when classes were small enough for teachers to observe all of the students at once. The discipline problem was compounded by the difficulty that the asylum had in hiring and retaining competent teachers. White teachers had trouble relating to the cultural differences of their charges. For this reason, the managers advertised for a black instructor in six issues of the *Colored American*. The paucity of educated African American women and the desire of many to teach in a black-controlled school made it hard for the asylum to hire one quickly. It was not until 1848 that a black woman, Mary A. Bodee, was employed. A popular teacher, she was ill for several years with a heart condition and repeated hemorrhages of the lungs. On her deathbed, Mary thanked God for giving her time to say goodbye to her children, Frances, Robert, and Edward, as well as the staff, teachers, and managers. She exclaimed, "o death, where is thy sting. O grave where is thy victory." She died with a "countenance . . . radiant with a sweet and heavenly smile." Secretary Anna Shotwell tellingly wrote that the institution's family loved Mary Bodee, despite her dark skin. Unfortunately, soon thereafter, Robert, Mary's twelve-year-old son, died of consumption. Anna Shotwell noted, "Robert had evidently found the pearl of great price; his mother's God was his God." Mary's daughter Frances had earlier been bound over to the institution until age twelve, but when she was ten, Mary had assigned her to be cared for by Mr. and Mrs. Edward Felix. The board of managers relinquished their claim and placed her in the foster home but retained oversight of her until she reached the age of twelve. Mary Bodee's son Robert had been learning the tinning business from

Edward Felix, and her other son, Edward, was indentured to a barber. Mary's death highlighted another segment of daily humiliation for New Yorkers of darker hue. The Rev. James W. C. Pennington heard of Mary's funeral an hour before it started, but he was unable to get public transportation because of racial prejudice. No carriage driver would take him for less than a then-astronomical fee of $1.50 (more than a day's pay for most laborers). Pennington had to walk on a humid day and arrived unfit for the service. Later, in 1855, he lost a discrimination suit against a railroad company.[33]

Community Support

The African American community in New York deeply appreciated the efforts of the Colored Orphan Asylum to care for their children. Despite the earlier misgivings of Samuel Cornish, the progress of the COA in its earliest years was facilitated by the efforts of clergymen who solicited funds and services from their congregations. A strong supporter was Peter Williams, the pastor of St. Philip's Episcopal Church. His death in 1840 was a major blow to the managers. The support of the black community reinforced the managers' belief that their mission was a holy one that had providential blessing and that kind New Yorkers would not let their fledging institution wither on the vine. They expected help from all quarters of political persuasion because they, from the beginning, never allowed the institution to ally itself with "the peculiar views and interests of any sect or party, or with the plans of any other benevolent organization." The managers declared in their fourth annual report "to place on a permanent footing an institution which shall no longer permit the helpless orphan to perish in his ignorance and wretchedness." They begged the public to support them in raising the black child "from his degradation . . . to elevate his character, develop his faculties and instruct him in . . . the knowledge of his obligation to himself, to his neighbor, and to his God." The response was heartwarming. Twenty-three patrons pledged to give annually fifty or more dollars at one time; seventeen life members vowed to donate twenty-five dollars at one time. Significant and timely gifts of dry goods, beans, crackers, potatoes, apples, Indian meal, buckwheat, shoes, and seven pairs of stockings knitted by a ninety-year-old colored woman in Rahway, New Jersey, were accepted with appreciation.[34]

The first few years proved to be a struggle for the female managers. Their heroic efforts kept the institution viable during this period and provided them with inspiration to continue despite future periods of financial insecurity and the devastating destruction of their building by rioters in 1863. Many of the details of their story for the period of 1841 through November 1846 has been lost to history, because the fires of the 1863 Draft Riots destroyed most of their records. The surviving records, however, reveal that faithful supporters kept alive the managers' hopes. The partial records indicated that throughout 1841 the ladies provided the children with a "good practical education" at a time when most Americans, children as well as adults, were illiterate.[35]

In 1842, a small fire started in a sleeping area, but thankfully during the day, averting a disaster. The children were temporarily sheltered on Fiftieth Street, then outside of the city's limits. This spurred the managers' effort to find a new home in an area of cleaner air. Their prayers and hopes were answered in June, when the Corporation of the City of New York provided them with twenty lots on Fifth Avenue between Forty-third and Forty-fourth Streets. There was space to build a home with a 140-foot front, forty-two to fifty feet of depth, and a cellar free of dampness. The prospect of a new home increased the urgency for renewed funding to pay for landscaping, to erect a fence, and eventually to grade the street. New supporters (there now were sixty-six) included Cornelius V. S. Roosevelt and his wife, Margaret, who became a manager in 1840. Margaret Roosevelt came from a prominent Philadelphia Quaker family. Cornelius Roosevelt, a wealthy banker, merchant, and philanthropist, was the grandfather of Theodore Roosevelt, the future president.[36]

The managers had over the years accumulated the twenty thousand dollars needed to erect the building, but in January 1843, Anna

Shotwell requested ten thousand dollars from the New York Manumission Society for the grounds, heating fixtures, and simple furniture. The Manumission Society quickly appropriated one thousand dollars. The managers eagerly looked forward to their new home, where they moved to on May 1, 1843.[37]

2 Fifth Avenue: Growth and Progress, 1843–54

The move to Forty-third Street and Fifth Avenue on May 1 was chaotic. The orphanage's staff had to transport furniture and household goods—along with children of various ages—through Manhattan streets clogged with private and public carriages and wagons ferrying goods around the island. This section of midtown Manhattan was not the glamorous area it is today, with banks, expensive shoe stores, jewelry stores, publishing houses, insurance agencies, and department stores. In contrast, the area, then outside of the city's limits, was described by Mary Murray as an inelegant neighborhood lacking paved streets. Winter storms brought endless mud, which forced the managers to place large stones in the road in order to cross Fifth Avenue. An advantage was the availability of water from the Croton Reservoir (the site of the present-day New York Public Library), located a block away. The new two-story building provided space for play rooms, coal and vegetable bins, a kitchen, dining room, bathing room, two infirmaries, and school rooms. The dining room, one of the infirmaries, and one of the school rooms were heated by hot water running through iron pipes. Friends of the institution aided their first year in their new home with donations of beef, mutton, fruit, crockery, furniture, carpeting, soap, books, tools, sheets, eating utensils, and pies and cakes. Good news came in early 1844, when the city provided twenty additional lots adjacent to their home. The extra space was used to keep several cows and to grow vegetables. Within a few years, the managers had earned income from the vegetable garden; they had built a brick stable and erected a garden fence. Unfortunately, the managers found out in

1847 that they had not been given legal right to the adjacent property, and it was sold.[1]

Prominent New Yorkers aided the institution. James Lenox, whose funds would immensely aid the future New York Public Library, was a major supporter of the Colored Orphan Asylum. Another supporter, John Jay, the son of the first chief justice of the U.S. Supreme Court, spoke on behalf of the orphanage on December 11, 1843. He noted that there were seventy children in a building that could accommodate 150. He called upon public support for the ladies who sought to follow Jesus Christ's admonition "to cherish the fatherless and to feed His lambs."[2]

By the end of 1845, 262 children had been admitted since June 9, 1837. The children helped to lower expenses by doing much of the housework (in preparation for similar work as indentures). The public appeals presented the bigoted view of the institution's physicians James MacDonald and James Proudfit, members of the American Colonization Society (which supported the removal of willing blacks to Liberia), that the children's high morbidity and mortality were due to environment, poverty, and their "peculiar constitution and condition."

The Fifth Avenue building at Forty-third Street, c. 1854. (Collection of The New-York Historical Society.)

The managers added that children would become vagrants, criminals, or beggars unless increased funding could bring them to the orphanage. This view of innate Negro depravity unless checked by benevolent paternalism was challenged by the black physician James McCune Smith, who informed the *New York Tribune* in early 1844 that proportionally there were more whites in the almshouses than blacks. Paradoxically, in light of the orphanage's paternalistic statements, the African American community aided them financially out of appreciation for the care provided their children. St. Philip's Episcopal Church contributed $99.71; a child, Charlotte Ann Seymour, collected $21.00 from her mother's friends; two black persons gave $2.00 each; another donated 50 cents; two friends from the West sent $3.00; and three donated four days each of work. The gratified managers exclaimed, "we would not omit the expression of gratitude to many of the colored friends of the institution for their kind offers."[3]

James McCune Smith, an educator, medical researcher, sociologist, political strategist, and first-rate intellectual, would be hired in December 1846 to be the orphanage's physician, where he remained until his death in 1865. Smith attended African Free School No. 2, where his classmates included the abolitionist Henry Highland Garnet, the actor Ira Aldridge, the educator Charles L. Reason, the clergyman Alexander Crummell, and the abolitionist Samuel Ringgold Ward. Racial prejudice forced Smith to go abroad for an education, after both Columbia College and Geneva Medical College denied him admission. He graduated first in his class while earning a bachelors, masters, and a medical degree in 1837 from the University of Glasgow in Scotland. Smith was scheduled to return to the United States in 1837 aboard the *Canonicus*, but the captain refused him boarding. Upon his return, the *Colored American* referred to him as one of the nation's brightest and no man's inferior in "moral worth and intellectual capacity." He treated both white and black patients at his private practice at 93 West Broadway in Manhattan.[4]

Smith's impressive pedigree did not protect him from discrimination. New York public carriers either excluded African Americans or relegated them to segregated conveyances. Smith had to walk six or

James McCune Smith, asylum's physician 1846–65. (Photographs and Prints Division, Schomburg Center for Research in Black Culture, the New York Public Library, Astor, Tilden and Lenox Foundations.)

seven miles round trip from his home at 151 Reade Street to the orphanage. At first, the managers allowed him to hire a conveyance at their expense during a period of disease in the building. Later, they arranged for a special dispensation to grant him a ticket for personal use. Upset by such blatant discrimination, the managers placed a notice in the daily papers complaining about the city cars denying riding privileges to colored residents. While this gesture was a departure from their vow not to get involved in the issues of the day, perhaps here they can be faulted for not making a greater effort. Many of the managers' friends were influential businessmen and attorneys, and some even supported equal rights, but the orphanage managers did not appeal to them to attack aggressively the racial discrimination that confronted African Americans daily. Blatant public conveyance discrimination persisted until 1858, when Maria Jenkins successfully sued for bias.[5]

The indignities that blacks faced in life often did not end with death. Just as many of their ancestors were buried in an area then beyond the city's limits known as the Negro Burial Ground, African Americans in the mid-nineteenth century faced difficult burial decisions. Many white churches would not bury them in their burial grounds, and unless they were members of a benevolent society, they might lack funds for a decent funeral. The managers' concern for the proper interment of their deceased charges was alleviated after Samuel N. Burrill offered to handle the asylum's burial arrangements at his own expense. However, his move to Brooklyn in late 1846 ended his near-decade of benevolence. Each burial at the Presbyterian Cemetery in Manhattan cost Burrill five dollars. His brother, who could not afford the whole cost, offered to bear half the expenses. The managers hoped that Samuel's friends would join his brother to defray the funeral costs. In early 1847, Samuel Burrill recommended that the managers apply to the trustees of Green-Wood Cemetery in Brooklyn for "a gift of ground." Burrill provided the names of brothers-in-law who had influence with the cemetery's board. On March 10, 1847, the managers were granted a Green-Wood plot of 37.5 feet. It would cost $2.37½ for each interment. Henry Stephenson, who died on February 13, 1850, was the first asylum child buried at Green-Wood. In later years, children would be interred at Trinity's cemetery in upper Manhattan and Kensico in Westchester County.[6]

Illness, Death, and a New Hospital

The managers' commitment to admitting needy children was tested during the winter of 1847, when an overabundance of children with infections or incurable diseases applied for admission. While not showing a willingness to admit diseased children, the managers thought it appropriate to admit scrofulous ones. However, a hospital was needed if the managers were to admit this class of children. Building a hospital would be costly, but Anna Shotwell argued that it was more costly to reject "this deplorably destitute and suffering portion of the human family." The advisers recommended on May 3, 1847, that the managers construct a hospital, perhaps on their Twelfth Street property. Later, in November, the managers decided to add a wing to the Fifth Avenue residence instead of erecting a separate building. They also changed their by-laws to accept children over the age of eight as long as they would not become permanent charges of the asylum.

This would prove to be a momentous decision, for it led to the admission of older children, whose age and background caused discipline problems. Dr. Smith noted that the main building had space for only fourteen sick children. A scrofulous condition, he stressed, was a product of poverty, not race. Many African American children lived in damp quarters, were exposed to inclement weather, and contracted the condition from their parents. Smith emphasized that a large hospital space would make it easier to control epidemics and noted that there had been twenty-four deaths in the orphanage in 1847 compared to fifteen in the previous four years combined. His appeal for funds to build a hospital wing added $121.37 to the treasury.[7]

Financial difficulties plagued the managers throughout 1847, but their prayers were temporarily answered in early 1848. The New York Manumission Society (inactive since the abolition of slavery in 1827) voted to dissolve its operation. Two advisers to the orphanage, William F. Mott and Mahlon Day, were president and first vice president respectively of the Manumission Society, and through their influence the society voted to turn over to the Colored Orphan Asylum all money, stock, bonds, and mortgages in their possession, provided the assets were used to educate and improve the condition of black New Yorkers.[8]

A hospital wing to isolate seriously sick and contagious children was needed. Smith's excellent medical skills could not prevent in 1848 the death of seventeen young children, deaths mostly attributed to some form of scrofulous condition. Smith noted in his report that isolation would have limited the deaths and provided an opportunity to carefully study the diseases "to which their hard life has condemned so large a proportion of them." The hospital became a reality with the receipt of a five-thousand-dollar legacy from Elizabeth DeMilt, who died on August 31, 1849. The managers used the unexpected funds to erect a thirty-by-sixty-five-foot building that corresponded "in height and architectural proportions with the main building," about fifteen feet apart from it. There were two large rooms for sick children, two additional rooms, a schoolroom for convalescent patients, an apothecary's room, nurses' apartments, a dining room, a playroom, and a basement room for drying clothes. The hospital wing opened on June 26, 1850, with thirty-two patients, mostly suffering from scrofulous inflammation of the glands. The managers praised James McCune Smith for "carefully seeking opportunity of marking the symptoms and of arresting the progress of disease, by judicial medical treatment." For the year ending November 22, 1850, eighty-two children were ill, thirty-three suffered from dysentery, and seven had died. Smith's physician report noted that a study, The Diseases of Infancy and Childhood by a Dr. West, reported that girls were affected more with whooping cough than were boys. This had proved true in London and in the New York orphanage as well, where 73.30 percent of the whooping cough cases were girls. Freedom to isolate the sick from the healthy allowed for better treatment of three typhus cases, and even though one died, it afforded the managers a "release from the pain of refusing applicant laboring under constitutional malady." But even Smith's exemplary medical skills could not protect all those who were sickly—not even his own children were spared. A few years later, he informed his friend Gerrit Smith of the deaths of Amy, Frederick, Peter, and Anna. The physician's lament, "oh it is so sad to have no children playing around the hearth stone," is shared by all parents who lose a child to disease.[9]

Indenturing

Indenturing children was a common practice in nineteenth-century orphanages, but race played a part in the assignments of children from the COA. Like girls in the Colored Orphan Asylum, educated girls in other orphanages were placed out as domestics until the age of eighteen. In 1809, the New York Orphan Asylum indentured educated boys until age fifteen, and then they were returned to the institution to be bound as apprentices "to virtuous mechanics of the community, and perhaps the future benefactors of the institution which nurtured their helpless infancy." The COA children remained until age twelve and, unless they were boarders, the girls were indentured as domestics and the boys as farm laborers. Few were permitted to work in New York City, which the managers deemed to be an unsavory place for young bodies, and fewer still were sent to mechanics or artisans. Most were sent to white families far removed from New York City, where many felt alienated and longed for contact with siblings in the orphanage or indentured elsewhere.[10]

Bigotry kept African Americans uneducated and untrained for trades. It was difficult for blacks to gain a bookkeeping position or to receive a carman's license. Left unsaid was the failure of New York's abolitionists and Quakers, many whom called for racial equality, to offer to teach the trades or business practices to African Americans. Samuel Ringgold Ward, a black abolitionist and clergyman, was deeply offended. He informed Frederick Douglass that even though Quakers were no longer slave owners nor did they join anti-Negro mobs, they never permitted youths of color to attend school with their children and that "whatever they do for us savors of pity, and is done at arm's length, on a sort of [do not touch me] principle. [T]hey would sooner put on a narrow brim or an unstraight coat [than] raise a negro boy to a clerkship or put him in a profession or fit him for anything more than a drudge." This was a serious charge, and it had more than a germ of truth to it. Only rarely during the sixty-odd years that the managers sent out indentures did they broach the subject of placing them with skilled artisans, and when they did, it usually was with a black barber or other skilled worker. One rare example was the placement of six-teen-year-old Sarah Williams, the first child admitted to the orphanage on June 9, 1837, who in 1849 left to be apprenticed to a tailor in Shrewsbury, New Jersey.[11]

Good and Bad Indentures

Those who were indentures had much in common: they left the or-phanage at age twelve, but not all were mature enough to accept the separation from the orphanage, for some the only home they knew, or from siblings. Some were physically too small or weak to perform chores to the standards of their employers, and some were unable to live by the moral guidance provided them in the asylum. Many did not complete their indentures, chafing under restrictions that initially confined them to an employer until age twenty-one, for boys (later, it was lowered to age eighteen). Those who left their assignments early did not receive the stipend money sent to the institution by employers.

T. H. F. (Thaddeus Henry Freeman) was indentured in 1843 to Wil-liam Demerest. Thaddeus wrote in 1846, "I learned catechism and hymn and Bible question." He had taught two young girls in his home to read. "They learn very nice," he proudly noted. "I am glad I have been taught [at the asylum] that nothing is sure to make me a good boy, but to believe in God." H. G. (Henry Giles) wrote from Sharon, Illinois, on February 10, 1846, "I send my love to sister, grandmother and mother, and let them know that I am pleased with the place." H. S. (Henry Smith) wrote on November 13, 1846, from Yorktown, New York, "I think I have a good home." He waited on tables, assisted the cook, cared for the cows, and read to the mistress of the house. Eager to please his new family, Henry added, "I try to be a good boy, and I hope no wrong deed will ever be coupled with [my] name."[12]

Some indentures were extremely fortunate to have kind employers who not only fed them properly but allowed them to go to school and oversaw their moral development by encouraging church attendance. George Coles was indentured on February 3, 1860, to William Henry Van Deventer, of Cranbury, New Jersey. On June 30, 1861, George wrote Superintendent Davis from Bald Mountain, New York, expressing loneliness and requesting a letter from his orphanage home. "For home it is; it was there w[h]ere I first l[e]arned the word of God; it was there where I first uttered my first prayer, and learned first my alphabet. My employer says that if I stay with him until I am twenty-one, he will give me a house and fifty acres of land; and I have now chose the place for the house. Now I want a little of your advice what to do about it, as I know that I can get good advice from you."[13] Undoubtedly, many a child heard these words and prayed for an employer as kind as Mr. Van Deventer.

Aaron Lewis, who was indentured on May 14, 1846, to Henry Roundtree of Cornwall, New York, was extremely pleased with his employer's kindness. Aaron wrote, on December 11, 1851, to "my kind benefactor," with thanks for being housed in the orphanage and for having a good master. "The darkness of my skin makes no difference in treatment of me," he added. The happy teenager concluded that every asylum boy should have a place as nice as his. Unlike most indentures, who worked in the home or on a farm, Aaron had learned how to take care of a steam engine and how to make stoves. He was pleased that his employer provided him with time and money to go to the state fair at Rochester, New York. Aaron, like most of the children, was indentured to a white family, and the record showed that there was little evidence of racial discrimination in either the housing or with neighbors.[14]

Some lacked self-discipline once they were removed from the constraints of the orphanage. James Gomes was indentured in Sullivan County, New York, in 1853. His loneliness prompted him to return to the orphanage, but the rules prohibited him from remaining there. The alternative was an assignment to the House of Refuge or a return to the streets. A thoroughly chastened James walked the one hundred miles back to the home of his former master, who accepted him as his prodigal son. In 1858, the twenty-one-year-old James wrote from Fallsburgh, New York, to the asylum children, "I warn you all as long as you have a good home . . . leave it not in a hurry to find a better. For if you do not you will find a hard road to travel, as I found when I left the asylum . . . before I reached my port, the way of the transgressor is hard. Take the advice of one who has tried it." James Gomes wrote to Superintendent William Davis, on November 15, 1860, "I am . . . striving to gain an honest livelihood which I owe to you. The only way I can show my gratitude towards you is by my future conduct and good behavior, and I can never forget my orphan home where I learned *what it requires* to make a man of good morals."[15]

By most circumstances, George Wesley Thompson could have been burdened by misfortunes. After the death of his parents, the thirteen-year-old boy departed Boston to be with his aunt in New York, who, unknowing to him, was buried the day before his arrival. He was indentured on April 15, 1845, but left his assignment without permission in 1847. Thirteen years later, the twenty-nine-year-old George wrote to the orphanage, "I am about to congratulate you upon the noble success you have had in training up those you have had and still are in charge of [for] many a child has been snatched away from poverty, cold, relentless grasp and placed in that happy home." The grateful man concluded, "the work you have begun will crown your brow with laurels and your hearts with triumphant satisfaction. Fire the zeal of love and plant the seed of righteousness." As a morality lesson for others, he added that he was a naughty boy who had "teased and taunted old men and women" until the asylum reformed him. "Oh! When will the children learn to honor their fathers an[d] mothers?" he lamented. Twenty-five-year-old George W. Potter wrote the asylum on Christmas Day, 1860. He reported that reading the Bible given him by the managers kept him from temptation. "I thank you for the kind attention given me. . . . To you I owe all that I am now, and [I plan] to act as a light of the institution. . . . It is with pride that I couple my name with the institution, and it shall be my care to bring no reproach, but . . . [to] retain the pleasant memory of my benefactors." George's brother, Frank, had completed his apprenticeship, and according to Anna Shotwell, the brothers were of "superior talents, strict integrity and persevering industry." William Isaac, whom George was indentured to in

1848, considered him a mechanical genius. Frank became a successful barber and hairdresser. He informed Superintendent Davis by letter on November 29, 1861, that he had shaved men and dressed hair for three months and was ready to cut hair. Frank praised the managers and hoped that they would receive his letter as a sign of his respect for them.[16] These and other success stories were highlighted in annual reports as fundraising tools to loosen the purse strings of New Yorkers.

Many indentured children failed to complete their assignment. For some, boredom led them to abscond from their placement, only to fall into a state of destitution or, worse, engage in mischievous or criminal behavior. Some came into the asylum bereft of common manners and lacking in morals. Their earlier exposure to vice and the managers' inability to develop a moral base in their lives caused some to commit acts of violence against their employer or the family that housed them. These incidents were hidden mainly in the minutes or indenturing reports, which were not available to the public. A few vicious acts appeared in newspapers, which caused embarrassment for the institution.

The oldest girl in the institution, Harriet Williams, an orphan, was placed on trial with James Montgomery of Charlton Street in Manhattan on April 15, 1839. Nine weeks later, she was deemed guilty of gross misconduct and sent to James Fuller of Skaneateles, New York, near Syracuse. Her age was between ten and twelve.[17] Phoebe Clark's father had died at sea. The twelve-year-old was indentured in 1854 to William J. Shurtleff of Winslow, Maine, who visited the asylum in 1855 to inform the superintendent that Phoebe had threatened to poison his family and set the house on fire.

Because most children were indentured as domestics or farm laborers, it was significant when one had the prospect to be assigned to a mechanic or tradesman. But it was extremely tragic when the youngster did not take advantage of the opportunity. Edward Moll, a resident of Germany, proposed in June 1852 that the managers allow him "to take a dark boy from the asylum, give him a thoroughly good education and trade or profession as he may choose and when of age provide him with [funds to return] to New York, should it be his wish, by a respectable conveyance separate from the steerage passengers." After verifying Moll's character, the managers allowed eleven-year-old David Shutt to travel abroad. This was an amazing gesture, which, unfortunately, the young boy did not or was not able to appreciate. He returned home for unknown reasons, but his age (over twelve) prohibited him from remaining in the asylum. He soon became a thief and a drifter. He died of fever at an unspecified date in a juvenile receiving home.[18]

Often, the young children did not realize how fortunate they were to be living in the Colored Orphan Asylum. Those who entered as infants were sheltered from the ills of poverty, food of poor quality and limited quantity, filth, and crime that hindered so many children of both races. Children in the asylum took for granted an education that many, including adults, were unable to receive. Elizabeth Thomas wrote the managers from Egremont, Massachusetts, on her fifteenth birthday, April 18, 1859. "I feel very sorrow to think I did not improve the opportunity which I had to learn while I was there now that it does not seem convenient for me to go. I have been to school nearly four months since I have been here, and hope to go more." Elizabeth had much to regret. Indentured to Mrs. Sarah Upton, Elizabeth wrote on April 3, 1857, nearly ten months after leaving the managers, that she liked her new home very much. The situation, however, changed rapidly. Mrs. Upton wrote the asylum on January 4, 1859, that the young girl had behaved improperly, which was the reason why she had delayed forwarding the stipend money. Mrs. Upton, nonetheless, saw some improvement in her fourteen-year-old charge. Elizabeth's misbehavior paled in comparison with the antics of some children. A representative of this group was Charles Henry Cisco. The orphan boy was indentured on September 30, 1859, to the Rev. Thomas D. Hoover of Cranbury, New Jersey. Hoover wrote in July 1864 that Charles had been worthless for over a year and had recently been intoxicated three times. The pious minister's kindness failed to turn Charles around. "I hope God will watch over him," he plaintively added. Not soured by this experience, Hoover requested that the managers send him a fourteen-year-old boy, for whom he promised to "do all I can for his moral and religious culture." Left unsaid in the correspondence was Charles's age. His restlessness and experiments with liquor occurred when he was about seventeen. Many indentures resented working until the age of twenty-one before they could earn wages, and drinking and smoking were their only expressions of reaching manhood.[19]

The depravity of some children resulted in theft, fires, poisoning, and even physical violence. Even the promise of unofficial adoption did not curb some misbehavior. Sophie Slossom was admitted in 1856 as a seven-year-old by a Mrs. Slossom, who agreed to pay fifty cents weekly for her board. Her parents were unknown. The managers agreed to turn Sophie over to Mrs. Slossom when she reached age twelve, "providing she lives in the country as she has taken so much

Teachers imparting moral guidance for successful indentures in the Fifth Avenue building, Good Friday 1861. (Collection of The New-York Historical Society.)

Children at play in a courtyard of the Fifth Avenue building. (Collection of The New-York Historical Society.)

interest in her and allows her to be called by her own name." Sophie, however, was indentured at age thirteen to Frederick Voorhies in Mill Stone, New Jersey. Mr. Voorhies wrote the managers on April 11, 1864 (two years after receiving Sophie), that four days earlier, she had burned down two barns, a hovel, the carriage house, and a pig pen valued at three thousand dollars. Sophie's excuse was that she did not think that straw would burn. It appears that the teenager was fooling around with matches and had no malicious intent to cause damage.[20]

Some children's mental instability was further eroded by their absence from the orphanage, the only home they knew or felt secure in.

Their inability to cope with new surroundings and their unwillingness to accommodate themselves to the standards of others led to tragedy for themselves or others. The effort of the managers to train the children to be morally upright sometimes, unfortunately, met with setbacks. Two incidents in 1868 reflected the difficulty of sending children, some of whom had troubled personalities and psychological issues, far from the institution without emotional support. These troubled teenagers did harm to themselves or to others. Seventeen-year-old Susan Solomons was unmarried and pregnant. The distraught child swallowed a dose of Paris green and died on September 18. This devastating information appeared in the *New York Times* but was conveniently left out of the minutes, the indenturing and admission records, and the annual report by the managers, who probably were embarrassed and ashamed. Fifteen-year-old Augustus Layton was returned from his first indenture because he ran away, wanting to be outdoors more. His second indenture resulted in him pushing his employer's daughter into the pond, in which she drowned. The psychologically disturbed Augustus was given a third indenture, which resulted in the teenager severely beating his employer's wife, Mrs. John Garrabrandt. The court sentenced him on April 30, 1870, to thirty months in prison. At a later date, Augustus committed murder. In 1881, the managers opted to petition the governor for the commutation of his sentence to life imprisonment instead of sharing some of the expense of an appeal for a new trial. In that same year, the children visited him in the Manhattan House of Detention for Men, where he told them to avoid the temptations that "had brought him to his present sad condition, which he little realized would be his when he was a boy at the asy[lum]."[21]

The emotional immaturity of some of the orphans caused them to rebel in destructive ways. William Neal entered the COA in January 1876 as an eight-year-old orphan; he was "delivered to friends" on October 5, 1877, but adopted at age twelve by a colored family in Middletown, New York. For unstated reasons, he set fire to a hardware store, only a few days after setting fire to a barn. His vicious acts sent him to the House of Refuge. Fifteen-year-old George W. Greene was indentured to A. J. Duncan, who wrote on August 3, 1881, that the teenager set fire to the barn; the conflagration killed horses and destroyed hay and grain, at a loss of four thousand dollars. He was placed in jail in New Brunswick, New Jersey. Fourteen-year-old William Beasley broke into a candy store in Kingston, New York. Six years later, the institution's records noted that the then twenty-year-old resided in Philadelphia and "look[ed] like a tramp." Some so-called bad children lacked the emotional maturity to deal with their separation from the orphanage. They simply needed guidance and love, which they did not receive from their employers, who wanted a good day's work from them. Eugene Mitchell abused a horse in 1882. He left his employer prematurely but by 1886 had saved twenty-five dollars in a bank. The following year, Eugene enrolled in school to study for the ministry. Asylum records noted that he visited on January 2, 1896, then as the pastor of Knox Presbyterian Church in Baltimore.[22]

Annie Williams was returned by her employer. Angry, she broke the matron's eyeglasses, which cost the impudent child $5.35. Sixteen-year-old Alice Price was reprimanded for wearing her employer's shoes without permission. Enraged, she used rat poison to sicken the family of J. Van Nest Stillwell, the postmaster of White Horse, New Jersey. The family recovered, unaware of the cause of their sickness. Alice then placed poison in the family's succotash. Four people nearly died, but Alice was still not suspected as the culprit. Alice next poisoned the fried oysters, which caused the family and guests to become deathly sick. Once Mr. Stillwell noticed the missing poison, he confronted Alice, who confessed. She was sentenced to one year in state prison. Alice's stipend money was never collected by her, and the account, which had grown to $71.03, was placed in the lapsed stipend fund on February 26, 1923.[23]

Proper moral guidance was something the managers firmly believed placed their charges on the right path. Another former boy, Andrew Rankins, reinforced this faith with his letter to Superintendent Sherwin. The twenty-seven-year-old Rankins was married with a steady job, earning ten dollars a week. "I know it will be a scource [source] of pleasure to you to know that I often think of you and your often told teachings and heed them. I neither drink, smoke nor chew [tobacco] and I have never had no desire for any of those habits."[24]

Mistreatment by Employers

Proper moral guidance helped many youngsters cope with temptation, but it was of no assistance when they were assigned to vicious employers who physically abused them. Prior to the formation of the Society for the Prevention of Cruelty to Children in 1874, employers treated children harshly, without fear of punishment. They, like society in general, believed that sparing the rod spoiled the child. The realization that animals were protected from cruelty before society deemed it necessary to protect children suggests that children were often at the mercy of their employers.

Before the Civil War, Edward Bennett of Southport, Connecticut, severely mistreated John Dolan for unknown reasons. Superintendent William Davis visited young Dolan and found him nearly frozen to death. He had "lost his fingers at the first and second joints, and [had been] unmercifully flogged . . . [with] 36 lashes all of which opened his skin." John visited the asylum in 1883 to inform the managers that he was now married and a seaman. In 1891, when he was forty-six years old, he visited the asylum requesting assistance, which he received. He visited again on July 21, 1895, this time seeking help because he was "very hard up." Six months later, Superintendent Sherwin wrote to Dolan asking him to locate witnesses to testify against Bennett. It is unlikely that he could find any after an absence of more than forty years. The trustees (as the managers were termed after 1900) voted in 1921 to assist Dolan with one hundred dollars from the lapsed stipend fund. They decided that John needed regular donations of coal, groceries, and other necessities. Seven years later, they decided to pay for home care for two months but then inform his family that he was their responsibility. But Dolan's health had declined so rapidly that the trustees informed the family that they would continue his care. He died soon thereafter, and the institution agreed to cover the $175 funeral expense. The asylum had paid $1,085.47 over the years to assist John Dolan, who was not the only former "inmate" to receive their benevolence.[25]

It was decided by the managers in May 1867 that, in the event of unkind treatment or failure to keep up with stipend payments, the superintendent or his representative would visit the person and learn the local laws of that state pertaining to masters and apprentices and impose necessary penalties. This decision had little bearing on the horrific torturing of thirteen-year-old Martha M. Rue, who was savagely and cruelly beaten by Mr. and Mrs. Charles McNeill. Described by the *New York Sun* as "The Monsters of Paterson," the New Jersey couple, believing that their indentured employee had stolen, sought a confession by tying her by her thumbs to an overhead beam with her toes barely touching the ground. For two weeks, the frightened teenager was beaten with a black rawhide and choked until she "confessed"— but could not say where the money was. The McNeills took her to jail, where she languished for two weeks. An appalled judge fined the couple two hundred dollars and refused to have charges of theft filed against Martha. The superintendent visited Martha and found her with "raw flesh rolled up from the bones of the thumbs." It is not known if the managers sought a civil suit for damages. Martha was subsequently placed in a position with Miss A. D. Fairbanks, at six dollars per month. Unfortunately, the managers learned on March 7, 1879, that Martha had died. She was twenty-three years old.[26]

The managers sought in early 1879 to eliminate potentially vicious employers by requesting letters of testimony, which were notes from a clergyman confirming their regular church attendance and including an agreement from the employer that he or she would not permit their indenture "to frequent alehouses, taverns or play-houses." They were to see that the child attend church regularly when practical, to read the Bible aloud, and "provide . . . sufficient meat, drink, apparel, lodging and washing . . . and cause [the child] to go to school three months in every year, until [age] sixteen." The indenture was provided with a Bible and suit of clothes at the end of their indenture. One hundred dollars was the stipend the employer sent to the orphanage for boys; girls received fifty dollars.[27]

Despite the intent of the managers and the superintendent to be more selective in choosing employers, mistakes in judgment occurred, from which the children suffered. Thirteen-year-old Patrick Hance, indentured to Miss M. E. Whitson of Westbury, New York, used vulgar language in the presence of the woman, which led to a severe beating by her brother on August 3, 1894. The Society for the Prevention of Cruelty to Children charged William Whitson, who was fined twenty-five dollars. The asylum decided that Patrick would be returned "if it is proved that the family are [sic] not *proper custodians* of the boy." They considered placing him in the Juvenile Asylum if they could not find his friends, "as he is too bad a boy to associate with the children of our institution." Patrick was reassigned on January 30, 1895, to Martin V. Higgins, of Kingston, New York, but the disturbed boy ran away on September 3, 1895. Regardless of the boy's machinations, it was the responsibility of the asylum to look out for his interest. All of the parties ignored or overlooked Patrick's need for psychological assistance.[28]

The Children's Aid Society and the Colored Orphan Asylum

While the managers sought to better look after their charges by insisting that the children write regularly and with visits from the superintendent, it was impossible to check on the progress or safety of those sent out West under the auspices of the Children's Aid Society. Founded in New York City in 1853 by Charles Loring Brace, the Children's Aid Society believed that the West offered unlimited opportunities. The farmer, he asserted, was the nation's "most solid and intelligent citizen." In the manner of a slave auction, families selected children. Unfortunately, many children were overworked and poorly fed or clothed. Most of the ninety thousand who left New York City were shifted from one placement to another and eventually returned to the East.[29]

The African American children were sometimes sent to live with black families, but many lived with white families who differed from them in culture and value systems. Approximately twenty-one children were sent from the Colored Orphan Asylum to the West between 1870 and 1886. The assignment to the West was a type of punishment for gross misbehavior. The change of scenery did little to improve their conduct, and most returned within two years or left their assignment to live temporarily with one of the few African American families in the area. J. A. W., age twelve, was sent to South Cedar, Kansas, where after a year he boarded with a black family named Wilson. The Children's Aid Society records indicate that "the colored people, some of them, report him a bad boy. Mrs. Wilson says he is a good boy." Within seven weeks, he was returned to the orphanage. W. F. L. went to Iowa in 1880. Ten years later, he wanted to know if his family was still alive. As late as 1925, he still was writing to the asylum to inquire about his family. The records showed that his father was an alcoholic and that his parents were separated when he was admitted in 1872. (Evidently, the orphanage did not divulge this information, and one can only imagine the pain of a middle-aged man wondering if he had a family or not.) C. B. went to Leonardville, Kansas. Reports indicated that he adjusted well, a remarkable change for one who entered the asylum as a "profane little fellow." C. A. W. was sent to Kansas in 1887, but the twelve-year-old lost several toes when a farmer banished him to a cornfield in freezing weather. The Children's Aid Society sent him to the poor farm, but he left there to live with William Allen, a man of color, in Holton, Kansas. At age sixteen, the dishonest boy was returned to New York. One child, A. E., was sent to the West, partly because he no longer was considered white. He was supposedly adopted as an infant, but "as he grew older it became apparent that he had colored blood in his veins." He entered the Colored Orphan Asylum at age seven.[30]

The West was a dumping ground for children that the orphanage basically found unmanageable. They admitted in the annual report for 1870 that some children were so tainted with moral depravity that it was extremely difficult to bring about a change in their behavior.

> Although not of this class known as reformatory institutions, still there are many received-infants in years but old in sin. [These children are] depraved in taste, and hardened by the continual contact of evil. If the moral taint can be effaced and even a portion of these fitted for usefulness, there is cause for much thankfulness, even with the discouragements presenting of occasional cases of misconduct. These however, are not frequent in proportion to numbers sent out, and may often be attributed to some unfortunate circumstance of life.

The managers faced the awesome task of taking children afflicted with many social problems and trying to provide them with moral guidance and an education "beyond the simplest element." A persisting problem was their inability or unwillingness to see beyond the common belief of innate Negro inferiority. They admitted that blacks possessed "disadvantages peculiar to their race, [and therefore] more certainly cannot be expected of them." These "disadvantages" the managers believed were caused not by poverty but by nature and evolution. Like many of this period, they accepted the belief that Anglo-Saxons were superior in intellectual attainments and that Negroes, as a race, were further back on the evolutionary scale.[31]

Despite efforts at reforms, the managers found indenturing to be impractical. By the end of the nineteenth century, reformers concluded that children were too immature to be sent long distances away from an orphanage that for many was the only home they knew. Additionally, many were often separated from siblings who were left behind in the institution or indentured elsewhere. Ellen Simpson cried whenever she thought about her brother, not knowing where he was indentured. "Every now and then when I am feeling real bad, I . . . say 'o Sammy, I want you.' Do you think I shall ever see or hear from him again?" Since their indentures ended nine months apart, with Ellen in Oneida, New York, and Sammy in Rutherford, New Jersey, it is not known if they were reunited. Sadly, the asylum made little effort to keep twelve-, fourteen-, or sixteen-year-old children informed about the location of siblings.[32] A 1923 law ended indenturing for children.

Early in its existence, the COA would try to keep children in the institution instead of sending them out as indentures. Later, promising children would be sent to Hampton Institute or Tuskegee Institute to study to be teachers. Bright youngsters were singled out for special consideration. The executive committee recommended in 1859 that four youngsters, Benjamin and Joseph Bowen, Sarah Brown, and Ann Eliza Hinton, remain in the asylum: "being children of uncommon promise it is hoped some arrangement may be made for their advancement." The fate of Sarah Brown is unknown. Her mother died in childbirth; her father was a respectable basketmaker in Nyack, a town near New York City. Despite his skilled position, a rarity among African

American men, he was unable to care for Sarah and her two sisters, who were admitted on December 23, 1843. Ann Eliza Hinton, a half-orphan, became an assistant teacher in the institution in 1852. A fourteen-year-old in charge of the infant school, she had the children's affection, "while she maintained unfaltering discipline." Her plans to enroll at Oberlin College were cancelled when a cold she caught in 1858 led to consumption. Near death, Ann told the nurse, "I am going home. I feel happy. I did not know I could feel so happy." On May 24, 1859, she "died in the faith." Benjamin and Joseph Bowen were admitted February 10, 1846, after their mother died of West India fever. Joseph was apprenticed to William Hodges, his uncle, on October 22, 1852, as a painter. Benjamin was staying with Anna Shotwell, the institution's secretary, who procured a position for him in England to learn a machinist's trade. A few days before sailing, Benjamin "was ungrateful enough to leave without [her] approbation." He ended up living with his uncle in Williamsburg (now part of Brooklyn), New York. Perhaps the fear of going to a foreign country, far removed from his family, caused him to abscond. Eight boys, four under the age of twelve, were learning the shoemaking business at the asylum. A trusty boy operated the steam boiler, and an older girl was in charge of the nursery. They were learning skills that the managers believed would bode well for them in the future.[33]

The vast majority of children had little hope of learning a trade, despite the inclination of some for mechanical skills. Institutional prejudice among tradesmen represented "an almost impassable barrier." The difficulty of gaining acceptance from white tradesmen was reflected in the 1850 census, which indicated that the majority of New York City's blacks were in menial positions and that skilled tradesmen were rare. For example, the census listed one African American blacksmith, three jewelers, one gunsmith, and only two mechanics. This blatant discrimination would continue for years, as most labor unions refused to integrate.[34]

In brief, the majority of children were indentured, but most failed to complete their assignments, at a cost of self-esteem and loss of stipend money, which eventually was used by the institution to pay for bills or to aid less fortunate individuals, such as John Dolan.

3

Disaster and Rebirth, 1855-63

All deaths are occasions for sadness, but some cause more grief than others. The 1853 passing of longtime Colored Orphan Asylum supporter Anson G. Phelps was an instance for lamentation. Phelps was president of the New-York State Colonization Society for twelve years and a prominent merchant. That institution eulogized him by noting that "the heathen, the pioneers of western population, the blind [and] the children of Africa have lost a friend and benefactor." The Rev. George Prentiss cautioned that "tears will trickle down the sable cheeks of scores of liberated Africans [in Liberia] when they learn that [he] who helped to purchase their freedom . . . is no longer among the living!" Phelps, who earned a fortune as a metal trader and merchant, provided in his will fifty thousand dollars to establish a theological department in a Liberian college. A timely thousand dollars was bequeathed to the COA.[1] Another setback for the institution was the resignation of Mary Murray, co-founder of the organization in 1837. Without any specific explanation, she informed the board of managers in April 1854, "in resigning my connection with you I need hardly express the warm interest I shall continue to feel in the objects of your care and your responsibility, or the unmingled satisfaction I have had on being associated with you."[2]

The Colored Orphan Asylum suffered a major blow on September 27, 1854, when tragedy struck many New Yorkers, some of whom were friends of the asylum. The passenger ship *Arctic* collided with the British steamer *Cleopatra* in severe fog. While 108 survived, a watery grave was the fate of several hundred prominent New Yorkers, including Mahlon Day, a founder of the *New York Sun* in 1832, former adviser to the Colored Orphan Asylum, and publisher of many of their earlier annual reports. His wife, Mary, a manager of the institution until 1852, also perished, along with their daughter. Mahlon Day's will stated that "the interest and income thereof" from the sale of real estate should benefit his niece Phebe Ann Crane "during her natural life," with the funds bequeathed to the orphanage upon her death. She died in 1857, and the Colored Orphan Asylum was a thousand dollars richer. The managers used the bequest to purchase real estate in New York City, a venture that would lead them eventually to purchase mortgages on houses and invest in railroads and other major corporations. As with all tragedies, the spirit moves forward in the hopes that tomorrow will bring gentler news. Financial crisis, deaths, and exotic admissions would make 1855 a bittersweet year for the overworked managers and staff of the Colored Orphan Asylum. Two prominent managers died six days apart in 1856. They were Ann Jay and her sister Maria Jay Banyer, the daughters of John Jay, the first chief justice of the U.S. Supreme Court. Both generously gave to the Colored Orphan Asylum as "a friend"; Anna anonymously donated to the institution five thousand dollars when the fledging asylum most needed funds. Ann died on November 13, at the age of seventy-three. A firm believer in philanthropy, Ann gave to charity nearly eight thousand dollars annually for the last nine years of her life. She provided one thousand dollars in her will for the orphanage. Samuel Cooke, the rector of St. Bartholomew's Church in New York, eulogized the sisters as witnesses for Jesus Christ. "The world is darker now that their lights are quenched." The rector added that poor widows, children, and missionaries, recipients of their generous grants, pray that others would imitate their charitable giving.[3]

The *Arctic* tragedy foreshadowed the year 1855 as one of highs and lows for the managers. In January, a badly needed legacy of five hundred dollars (a day laborer's salary for two years) was granted to the asylum from the estate of Susan B. Morrison. This good news was undermined by a shocking and potentially devastating assessment in February, when the city presented them with a bill for $2,100. Just over half, $1,200, was due promptly, "to prevent an immediate sale." Distraught, they turned to their adviser William F. Mott, but he was unable to get the authorities to waive the amount. Determined to extricate themselves from this financial burden, the managers issued a public appeal, but in a manner "as not to reproach the public functionaries." A public appeal for aid appeared in the March 3 issue of the *New York Times*. Fortunately, the city cancelled the assessment bill, and a grant from the state legislature of $2,780.18 erased their debts, at least for a short period.[4]

The fluctuating periods of solvency and insolvency pushed the managers to find more sources of revenue and cut expenses whenever possible. Superintendent William Davis was able to save on some food expenses after Ezra Towne, a friend of the institution, agreed to sell them rice, flour, potatoes, Indian meal, salt fish, and other foodstuffs at favorable rates. The Colored Sailor's Home and thirteen individuals contributed a combined $24.38 for the children's Christmas dinner. A spring fair held by the Bridge Street African Wesleyan Church in Brooklyn netted $772.16, after expenses. Other black churches in Brooklyn aided the treasury with donations totaling $4,205.54. The treasurer aggressively sought to have the Seaman's Savings Bank turn over to the asylum the unclaimed deposits of deceased seamen. Additional African American support came in 1856, when a fair brought in a profit of $761.13. Three schoolgirls held a fair and raised $68.77 for the orphanage. More money was received in 1855 than in the previous year, which gave credence to George Templeton Strong's observation that in recent years the upper class had been more generous in their charitable support. He concluded that it was more fashionable to be generous, which he decided was "an indication most encouraging of progress toward social health."[5]

Increased funding was needed to care for the growing institution. Besides the usual admission of neglected and abused children, orphans, and half-orphans, in late 1854 the asylum admitted two African boys. In October, a French ship wrecked off the coast of Long Island. The two boys came to the attention of Mr. and Mrs. James Wright, who, assisted by the captain, brought them to the orphanage to be admitted temporarily as transient boarders. The two Africans, without any knowledge of English or American culture, were viewed as exotic creatures by all in the institution, including the black children and staff, who saw, perhaps for the first time, someone from "darkest" Africa. Dongo, the oldest and reported to be a prince, "was the most ambitious to learn and discovered a remarkably intelligent mind." He was writing and reading within a few months, but the younger child, Kelso, was feeble and died of measles within four months. The managers wanted to place Dongo in a boarding school, where he would be trained as a missionary to return to help "his benighted countrymen." No longer having any one who shared his language and culture and fearful that indentured children were sold when they left the institution, Dongo adamantly refused to go to any school (it is not clear why he did not attend the asylum's school) and threatened suicide if he had to leave the asylum. Finally, a former missionary who spoke his language convinced him that he would not be sold if he left the building. Not reconciled to his new life and suffering from depression, Dongo's desire to return to Africa was honored by the managers.[6]

The managers' intention to train Dongo to be a missionary was reflective of the era: it was the Christian duty of Anglo-Saxons to "civilize" exotic people. It was the managers' desire to make all their charges fervent practitioners of Protestant beliefs that dictated their decision to have them occasionally attend Sunday services at Joel Parker's Bleecker Street Presbyterian Church, at the corner of Fourth Avenue and East Twenty-second Street. On most Sundays, however, religious meetings were held in the institution, which drew members of Henry Belden's church, Broadway Congregational, located at 1104 Broadway. These services had the effect of inspiring some of the older girls and even several officers "to serious reflection and [to become] concern[ed] for their eternal welfare. No excitement . . . prevailed but it is earnestly hoped that good seed has been sown," reported the secretary.[7]

The managers, many of whom were Quakers, eschewed fancy dress and food, but they appreciated comfort. They had gas pipes installed in the building in the fall of 1855, perhaps becoming among the first in the city to improve a building's heating system. A satisfied Anna Shotwell wrote that gas was "promotive of cleanliness and comfort, and as a reduction of labor and care to the officers employed."[8]

Education in the institution was in a state of flux. The managers decided in April to suspend whipping for three months, which improved behavior in School No. 2. The minutes indicated mixed results. Many children entered the asylum without knowledge of the alphabet, let alone possessing reading or writing skills. The children received no more than about six years of education before they were indentured or returned to family or friends. It was reported in April that the reading level in School No. 1 was unsatisfactory; geography was well recited, and spelling and vocabulary showed improvement. "Grammar recitation as an effect of memory creditable, writing much neglected," reported the teacher. Students in School No. 2 performed well in reading, spelling, and arithmetic up to long division. The infant school showed success in reading, spelling, and the multiplication tables. A superintendent was needed to take over the supervision of schools and teachers and to write reports, and one was hired in 1857 at four hundred dollars per year. The children who attended the asylum school learned in a well-ventilated, heated environment. Donations of books enhanced their reading interest, and they encountered informal learning from managers who had traveled widely in the eastern United States and western Europe. The public schools for black children in Manhattan paled in comparison. The description of the six colored schools ranked with some of the worst in the city's history. Children had to learn in neighborhoods described as "degraded," "vicious," or "full of filth and vice." Colored School No. 6 at Broadway, near Thirty-seventh Street, had "four feet of water in the cellar" during rainy periods. In contrast, the *Anglo African Magazine* described Manhattan's white schools as "splendid, almost palatial with manifold comforts, convenience and elegancies."[9]

In 1856, the managers celebrated their first twenty years of existence. Surely during the preceding years, they must have had periods of doubt that they would last for two decades. Anna Shotwell looked back on twenty years and noted a pronounced a shift in public opinion. "Hitherto the managers found it expedient to urge [our] claims . . . in the annual report; but they now feel that the institution can no longer be considered experimental, and that by its successful operation, it has gained the confidence and approval of the public." This she attributed to God, who "did not permit them a barrel of meal to waste, or the cruse of oil to fail." This sentiment reflected Shotwell's optimism, but the Colored Orphan Asylum would be forced by adverse circumstances to continue well into the twentieth century to solicit the public's confidence, approval, and finances.[10]

The running of an institution with children from diverse backgrounds would tax the patience and child-care skills of teachers and staff alike. Corporal punishment was a topic that sparked internal debate throughout the existence of the Colored Orphan Asylum. The managers agonized over whether it should be administered, and if so, what manner was preferable. They discussed whether it was better to use the rod or to place children in closets as fit punishment. The minutes for December 1857 indicated that the managers decided to discontinue whipping unless absolutely unavoidable. Only the superintendent, matron, or head teacher was to apply corporal punishment to the older children in School No. 1. The superintendent had jurisdiction over the boys, and the matron was authorized to whip girls for house offenses. The head teacher could whip girls for offenses committed in the classroom. In a "humane" gesture, they noted that "no children are to be shut up [in seclusion] to exceed two hours." Some children, especially the younger ones, probably dreaded staying in a dark locked closet more than a few swipes of a belt or razor strop. The teachers' complaints about taking care of children outside of school hours were a source of contention that contributed to discipline problems. Not unlike modern teachers who resent lunch-room duty or hall patrol, the asylum's teachers wanted relief from "a laborious and exposing duty." Their complaints were answered when the managers gave this responsibility to a man in the shoe shop and a woman in the sewing room.[11]

As pressing as the discipline issue was, the managers were constantly confronted with the perils of proper financing. Funds from the city, donations from the black community, and legacies from friends, supporters, and deceased managers generally were not enough to keep them financially solvent. In 1857, the managers faced a deficit; this time it amounted to $2,854.39, primarily because of a Central Park assessment and the grading of Fifth Avenue. The magnificent park was still under construction, and even though it was nearly a mile away, the city expected nearby residents to help with the expenses. They ended the year 1858 with $4,256.01 of debt, in part because the city assessed them $371 for Central Park and $2,642.29 for grading, paving, and installing sewers on Fifth Avenue. The following year, their assessment for Central Park and Fifth Avenue totaled $4,422. Public appeals to aid the orphanage were printed free of charge in the New York papers: the *Times, Tribune, Sun, Evening Post, Express,* and *Journal of Commerce.* Financial deficits remained a constant irritant to the managers. It was such a nuisance in 1859 that the matron Jane McClelland suggested that the workers "subscribe the value of two weeks labor towards its liquidation." Most of the staff complied, which reduced the debt by eighty-four dollars. As in past years, the economic needs of the asylum taxed the limited resources of the ladies, who faced unpaid bills amounting to $2,591.27 as of December 1, 1860. The dire financial situation forced the managers to lower salaries by 6 percent. The staff's acquiescence was considered "truly gratifying to the [finance] committee." In the annual report the ladies again appealed for more generous funding to cover the cost of repairs, salaries, fuel, clothing, and other expenses. They cited themselves as standing nearly alone in helping the colored race. Anna Shotwell commented, "but when it is remembered that the colored people are excluded from most lucrative employment, that little encouragement is given to raise their condition, and that a small comparative amount is afforded to relieve their distress . . . may we not hope that this appeal will awaken attention to the subject, and that the claims of the colored orphan will be remembered?"[12]

The appeal, while earnest, overlooked some important considerations. First, it dismissed the efforts of the black community to support the orphanage consistently since its founding with money and volunteer work. This was in large part because of James McCune Smith's prominence as the orphanage's physician and his role as an active liaison to this community. While they could not make a large dent in the asylum's deficit, black New Yorkers, not unmindful of the ladies' efforts to save their children, responded with their meager funds. Members of Brooklyn's Bridge Street African Methodist Wesleyan

Church, Manhattan's Shiloh Presbyterian and St. Philip's Episcopal churches, and the residents of the Colored Sailors' Home gave donations in the late 1850s. Ten dollars came "from a lady who saw the children going to church." James McCune Smith gave two dollars, "a donation of drugs at different times, also $3 to purchase apples for hospital children." Proceeds from an 1860 colored fair in Brooklyn yielded $1,112.03 for the managers, in addition to $11.37 contributed by the black crew members of the steamer *Plymouth Rock*, and $36.08 came from the parishioners of St. Philip's Episcopal Church. In 1861, the black community was equally supportive. St. Philip's Church collected $48.65, Shiloh Presbyterian Church added $48.89, the Society for the Promotion of Education Among Colored People contributed $45, and Jane Francis, a child in the orphanage, gave one dollar. Following tradition, James McCune Smith donated two barrels of apples as well as medicine. Jacob Day donated two dollars; Charles Reason, the principal of Colored School No. 6, donated $5.50; and a collection in Colored Schools Nos. 1–5 added $33.36 to the asylum's treasury.[13]

Second, Shotwell's words gave the mistaken impression that the African American community had no or little interest in their advancement as a group, and, more significantly, that they lacked refinement and intelligence. Unfortunately, the white women were dismissive of the African American community and displayed a woeful lack of cultural sensitivity. The year 1862 began on a promising note, when African Americans in Brooklyn and Manhattan raised $1,464 at a fair. This so pleased the managers that they wrote in the annual report that the fair "was carried out on strictly mercantile principles. The articles were selected with taste and judgment; an appropriate location secured for their sale on Broadway; a moderate price charged; correct change given; raffling and other species of lottery avoided." While the writer believed that her praise was well directed, it was just the opposite. The organizers of the fair were not children who needed praise for their ability to make the correct change. The managers would never have made such condescending and patronizing comments about a successful "white" fair. It is not known if James McCune Smith or any other race leaders challenged these remarks. Another fair organized by the black community netted $14.64 in profits. The Colored Sabbath School of St. Philip's Church raised $3.30, and the Ladies' Emancipation Society of Scotland contributed $24.20. The managers would have better understood the community had they read important African American publications such as the *Anglo African Magazine*. Two important pieces published in New York's *Anglo African Magazine* in 1859 expressed a concern for self-betterment. Frances Ellen Watkins (later Frances Ellen Watkins Harper), an antislavery poet, stated in "Our Greatest Want" that her people needed "not gold, silver, talent or genius, but true men and true women . . . whose hearts are the homes of a high and lofty enthusiasm." She urged the black population to use their money and talents to serve the cause of humanity in the struggle for justice and equality. J. M. H. Freeman called upon African Americans to avoid negative influences and to achieve self-respect and self-reliance. He argued that too many young people were victims of self-hatred. "The great want of the free colored race . . . is not science, but self apprecia-tion, not the higher mathematics, but a higher manhood." While one may argue with both of these theses, it was clear that the black commu-nity sought to aid itself and that Anna Shotwell misrepresented or misunderstood the willingness of this community to do just that.[14]

Finally, Shotwell's contention that blacks were excluded from lucra-tive employment unwittingly indicted influential Quakers and others who openly abhorred slavery and racial bigotry. While it was true that the managers preferred to have children indentured out of urban areas to avoid temptation and vice, they made no effort to get their influen-tial advisers, who were industrialists, bankers, merchants, entrepre-neurs and businessmen, to aid promising boys as indentures or to provide training and jobs for those young men after they had com-pleted their indentures. Certainly, some of them had the intelligence and strong work ethic to succeed as clerks or apprentices. Instead, they kept insisting in their annual reports that they were training their charges for their life's work as domestics and farm boys, with rare exceptions later sent to Hampton or Tuskegee for industrial training.

While the issues of running the orphanage from day to day, along with the immense and perpetual problem of raising funds, would con-tinue, the issue of slavery and the coming of the Civil War would have a monumental effect on the institution. Although the managers had vowed to refrain from joining forces with any political faction (so as to not antagonize potential donors), they were tacitly allied with the antislavery group. Some of their male relatives belonged to the various antislavery organizations, including in earlier years the New York Manumission Society. Anna Shotwell and other managers supported the abolition of slavery. This sentiment gave them a great interest in admitting enslaved or recently freed slave children into the institution. From 1837 to the eve of the Civil War, approximately thirty children came from an enslaved background. Six children, out of eight hundred to one thousand slaves owned by Estevan Santa Cruz de Oviedo, in Cuba, were admitted on February 23, 1857. The children were the offspring of Oviedo and six different mothers. A guardian, Juan Elichery, brought them to the institution to be educated. He agreed to pay sixty dollars annually for each child to cover board, tuition, and clothing. (This was a significant amount, as boarding children's parents paid twenty-four dollars annually.) The children did not remain in the institution very long, as the severe climate change adversely affected their health. Two died of scarlatina (scarlet fever) within weeks of admission, and the others were returned to Elichery within seven weeks of their arrival. It is not known how Oviedo had learned of the institution, but perhaps Elichery, a Brooklyn resident, had informed him. Mary Ella Williams, a six-year-old who was admitted on June 26, 1856, after Nathaniel Parker Willis, a journalist, poet, and editor, raised eight hundred dollars to purchase a mother of two children from a lewd master. "His slaves' sense of virtue and propriety [incensed] him against her and led him to sell her for revenge but God has overruled it for good," comments the admission record, cryptically. After the death of the mother, Mrs. Willis brought Mary to the asylum. The fate of her sibling is unknown. These admissions were not mentioned in the annual report that was sent to elected officials and made available to the general public. Obviously, the managers preferred not to have the public believe that the asylum was a sanctuary for runaway slaves or recently emancipated ones.[15]

It was this concern that prompted the managers to avoid commenting directly on John Brown's ill-fated attack on the federal arsenal at Harpers Ferry, Virginia (now West Virginia), in 1859. The excitement over the attack inspired Anna Marie Piner, a thirteen-year-old indenture, to write to the institution. For inexplicable reasons, given the managers' eschewing of politics, they published her letter in the twenty-third annual report. Anna was indentured on May 17, 1859, to a colored man, Henry Gardon of Philadelphia. On December 1, 1859, she wrote to "my dear young friends," expressing her viewpoint on Brown's October 16 aborted effort to arm slaves to rebel against their owners. She asked, "do you think it was wise for him to lay down his life for these slaves? Why did not he do what he intended and been done with it?" Acting as a military strategist, she stated, "he ought not to let the train gone on, and then he could have done what he wanted and fled to the mountains." She added that the people in Philadelphia were against Captain John E. Cook for confessing but that others who remained silent were to be executed anyway on December 16.[16]

James McCune Smith had no overriding reason to keep silent on the Harpers' Ferry situation. For one, it was a sensational story that helped to widen the division between the slaveholders and abolitionists. Many considered Brown a fanatical deranged person; others viewed him as a martyr to the cause of human equality. Besides being a well-respected physician with a private practice and pharmacy in Manhattan, Smith was an active abolitionist who became the first African American to chair a political convention: the Radical Abolitionist convention, which met in Syracuse, New York, in June 1855. Smith broke with those abolitionists who advocated moral suasion as the only effective way to eradicate slavery; instead, he joined with other radicals to organize the New York City Abolitionist Society to end slavery "by means of the Constitution *or otherwise*." Smith openly embraced violence, if necessary, as a justified means to destroy slavery in the American South. He added that it would be necessary for men of color to knock down bigoted whites before they would "hug us as men and brothers." Undoubtedly, the managers privately disapproved of Smith's radicalism, but, to their credit, they did not make an issue of his views. As a radical abolitionist, James McCune Smith denounced William Lloyd Garrison and others for their unwillingness to accept violence as a weapon in the fight to destroy American slavery. The physician wrote in the July 30, 1859, *Weekly Anglo African* newspaper that a forthcoming slave rebellion meant that "no power of the tyrant, no chain of the oppressor, no skill or craft of the diplomat, can [stop it]. Come on it will, and come on it must."[17]

Like Frederick Douglass, James McCune Smith mourned the death of William Jay, the second son of Chief Justice John Jay, who was an author, judge, and moral reformer who helped to establish the New York City Anti-Slavery Society. Unlike some of the asylum's abolitionist friends, William Jay, an adviser to the orphanage, opposed the colonization of freed slaves to Liberia and gradual emancipation and insisted that there be "immediate emancipation or continued slavery." Frederick Douglass eulogized him with a moving tribute. "I wear the hated complexion which [he] never hated," noted the black leader. Douglass added that "the black man should weep, when the black man's friend is no more!"[18]

The Civil War and the Draft Riots

The election of Abraham Lincoln in November 1860 pushed the nation closer to violent separation, which finally occurred when the newly formed Confederate States of America fired upon Fort Sumter in Charleston's harbor, in April 1861. Although the managers eschewed political affiliations, Anna Shotwell's abolitionist sentiments could not publicly remain silent. She wrote in the annual report that "war with its attendant calamities, is now absorbing the attention and interest of the community, and is threatening to revolutionize this great Republic; foreshadowing, as is believed, the liberty of the captive and the freedom of the oppressed."[19]

The four-year Civil War was America's bloodiest war to date, killing 618,000 and maiming hundreds of thousands. It would have a tremendous effect upon the Colored Orphan Society. About a dozen children would enter the orphanage either because their fathers had died in combat or because the fathers' prolonged absence caused a hardship on the mother, who was forced to seek relief in the asylum. Some of the former asylum boys would wear the Union blue in combat, and one, James Henry Gooding, would achieve national prominence. The war's greatest effect upon the asylum, however, was its total destruction by a raging mob in July 1863.[20]

The Civil War, while not cited in the minutes or annual report in 1861, came to the attention of the managers in a personal way in 1862. At least nine former boys were serving in the war. One of the unusual indentures was Charles Henry Thompson, a name he shared with three others in the asylum, who was an indenture at Camp Hernanary. He wrote to Superintendent Davis on February 22, 1862, that he was earning seventeen dollars a month and board working for Sgt. Joseph D. Osborne of the New Jersey Fourth Regiment Volunteers. Charles described his duties as washing clothes, caring for a horse, cutting wood, and cleaning officers' boots. He described the capture of two enemy soldiers. His assessment of the war would prove incorrect. "I think the war may be over with befor[e] five months is ended; we are going into it pretty strong; they will find themselves whip[p]ed before long I am thinking." Evidently, Charles wanted to be there when the Confederates were beaten, because he enlisted in company D of the Twentieth United States Colored Regiment on December 4, 1863.[21]

Although this young indenture could witness the war, the nation was not ready to accept black recruits as soldiers until January 1, 1863, when Abraham Lincoln's Emancipation Proclamation called for their recruitment. Before the war ended in April 1865, nearly two hundred thousand African Americans, slave and freed, would help to preserve the Union and to destroy American slavery. The efforts of the Union League Club (which included some supporters of the Colored Orphan Asylum) led to the formation of the Twentieth, Twenty-sixth, and Thirty-first United States Colored Troops in New York State.[22]

Lewis Henry White enlisted in the Twentieth Regiment on November 2, 1863. He wrote Superintendent Davis from Camp Parapet in New Orleans on July 10, 1864: "when I was 14 and under your care never did I think I would have all this hardship to go through. Ah I have a heavy burden on my shoulders which I will not be able to get off in 3 years time unless I die or get shot. I am 4 sargent in D company." Lewis, who had not yet been in battle, added, "I hope we will all live to see our homes once more. Give my kind respecks to . . . my kind and benevolent school teacher [Miss Young] who worked so hard to give me a good common school education." Lewis had just turned eighteen when he wrote this letter and served unharmed until the war ended. Other orphanage boys known to serve in the war were Charles Taylor, James W. Slater, Charles H. Thompson, Hannibal Francis, Edward Benjamin, Frank Kipp, Edward Daniel Hall, and James Henry Gooding.[23]

Edward Daniel Hall's military experience could not have been anticipated a few years earlier, when he was returned from his indenture for stealing money from his employer. Efforts to reform the fourteen-year-old failed. Superintendent William Davis complied with Edward's request to send the youthful offender to the House of Refuge for rehabilitation. At seventeen, in the fall of 1863, he joined the army. He wrote "a reminiscence of my life after leaving the colored orphan asylum," which was published in 1866, in the asylum's thirtieth annual report. He reported that he was assigned to the Army of the Potomac and witnessed every battle from their departure from the Rapidan River until Robert E. Lee's surrender at Appomattox Court House, in Virginia. Edward was evidently extremely fair complexioned, because he wrote that a colonel had complained to the general that Edward was a descendant of Africans. His name did not appear in a search of soldiers in the United States Colored Troops, but an Edward Daniel Hall is listed with a white regiment, the Twenty-third New York Infantry, which was assigned to the Army of the Potomac. Edward suffered a minor flesh wound, and he wrote that "I have had balls come so uncomfortably near me that they gave out disagreeable effluvia."[24]

The most famous black Civil War soldier was James Henry Gooding, who was born a slave in North Carolina on August 28, 1838. Henry's freedom was purchased by James M. Gooding (who may have been his father), who brought him to New York, where he gave him manumission papers. James was admitted into the asylum on September 11, 1846, and indentured in 1850 to Albert Westlake, but he left his employ on July 15, 1852. His personal history from 1852 until he joined the army became a work of fiction. In 1991, Virginia M. Adams edited *On the Altar of Freedom: A Black Soldier's Civil War Letters*, an examination of the extraordinary forty-eight letters that Gooding wrote to *The Mercury* in New Bedford, Massachusetts, between March 3, 1863, and February 22, 1864.

For unknown reasons, Gooding hid both his slave background and his years in the orphanage. He fabricated a history that had him born in Troy, New York. This misinformation was cited in his seaman's papers, his marriage certificate, and military records. Understandably, Adams could not locate records for the Gooding family in either the New York State census or local upstate records. She was struck by his familiarity with the classics, history, and literature, and while she could not locate his school records, it is clear that he was educated in the asylum. Gooding worked as a seaman from 1856 to early 1860 and then again in 1861, in both the Indian and Pacific Oceans. He was described by a contemporary as "a person of intelligence and cultivation much in advance of a majority of his race," and indeed, it could be added, much in advance of many whites of the period. The erudite Gooding wrote six poems while at sea that were eventually published. His most famous writing, a December 28, 1863, letter to President Lincoln, was prompted by the military paying black soldiers less than their white counterparts. Gooding, who had joined the Fifty-fourth Massachusetts Regiment, the first colored regiment raised in the North, asked for equal pay for black men, some of whom had known "the cruelties of the iron heel of oppression [of slavery]. . . . [Pay us] as American *soldiers*, not as menial hirelings." He asked his commander in chief: "are we *soldiers*, or are we *labourers*?" It is not known if Lincoln saw Gooding's letter, but the government decided in 1864 to equalize salaries, some eighteen months after men of the Fifty-fourth Massachusetts Regiment refused to accept an unequal salary. During the Battle of Morris Island at Fort Wagner (dramatized in the film *Glory*), near Charleston, South Carolina, Gooding heroically planted the regimental flag. (The asylum records mistakenly noted that he was killed during the battle.) Gooding was wounded in February 1864 at the Battle of Olustee and was taken prisoner. He died six months later in the infamous Confederate prison camp at Andersonville, Georgia, which was so notorious for its mistreatment of Union soldiers that its commander was executed after the war ended.[25]

Tranquility in the asylum and in the city would soon end: the Draft Riots from July 13 through July 16, 1863, engulfed the city in mob violence against policemen, abolitionists, and the most sought after target, African Americans. The rage of the mob did not spare the Colored Orphan Asylum. Irish immigrants made up about a quarter of New York City's population. Economically, they were at the bottom, mired in poverty and held in contempt by the Protestant white elite. George Templeton Strong, a representative of the elite class, viewed the Irish as "brutal, base [and] cruel."[26]

The Irish despised the Negro, with whom they often competed for the most menial positions. Tensions between the groups often led to violent clashes. On August 4, 1862, four hundred Irishmen attempted to burn a factory that employed black women and children but were prevented from doing so by the police. The *New York Times* urged Catholic priests to admonish their Irish parishioners to behave as better Christians. Poverty forced many Irish to serve in the Union army because they, unlike wealthier persons, could not hire a substitute for three hundred dollars. Often drafted, they served and died in disproportionate numbers. Several Irish firemen resented being drafted, because they believed that their service in the militia exempted them from the draft. They went on a rampage and destroyed the draft office in Manhattan's nineteenth ward. It was falsely believed that the riot was precipitated by Negro strikebreakers who had taken stevedore jobs. Recent research indicates that only three rioters were identified as longshoremen and that they were not known to have engaged in antiblack violence.[27]

The mob pillaged the mayor's home; attempted to destroy the office of the *Tribune*, an antislavery newspaper; and tried to kill prominent African Americans including Henry Highland Garnet, the pastor of Shiloh Presbyterian Church. Superintendent of Police Kennedy, "a man of powerful physique," was so savagely beaten that he became "disfigured as not to be recognizable." According to the eyewitness Charles Chapin, "Negroes [were] hunted . . . as if they were wild beasts." Chapin reported that on the third day of rioting, he spotted a black man trying to get on a ferry to Long Island. "For once I saw a black man turn white from fear and as I sank my hands on his shoulder he sank to his knees with the piteous cry of 'for God's sake massa don't kill me.'" Chapin escorted the frightened man to safety.[28]

The mob was so intent on killing blacks that neither gender nor age mattered. The Colored Orphan Asylum became a target because the majestic building underscored the success of blacks over the Irish. The children had clean linen to sleep on, food was plentiful, and meals were regular. The Irish complained that the wives and daughters of New York's swells provided them with the comforts of life. There were 233 children in the asylum on that fateful day, July 13, when the mob came. After looting bedding, furniture, dishes, and any usable item they could carry, they soaked the floors with an inflammable substance. Just before the attack, a light-complexioned man (later identified as James McCune Smith's son) mingled with the mob and warned Superintendent Davis of their designs. The assembled children were asked by a teacher, "do you believe, that almighty God, can deliver you from a mob?" They were told to pray for God's protection as they silently left the building. Mary Murray noted that only five employees—the nurse, a teacher, a shoemaker, the superintendent, and the matron—remained in the building with the children. But when they exited "the sight of a helplessness so absolute stirred in the hearts of the rioters a feeling akin to pity, cursing was turned to blessing and then a hush felled over the crowd, the seething mass fell back upon itself, and a passage was opened for the children. It seemed as though a mighty hand was holding them in control." This may have been an invented scene suggested for its effect on a sympathetic city that believed that the hand of Providence had saved the children and that they should aid the rebuilding of the orphanage. An Irishman on the street was severely attacked for telling the rioters, "if there is a man among you with a heart within come and help these poor children." The children managed to get to the police station on Thirty-fifth Street, nearly a half-mile distance, where they were left uncomfortably close to incarcerated rioters. Thomas H. Barnes, who wrote an unpublished autobiography in 1924, recalled that the "prisoners would strike at [the children] through the bars of the doors. They would let the water run on the floor, compelling us to stand in the filthy water from their cells. It was nearly twenty-four hours before we got anything to eat." Barnes praised a German woman who brought in bread and meat "secreted in her clothing." This she did on several occasions, which

Barnes believed would have led to her demise had she been discovered by the rioters. The frightened children remained for three days, fearing that the mob would break into the police station and massacre them. On July 16, the asylum's children left for Blackwell's Island under the guarded protection of forty policemen and fifty Zouaves carrying fixed bayonets. They were placed on boats that took them to Blackwell's Island (Roosevelt Island), where confusion reigned: approximately a thousand refugees were on the island searching for lost relatives and fearful that rioters would board boats and storm their sanctuary. Blackwell's Island housed the insane, criminals, and paupers, and the sight of them provided the children with unexpected lessons about the vicissitudes of life.[29]

Before the rampage ended, many African Americans were viciously beaten and lynched regardless of gender, age, or race. One victim, Peter Heuston, a Mohawk Indian, was killed because rioters thought he was a black American. Seven-year-old Joseph Reed was beaten with sticks

Destruction of the Fifth Avenue building during the Draft Riots, July 13, 1863. (Collection of The New-York Historical Society.)

and cobblestones before John F. McGovern, a fireman, rescued him. The boy was cared for by a German woman, but he died of his wounds a few days later. Irish women who were married to black men were viciously beaten for "crossing" over. A white woman, a Mrs. Derickson, died a week after receiving a severe beating.[30]

George Templeton Strong condemned "the unspeakable infamy of the nigger persecution," which he deemed worse than the "Jew hunting of the middle ages."[31] In Boston, the abolitionist William Lloyd Garrison wrote to Oliver Johnson, co-editor of the *National Anti-Slavery Standard*, of his fear that the riot may spread to other cities: "the whole North is volcanic." He added, "my heart bleeds to think of the poor unoffending colored people . . . outraged, plundered, murdered by the demons in human shape."[32]

There were many acts of heroism during the rioting. One of the most remarkable was rendered by an unidentified eight-year-old girl, who saved the asylum's Bible before the children evacuated the building. The Bible is now in the possession of the New-York Historical Society. An Irish family, at great peril to their own safety, hid a dozen blacks in their home for several days until a police escort could take the frightened souls to the station house. A six-year-old boy became separated from the fleeing asylum children. An Irish woman who worked in the asylum for eleven years took him to the home of Allen Griffin, the colored shoemaker at the asylum. Eight black women on Thompson Street vowed not to be sacrificial lambs for the mob's blood lust. They boiled a mixture of water, soap, and ashes to pour on anyone who attempted to break into their homes. The aftermath of the riot saw the dispersal of about five thousand African Americans, who fled Manhattan for the New Jersey swamps or to the black community of Weeksville, in Brooklyn. Manhattan's black population declined to 9,943 in 1865, from a high of 12,574 in 1860.[33]

Five days after the riot ended, New York City's merchants organized a relief committee to aid black victims. Assistance was provided for 6,392 persons who lost property during the three days of rioting. On August 22, Henry Highland Garnet and seventeen prominent blacks wrote and thanked the merchants. "You bound up our wounds and poured in the oil and wine of Christian kindness and took care of us. You also comforted the aching hearts of our widowed sisters and soothed the sorrows of orphan children."[34] The children were temporarily housed at Blackwell's Island until early fall. A girl died there of consumption on October 7. Two boys who disobeyed instructions not to swim in the East River drowned.[35]

African Americans in New York and throughout the nation quickly came to the aid of the distressed ladies. Maria Barnes contributed $225.25; Three hundred dollars came from San Francisco, and $126 was raised by six women in St. Louis. The New York Merchants' Relief Committee contributed one thousand dollars, and $1,600 was raised through the efforts of Theodore Roosevelt Sr., the father of the future president and a COA adviser. Six African American churches in Manhattan donated $75 in gold through James McCune Smith.[36]

Outrage over the mob's actions against defenseless people and angry at New York Governor Horatio Seymour's undisguised sympathy for the rioters inspired an individual or individuals to produce a card 5.5 inches in length and 2.75 inches in width, which was printed as a bookmark or as a fundraising item. It read in bold letters, punctuated with capital words:

SACRED

To the Memory of the

COLORED ORPHAN ASYLUM

of

New York

Which was

BURNED TO ASHES JULY, 1863

By a

RUFFIANLY MOB

Who were acknowledged and addressed by

HORATIO SEYMOUR

Governor of New York

As being his

"FRIENDS"

God save the State of New York![37]

The death of African Americans in the riots left surviving family members with no choice but to seek assistance from the orphanage. Sarah, Ann, and Margaret Richards were admitted on October 27, 1863. Their ages and the names of their parents were unknown. L. Kollock, overseer of the poor in Red Bank, New Jersey, informed the asylum that their mother brought them to be boarded by Jane and Elizabeth Jobes but quickly abandoned them. The children were destitute and helpless and had no knowledge if their father was dead or alive. Red Bank law required a year's residence before they could be wards of the community; Kollock concluded that the Colored Orphan Asylum might be able to locate the children's mother or that at least they would be better off there than they would be in New Jersey. Nearly three-year-old Elizabeth Robinson was admitted on November 4, 1867. Her father, Jeremiah Robinson, was killed during the riot when he, dressed as a woman, tried to escape with his wife and a female friend. The mob noticed his beard and their atrocities upon him were "so indecent, they are unfit for publication," noted the Merchants' Relief Committee. The mob killed Robinson and threw his body into the East River. The two women were able to escape to Grand Street, where a ferry took them to Brooklyn. Lewis Yates or Gates was admitted on August 22, 1869. His father was killed in a Brooklyn riot in 1862, when over four hundred Irish assaulted a factory employing African American women and children. The particulars of his demise are unknown.[38]

Indentured children were understandably appalled when they heard about the destruction of their beloved former home. Jane Guise, on the day before her nineteenth birthday, April 17, 1865, wrote Superintendent Davis: "Oh! When I think of our noble asylum burnt to the ground . . . if seems as if my heart would break." She shed tears when she realized that she would never again "walk through the school rooms, sleeping rooms, dining rooms and nurseries, nor the hospital or even the laundry." She viewed the ruins of the asylum and declared that it was "far dearer to me than the handsomest asylum they would possibly build." Sixteen-year-old George Allen McIntyre wrote to Sarah Murray on May 9, 1866, that if he had his way, "terrible indeed would have been the punishment of those hard hearted wretches had it been meted out to them according to my jurisdiction." John Hicks, about twenty-one, wrote to Miss Mary Young, a teacher, on August 29, 1866, that he could not stop crying when he heard about the demise of the asylum. Like Jane Guise, he could not sleep because he would never be able to see again the rooms that had provided so many good times.[39]

At Blackwell's Island, adjacent to Manhattan, a committee of John Campbell, James Roosevelt, Samuel Willets, Benjamin Latham, and Daniel W. James was formed to find a temporary home for the children. In mid-September, they inspected the former home of Hickson Field, a longtime supporter, in the Carmansville section of upper Manhattan. The managers resolved to meet the challenge and rise from the ashes. They took temporary possession of the home on October 9, but it was in disarray. It had been closed for twenty years, with a caretaker living in a few basement rooms. Most of the furniture had been removed; what remained was of "little account." The bowling alley on the grounds was converted into a school. The land occupied thirty acres between 150th and 152nd Streets, facing Broadway. Despite the efforts of the managers to air out the building (weeks before the children's arrival), Thomas Barnes recalled that the air "was poison, foul, with gasses from decay, a veritable pest house." The managers had no choice but to make the old mansion livable. It was costly to find a building large enough to accommodate several hundred children. The managers wanted to rebuild on lots on Fifth Avenue unless the city gave "them a clear deed for the same." Fifth Avenue neighbors, fearing further reprisals, were in strong opposition, which resulted in the orphanage making do at Carmansville until May 1868, when they were able to relocate to their new home, built at 143rd Street and Amsterdam Avenue, in an undeveloped section of Harlem, near the historic home of Alexander Hamilton.[40]

The managers faced the new year of 1864 with a great deal of anxiety. Some of the younger children had been traumatized by the sacking of their home. Less traumatizing but still problematic was the reality of rising operational costs. The ladies were allocated sixty cents a week per child for the maintenance of 180 children, which was "the average number in the asylum as ascertained by the Board as proper subjects for public support." Unfortunately, it cost them in excess of $1.50 per child per week to sustain them while at Blackwell's Island. They requested that the commissioner of the almshouse grant them a dollar per child per week to care for the children on a "rigid economy." Now, at the beginning of 1864, the managers had to care for over two hundred children, ranging in age from two to twelve, in an old building in dire need of repairs. They had already spent $1,346.25 since October 1863 for repairs and $312.50 on the rent for the Carmansville home. Now, in early January 1864, they faced a debt of $1,960.97.[1]

The advisers William F. Mott, Samuel Willets, Christopher R. Roberts, and Daniel W. James met, at a special meeting on January 12, to request compensation from the city for the property destruction during the Draft Riots. They suggested that the managers sell their Fifth Avenue lots and invest the proceeds. By March, the riot claims committee of the Board of Supervisors granted the orphanage $73,089.26— just five dollars less than the managers claimed for damages. Funds could not be disbursed, however, until the state legislature authorized the city comptroller to borrow funds to pay off all the claims. In October, the advisers Theodore Roosevelt Sr., William F. Mott, Christopher R. Robert, and Samuel Willets informed First Directress Rachel Phelps that the comptroller's payment would be in 6 percent "bonds of the city having about 18 years to run, at 3 per cent premium." Although the managers could have held out for a cash payment, the advisers recommended that they accept the comptroller's offer rather than "risk further loss of interest by longer delay although the bonds are barely worth par in the market and must be taken in full payment of all claims for damages." Others, too, inundated the city with damage claims, and eventually the comptroller settled 1,596 claims at a cost of $1,200,609.33.[2]

The managers wanted to build an office and a depot of materials for the institution on the site of their destroyed home, but their plan to rebuild on the Fifth Avenue site was met with opposition from their neighbors, who feared further mob action against the orphanage. In 1865, the city-owned lots were sold by a quit-claim deed and earned a profit of $170,000, after legal fees. (In 1889, the valuable land became the site of the Century Club.) The sale of the Fifth Avenue lots led to some changes. The managers were no longer restricted to admit children only from Manhattan, a stipulation that was binding as long as they remained at the Fifth Avenue location. On the advice of their advisers, the managers used this money to purchase U.S. bonds, New York County bonds, and New York State bonds for $162,247.18. An investment in bonds was a pattern they would use for the rest of their existence as a way to increase their financial portfolio, selling only when they needed funds for emergencies. The city gave them an additional ten thousand dollars under a riot law. The ladies decided to purchase land and erect a new building north of 110th Street, then a little-developed area.[3]

Individuals throughout New York and elsewhere, shocked by the dastardly destruction of the asylum, aided the ladies with their financial support. In 1864, the Ladies Union Bazaar Association, comprising wives of prominent African American men, placed an announcement in the *Liberator* that read: "Driven from their pleasant and comfortable asylum by a wicked unprovoked attack of the ruthless and infuriated mob . . . should not our sympathy for them be doubly increased and more strongly manifested?" The May fair raised $2,200.17, which was used to purchase supplemental clothing for the children. These same women had raised $1,464 in 1862 to benefit the asylum. Chauncey Rose donated twenty thousand dollars from the estate of John Rose, his brother. A fair in Hartford, Connecticut, hosted by three girls added $27.50 to the treasury. One hundred and twenty-nine patrons and life members contributed an additional $3,316.18. Proceeds from wills brought to the treasury $948.39, donors and subscribers contributed $3,533.04, and Charles Francis, a former resident, donated five dollars. "A class of little girls attached to the Presbyterian Church, Cooperstown, NY" gave sixty dollars from the proceeds of a fair. The managers received $3,111.18 from selling the brick from the demolished former home. The annual report for 1864 noted that "adversity has stimulated exertion, and many, who in prosperity were indifferent, have been induced to extend to us a generous support." Still, the financial crunch forced the managers to dismiss several domestic workers, and four teachers now did the work of six.[4]

Under these trying conditions, it was understandable that they refused to accept their adviser Theodore Roosevelt Sr.'s resignation. He changed his mind after the managers reminded him of the contribution of his mother, Margaret Roosevelt, to the development of the institution during its nascent years. However, their pleas were not strong enough to prevent the resignation of Anna Shotwell, a co-founder of the orphanage. The devoted Shotwell had missed only one meeting in twenty-eight years. She was widely respected in New York, and her contacts were highly supportive of the asylum, which made her departure all the more difficult for others to accept. She had been for forty years the public face of the institution; she had also served as secretary for twenty-eight years, which makes it all the more surprising and shocking that her death in 1875 received scanty reference in the minutes and annual report. Younger souls, perhaps in a timeless custom, minimized the sacrifices and contribution of their elders. More devastating was the declining health and death of James McCune Smith, the asylum's attending physician for twenty years. Smith's death in 1865 meant more than the loss of an outstanding physician's services; he was also a major liaison to New York's community of color. His friends and associates provided funding because he was closely associated with the asylum, and he was able to allay their suspicions of white control over black children. It would not be until the 1940s that African American community involvement would again be of significant aid to the managers. Smith was replaced by Dr. William Frothingham, who was described by Thomas Barnes as "rough and gruff," and with him it was "kill or cure." The spacious grounds of Hickson Field's former home encouraged the children to play outside in the woods, where there were stagnant pools and swamps. As Barnes remembered, the children, excited to be away from the confines of their former Fifth Avenue home and Blackwell's Island, explored the woods, which was filled with poison ivy. They foolishly drank water from the stagnant pools, which caused throat problems and typhoid fever.[5]

Frothingham's physician report for the period ending November 30, 1864, indicated that there were forty cases of diarrhea resulting from eating green apples, thirteen cases of remittent fever, thirty cases of eye infection, twenty cases each of whooping cough and intermittent fever, and twenty-five cases of scrofulous infection. The sickness and death of fourteen children led to the physician's recommendation that a good diet would prevent scrofulous diseases. The managers agreed to provide meat five times a week instead of the former three days and "fish one day & beans one day, the latter occasionally boiled with the beef." Frothingham feared that eventually the crowded conditions of the temporary home would "exert an influence in depressing the vital powers of the inmates," a description that was commonly applied to anyone in an institution.[6]

Carmansville and Racial Opposition

The managers adjusted as best as possible under the circumstances to accommodate over two hundred children in a poorly heated house. The rooms on the lower floor remained untidy (an abomination to Quakers), because of a scarcity of water. The dormitories were overcrowded, but the managers lacked sufficient funds to purchase land and buy building materials, which were both at high prices because of the Civil War. Friends of the asylum made clothes for the children "at a time when the high price of all such articles made their purchase a heavy drain upon the Association." Superintendent William Davis caught the managers by surprise when he, disturbed by the confinement at Carmansville, decided to retire to a farm in Michigan.[7] Unfortunately, other problems confronted the managers' patience and the asylum's bank account. The milk cows went dry, so they were slaughtered for meat for the children. Previously, they had watered down the milk to make it last longer. Lack of funds forced the cooks to substitute molasses for supper twice a week. The house was in a "miserable condition." The teachers lacked heat in their rooms. The managers relented and permitted them to have a private fire from Saturday afternoon through Sunday. At other times, the teachers would congregate in the warm dining room.[8]

Again the managers were forced to appeal to the public for charity. They requested in the annual report for 1865 that "past prejudices may be removed, and that this class upon whom still rests the stigma of a long enslaved race, may be admitted into a common brotherhood, if not of social equality, at least of Christian fellowship." Unfortunately, racial prejudice remained a presence in New York, a city with many citizens sympathetic to slavery, a major contributor to the wealth of individual New Yorkers. Racists labeled Republican politicians lustful embracers of miscegenation, much in the same manner that Southerners a hundred years later referred to interracial civil rights activists as being part of a communist plot to destroy America. A satirical sheet, *Black Republican and Office Holder's Journal*, edited by Pluto Jumbo, declared that "some traitors fuse to ride in de same cars wid cullud pussuns. Dem people are disloyal to the Bolition Siety . . . if dey don't like de smell of cullud pussuns, dey hab got to get use to it, and if dey fuse to get use to it, dey must suffer de consequence. . . . De black cars muss be put away, so dat cullud pussons can ride wid white folks." An equally odious publication was *Niggerhead and Blue Law Advocate*, edited by Peter Pecksnipe and allegedly assisted by the agents Henry Ward Beecher, Horace Greeley, Theodore Tilton, Wendell Phillips, and Oliver Johnson, who were all prominent abolitionists. The masthead for this antiabolitionist and negrophobic publication displayed a black man holding up a Ulysses S. Grant–Schuyler Colfax presidential banner while standing on the shoulders of two white men. The paper's motto was "Down With The Constitution. Up With The Nigger. De-voted To Great Moral Ideas Published By The Free Love Society."[9]

Miscegenation was certainly not endorsed by the managers, many of whom were probably personally appalled by the idea of black men sexually embracing white women. Nevertheless, regardless of their personal views on this delicate subject, they were painfully aware of the consequences of racism. In fact, the asylum had initially been founded because of white bigotry, and the aftermath of the Draft Riots affected admission rates. The annual report for 1865 noted that "many entire families, orphaned by the late war, seek our protection." Seventy-four children, a higher-than-usual number, were admitted during the year. As usual, the majority, forty-eight, did not know the alphabet. The crowded conditions at Carmansville affected the children's health; fifty suffered from conjunctivitis because of a lack of water and clean towels. The epidemic was halted when children were taken to the brook to be washed. Twenty-eight children suffered from some form of fever; twelve were afflicted with either diarrhea or dysentery. Eleven children died in 1865, with four succumbing to phthisis pulmonalis, two each to scrofulous cachexia and pneumonia, and one each from phthisis abdominalis, hemorrhaging from the heart, and dysentery.[10]

In 1866, the primary goal of the managers was the acquisition of land for a new building. But first, they opted to lease Hickson Field's property for one year at $2,400, with the asylum responsible for repairs. In May, after selling some stocks, the managers purchased for $45,000 forty-eight lots from 143rd to 144th Streets, between Amsterdam Avenue and Broadway. They started to build but lacked money to finish the building. Funds were so low that children could not attend church, until an emergency expenditure of $172.50, aided by individual contributions from managers, enabled some children to attend church properly dressed in shawls, hats, and caps.[11]

The managers were eager in early 1867 to get out of Carmansville. They feared that the rent would increase beyond the current $2,400 per year, which they considered exorbitant. Managers Mrs. William Onderdonk and Miss Mary Jane Underhill traveled to Albany to lobby the legislature for $100,000 to erect a building, but their efforts proved unsuccessful, as "no encouragement was given that their petition would be favored." The house at Carmansville was in a state of disrepair and difficult to clean. The managers decided that four eleven-and-a-half-year-old girls be kept out of school six months before leaving the asylum to engage in housework. The girls were taught personal cleanliness and given moral and religious instruction. After they were indentured, they were replaced by other girls "of the same age and chosen in the same manner." It was interesting that the managers, who stressed education, were willing to deny the girls six months of formal education to give them practical experience in the work that would dominate their adult lives.[12]

Home to Harlem

Good news came to the managers in May 1868. The nuisance of making do at Carmansville ended with the opening of their new home in Harlem, next to Hamilton Grange, the home of Alexander Hamilton. Their property was situated in a hilly section of Manhattan, with a clear view of the Hudson and Harlem rivers and far removed from the pestilence and filth of lower Manhattan. Here, the health of the children would flourish. Dr. William Frothingham attributed the good health of the house to its high elevation in the Hamilton Heights section of west Harlem. He wrote that it was remarkable that there were "no cases of secondary or tertiary syphilis." The context of this remark is unclear, because syphilis is not cited in any previous physician's reports, either of James McCune Smith or Frothingham. The illnesses were primarily measles (118 cases). The three deaths were one each of measles with capillary bronchitis, measles with pulmonary consumption, and measles with tubercular meningitis (scrofulous infection of the brain). Ironically, the nearly three hundred children arrived in the area nearly four decades before other African Americans left lower Manhattan for the "promised land" of Harlem. The building, designed by Carl Pfeiffer, was built in the Rhenish style, with a mansard roof covered with slate. It was steam heated and had fireproof stairways. The three-story building had a frontage of 234 feet, a depth of 125 feet, and three octagonal towers. The author J. F. Richmond described the view from the observatory as "so rich and extensive that one cannot visit this peerless place and contemplate its saintly character, without feeling himself improved and drawn perceptibly nearer to heaven." A lack of funds only permitted completion of half of the buildings. The superintendent reported that costs had escalated to 12.5 cents a day in 1867, compared to seven cents a day in 1850. Inexplicably, the managers' appeal for funds again misrepresented the black community. The annual report noted: "although for many years the work was greatly retarded, not only by the indifference of those who should have been its earliest supporters, but by a want of confidence on the part of the very race it designed to benefit."[13]

There was no basis for this accusation. The African American community faithfully supported the Colored Orphan Asylum from its inception through the end of the Civil War. Perhaps the managers

The COA building on Amsterdam Avenue at 143d Street, 1869. (Collection of The New-York Historical Society.)

resented the support some in the black community had shown toward the Home for the Children of Freedwomen, later known as the Brooklyn Howard Colored Orphan Asylum, established in 1866 with financial assistance from the Freedmen's Bureau. Unlike the Colored Orphan asylum, the Howard Colored Orphan Asylum had black managers, an achievement its counterpart would not accomplish until 1939. If this interpretation is true, it was a recent decision and does not explain the dismissive tone of the managers' appeal. Perhaps, as suggested by Michael Katz's research, the evangelical feminine motivation of the earlier managers (personified by Anna Shotwell, Mary Murray, and the Jay sisters) shifted to "a harsher, moralistic, bureaucratic male proto-professional campaign aimed more at the behavior of the poor than at their souls." Although this was a reference to the poorhouse, it was applicable to the orphanage. The earlier managers' connection to the antislavery movement made them more sympathetic to the black community and more willing to work with them.[14]

The managers' emphasis on improving the morals of the children clouded their judgment. Overly generalizing, the 1868 annual educational report declared "that for this race there is not that stimulus to a mental exertion, which would secure for a white child an entrance into the higher professions, or ensured a privileged association with the educated and gifted of his country."[15] It was emphasized that their former servitude made it difficult to "awaken the dormant energies, stimulate the habit of self assertion, and develop the large possibilities of the race." The annual report for 1878 considered African Americans to be "gentle and amenable to authority, [but] especially deficient in the power of vigorous, independent thought and action." More so than others, the managers should have held a more enlightened viewpoint. They knew that poverty, disease, and the lack of civic support for equality made it extremely difficult for African Americans, particularly children, to achieve on the same level as whites. They knew from past experience that ambitious children such as Edward Bodee, who used his indenture to establish his own barber business, or the Civil War hero James Henry Gooding were self-motivated achievers. Certainly they should have understood that other children could and would achieve if the managers held greater expectations for their potential.

A voice of racial reason was removed with the death of James McCune Smith. His successor, Dr. Frothingham, described the children in a manner consistent with the pseudoscientific beliefs of the late nineteenth century. Frothingham noted in his physician's report for 1868 that "with the exception of a strongly marked scrofulous tendency, inherent in an exotic race, the health of the house had been such that there could hardly be a change for the better." "Exotic" was obviously not a description that James McCune Smith would have applied to the children. Frothingham's use of the word reflects that he was judging the morality of African Americans: one dictionary meaning of scrofulous is "morally contaminated." The other definition of scrofulous is "having a diseased appearance," which could apply to whites also. The lack of consumption cases in 1876 elicited from Dr. Frothingham the erroneous observation that the disease was common with mulattoes, who were considered genetically inferior to whites and "pure" Negroes.[16]

The managers' embrace of white supremacist views was all the more perplexing in light of other whites who resented the asylum's role in caring for African American children. On January 19, 1869, a worker found an explosive missile on one of the boilers. The approximately ten-pound shell was "capable of igniting and doing great damage." The police advised secrecy in the matter and recommended that in the future the institution not have any Roman Catholics on the premises. The reference to Roman Catholics was a reminder that it was Roman Catholic Irish who had destroyed their Fifth Avenue home. Prior to this incident, police surveillance protected the property from attacks. The boilers were a problem even without the explosives. One boiler stopped in late 1868. A survey by an engineer revealed that it had been "badly built and miserably planned." A secondhand boiler was purchased for nine hundred dollars. The boilermaker eventually acknowledged defects in the works and offered to install one free of charge.[17]

The boiler system was symbolic of the problems inherent in running an institution that constantly needed funding. Donations from supporters were always problematic but became more troublesome

with the financial panic of 1873, which had been initiated by the failure of Jay Gould's financial house and the collapse of railroad specula-
tion. The resulting bankruptcies led to a decreased amount of giving
to charitable organizations. Only $362.51 was contributed in donations
in 1873, compared to $741.00 raised in 1871 and $842 donated in 1872.
The Colored Sabbath School in New Jersey contributed $23.23, the first
funds sent by African Americans since the end of the Civil War. The
managers pleaded for funds to rescue children from godless immoral
homes before their souls became "seared with the moral miasma
around" them. The managers had on hand $2,265.01 at the end of
1873, partly from the receipt of $58,296 in legacies from 1838 through
1871. Donations increased to $481.14 in 1874, because of an exaggera-
tion about the dismal state of black life in New York. Sarah Murray
wrote in the annual report for 1874 that charity was immediately
needed for "a class so helpless and so little self helpful as the colored
race." This self-serving statement overlooked the efforts that blacks
were making for their own self-improvement in the years following the
demise of slavery. They had built churches, established newspapers,
maintained fraternal and benevolent societies, and formed social, economic, and professional organizations for advancement. African
Americans had allied themselves with progressive whites to combat
prejudice and discrimination. However, the managers were still view-
ing African Americans as freed persons instead of as free men and free
women. Their mission, therefore, remained the same as it had been
since antebellum days: uplift the degraded Negro child to save a generation from the degenerate practice of their foreparents. Even when
they reached out to the black community, they did so without any
sensitivity to the cultural differences between the races. Fifty colored
residents of New York were invited in 1878 to the asylum's forty-
second anniversary. Presumably, these invitees were educated individuals who probably did not appreciate hearing the children sing plantation hymns. The managers did not realize that the postemancipation
generation was highly sensitive to reminders of slavery and that plantation songs were embarrassing to them. It certainly did not help that
the New York Times used a disparaging term in mentioning that the
institution cared for three hundred children, with all but fifty in school.

The "remaining fifty pickaninnies . . . are sheltered in the nursery department."[18]

The managers' belief that they were, indeed, helping the "helpless" led to more admissions. To achieve greater economic freedom, the managers sought Albany's approval to accept real estate via bequest and to receive destitute nonorphans, after learning that the legislature allowed an asylum to hold only fifty thousand dollars' worth of real estate. Albany permitted them to change their charter to accept destitute nonorphans if poverty or sickness prevented a parent from caring or if a parent was "a shame and disgrace" to a child. In March 1872, they complained that they received from the city "less *pro rata* than other institutions." The city had paid up to May 1 but declined to give more until they were notified under what authority had the institution originally been given funds. Records detailing the agreement had been destroyed during the Draft Riots nine years earlier. But since the managers were determined to assist black children in need, they pestered the city for more funds. Samuel Van Dusen, the husband of a manager, requested in January 1874 that the Board of Apportionment grant a per capita increase of $36.50 per child for 180 children. He argued that the same number would cost the Commissioner of Charities and Corrections $85.36 per child in a reformatory. Van Dusen added that, since the Department of Pauper Children refused to aid black children, if not for the Colored Orphan Asylum the children would be vagrants or criminals. The managers wanted funding to establish a home for infants and small children. Their plea was no trifling matter: the October minutes noted that city funding had decreased by half. Eventually, the commissioner of charities contributed $6,570.[19]

Unusual Admissions

The managers' belief that it was their duty to help those in need as long as they were "colored" by American standards led to the admission of Native American children. Seven-year-old Mattole Bronson, a full-blooded Indian orphan from Humboldt Bay, California, was brought to the orphanage by a Dr. Bronson of New York, who had cared for him for the past four years. Mattole's father was killed in an Indian war. Sherman Coolidge was admitted in 1871. He and his brother, a Howard University student, were full-blooded Arapahoe who were brought from Wyoming by Captain D. F. Larralia Portland. Another child, Minnie Greene, who was admitted in 1880, was described as having "Indian hair and complexion." These Native American children, like their counterparts who went to the Hampton Institute, were trained in the ways of "civilization" and were encouraged to discard their "primitive culture" for that of Anglo-Saxon behavior. The dire economic situation also led to the admission of a number of children of former residents. While the cases varied, the circumstances were similar. A parent died or deserted, the surviving spouse was in service and could not care for a child or children, or a parent was in jail or prison. Joshua and Charles Jenkins were admitted in 1869 after their white father neglected to care for them. Their unidentified mother was listed in the admission records as a former destitute admission. Anna Stewart, admitted December 14, 1860, gave birth to John Andrew Lewis on March 3, 1869. He was admitted on January 30, 1872. An interesting admission was that of Sarah Hinton. Sarah's mother, Keziah Hinton, was admitted in 1842 and in 1845 indentured to Dr. George Janeway of Piscataway, New Jersey. Later, Keziah poisoned her employer's family. She had been in prison for eight years when a Mrs. McDowell brought Sarah to the institution on November 2, 1870. For obvious reasons, Mrs. McDowell did not want Sarah to know about her mother's history.[20]

Discipline

Institutional discipline was a problem that would concern the asylum managers for years. Increased enrollment made discipline that much more difficult. The January 1869 minutes reported that the children should be washed every morning and that they should not wear during the day the clothes they had worn at night. Teachers complained about the children's body odor. Managers declared that untidy boys be sent to Allen Griffin, the shoemaker, and girls to Miss Hardwood, "to be immediately put into a cold bath." To minimize expenses and to provide children with practical work experience, the managers decided to keep children in the asylum until age thirteen or fourteen, "to be employed in the house for the last year but only such as are in the first class of school No. 1." The children were employed as follows: one boy each for the children's dining room, kitchen, and bakery; one girl each assigned to the hospital, nursery, and sewing room and to wait on the table; two boys were to assist the shoemaker; and four girls to assist the matron. Perhaps some children resented their assignment, which called for the superintendent to submit to the managers the names of those "he . . . found necessary to whip through the month." The year 1874 was a milestone for the institution for two reasons. Two thousand and fourteen children had been admitted since June 9, 1837, and there were currently 284 children in the house, the largest number to date. The packed house would become even more crowded in 1875, when a state law ordered that children in county poor houses be placed with foster parents, orphan asylums, or appropriate charitable or reformatory institutions. The law was amended in 1878 to include children past the age of two. Additional children were admitted by an act passed on January 13, 1876, which allowed the orphanage to accept children from bordering counties' almshouses. Some fourteen-year-olds were committed by police justices. These children were indentured as soon as places were located, but their unsavory backgrounds caused discipline problems for the staff. A four-year-old was "so low and vicious in all his tastes that he had to be removed from contact with his little associates." Three children of an African American father were forced by him to beg in the streets or steal. They would be beaten for a failure to comply or if they did not bring in sufficient money. This man had killed his Caucasian wife in a drunken brawl. His children were highlighted in the annual report as examples of the saving grace of the institution. The girl later became a valuable worker for her employer, one boy became a student at a Southern black college, and the other boy became an engineer's assistant.[21]

Part of the discipline problem was attributed to poor management—in particular, Superintendent William Davis, whom the managers notified in January 1870 by letter that he must correct deficiencies.

The following month, the decision was reached to replace him at the end of the year with an option to remain for an extra three months "if no other position immediately offers." This action was warranted because the asylum needed a younger and more energetic man to handle the duties of the position. The managers considered hiring Matron Jane McClelland as a replacement for six months. In April, an unidentified black man, employed for twenty-two years in the Deaf and Dumb Asylum, requested the superintendent's position, but no action was taken. The following month, the managers hired Orville Hutchinson to be superintendent for an annual salary of one thousand dollars and board for his wife, commencing June 1. It appeared that the children might have a role model when Superintendent Hutchinson hired a colored engineer "with excellent credentials, both of his moral character and his proficiency in his business." This unidentified man began employment on February 13, 1870, but was dismissed a few months later when his carelessness caused a boiler to break down. To add to their problems, the managers were dissatisfied with the matron and considered removing her from her position. They decided in October that Jane McClelland would remain, but at a reduced salary, and she was relieved of charge of the clothing department. In late 1874, the managers decided to keep her services until spring 1875. In March 1875, they gave her silver and cash in appreciation of twenty-two years of service. She was replaced by Jane Pearson, at an annual salary of three hundred dollars.[22]

Perhaps having more African Americans employed in positions beyond washers or cooks might have improved discipline, but sometimes they were just as impatient and harsh with the children as were the white employees. A case in point was Charlotte Yorke, whom the managers decided in the spring of 1878 to dismiss as the girls' caretaker, because "she had assumed work outside the institution taking in sewing and sitting up late using the gas [lamp]. She is very rough with the girls and her influence is not what it should be." Charlotte Yorke's replacement proved unsatisfactory, and Yorke was rehired in early 1879. Her salary was increased in 1881 to fourteen dollars per month, because "she is a very valuable person to the institution." Charlotte would remain with the asylum into the early twentieth century. Adelaide Butler was another long-serving black employee. She had served the children for twenty-five years as a nurse. A childless widow, she displayed a natural devotion to the children, even to the point of not abandoning them during the Draft Riots. She hummed with her last breath "that gate afar stands free for all who seek through it salvation; the rich and the poor, the great and the small, of every tribe and nation." She died on June 4, 1878. Her funeral at the orphanage on June 7 was a sad occasion for the managers, staff, and children. The Rev. Henry Highland Garnet noted on June 14 that "her superiors never once had to suggest to [her] the performance of any duty devolving upon her." *Harper's Weekly* commented that "it is the hard fate of every person of her race to be born into a society that associates them with servility and inferiority."[23]

While discipline would remain a constant in the institution, both because of the various ages living in close quarters and because some came to the institution from depraved backgrounds, the managers were generally pleased that the ending of slavery "has elevated their general tone and had a deciding bearing upon the character of the children indentured from this institution." They happily noted that William Spelman, the pastor of Abyssinian Baptist Church in Manhattan, had a number of former asylum children as congregants. Spelman considered them "among the most respected and consistent portion of his congregation." The managers resolved that "to make this institution a home, more than an asylum, is a constant aim!" With this as their goal, they sought to guide the children with examples of moral behavior rather than control them solely with "the sterner rule of law and force." Most of the children appreciated the effort of the managers to provide them with moral guidance. Asylum records reveal letters of appreciation as well as small monetary gifts from the former "inmates" years after they left the institution. Letters from successful teenagers delighted the managers, because it proved that their moral guidance had saved them from a life of crime or depravity. Equally important, it informed potential donors that their contributions would not be wasted. Twenty-three-year-old Sarah A. Guilder viewed her life as "useless and friendless." She still, however, believed that God would provide, because the managers had taught her to love Him. Mary Keenan, nineteen, regretted that her mother ruined her brother's life when she took him away from the Juvenile Asylum. She was glad that she "was plucked as a burning brand from the fire" and placed in the Colored Orphan Asylum. Eighteen-year-old Edwin Maynard wrote that he was a follower of Jesus Christ. "We poor children," he noted, "did not know the good of the asylum. Where should we poor children be today if it had not been for that asylum; may the asylum be the means of converting many of the poor colored orphans." George W. Potter, thirty-five, informed Anna Shotwell in 1870 that he remembered the Fifth Avenue home so fondly that he desired an illustration of the building "to have it photographed to a large size for framing." Three years later, Potter's wife deserted the family, which led Potter to place his seven-year-old son, George W. Potter Jr., in the institution.[24]

Potter's willingness to entrust his son to the orphanage was not unusual; many former residents held fond memories of their "home." Even strangers knew that the COA was a place that they could send their children if adversity struck their family. Of course, many were unaware of the racial politics that defined the institution during the aftermath of the Civil War. Two of the children admitted in 1872 and 1873 were unlike the usual cases of poverty, neglect, or desertion. These two reflected the dissatisfaction of African Americans who emigrated out of the United States for a better life abroad. Eleven-year-old John D. Johnson was born in Africa, where his parents had chosen to live. His merchant father died in Africa of fever in 1867. Louise and Annie Taylor were born in Haiti. Their American-born parents had left the United States probably under the auspices of the Haytian Emigration Bureau on the eve of the Civil War. The death of their father by fever led to their sudden admittance to the COA, and after a few months they were returned to their mother. A reverse situation occurred when Alexander Campbell left his indenture early in 1876 to go live with his father, an expatriate African American businessman in Lagos, Nigeria.[25]

The admission of more children caused more illness, which demanded a modern hospital to replace the old frame house that had served that purpose. A committee decided in April 1875 to determine the cost for a hospital building "to include a boys' room, hospital apartments, a school room and dormitory." It was agreed upon in June to repair the current decrepit hospital building, but at an expense not to exceed five thousand dollars. Lacking available funds, the treasurer sold five thousand dollars of U.S. bonds to erect a brick building at cost of $5,738.13. Circumstances forced the managers to retain the services of an incompetent nurse "until the presence of more sickness necessitates more competent help." The managers also decided to make children healthier by providing daily ten pounds of meat and fish and substituting cold meat for bread and butter for Sunday dinners. Extra vegetables were supplied three times a week. Butter was even added to tea, because the sweetened water for the children's breakfast drink lacked sufficient nutrients. Dr. Frothingham treated in 1875 twelve cases of malarial fever, four cases of typhoid fever, nine cases of pneumonia, thirteen diphtheria cases, and five cases of bronchitis, which resulted in nine deaths. Most of these diseases were the result of poor drainage systems: sewage gases backed up into water pipes and polluted the drinking water. The *New York Times*'s editor suggested that bathroom drainage pipes be directly connected to the city's sewers. The *Times* estimated that 2,500 children under the age of five in Manhattan had died of diphtheria or cholera during the month of July 1875.[26]

The year 1876 was pivotal for the managers, who formed a close relationship with General Samuel Chapman Armstrong, the founder in 1868 of the Hampton Normal and Agricultural Institute, in Hampton, Virginia. Armstrong visited the orphanage in December and agreed to accept fourteen-year-old children at the cost of sixty dollars' tuition for eight and a half months. Hampton offered a three-year course of common school curriculum, agriculture, chemistry, agricultural business methods, tinsmithing, bricklaying, and mechanical arts. By the early twentieth century, the Hampton Institute—and the Tuskegee Institute, under the direction of a Hampton graduate, Booker T. Washington—would be criticized for making Negroes and Native Americans docile and bereft of higher education. Nevertheless, for decades the managers were happy to send their brightest young charges to both institutions, as they saw in industrial education hope for those shunned by white

tradesmen. They would continue this practice even after industrial education came under attack from black militants who questioned its
value in a racist society. Josephine Brown, a former asylum girl, informed Matron Jane Pearson on January 3, 1876, that General Armstrong was popular among the colored people. She, too, considered
him a good friend of the race "and DARE say there is none better than
he." The twenty-one-year-old Josephine wrote the following year that
she was teaching in Butt's Road, Virginia, but "the people think I am
too young to manage the big boys." Sixteen-year-old Ezra Wright informed the COA that his schedule consisted of classes from 8:30 to
10:15, 10:30 to noon, and 12:45 to 3 o'clock. He had one and a half
hours of study in the morning and evening. Wright, like other students, could work if he chose on Saturday for forty cents. He attended
church on Sunday at 11:00 and Sunday school from 2:00 to 3:00 in the
afternoon. Twenty-one-year-old Charles H. Minnie informed Manager
Mrs. James Stokes in late 1879 that he was a sophomore at Williston
Seminary in Easthampton, Massachusetts. He had sufficient funds to
pay his tuition until the spring of 1880, but he lacked money to purchase an overcoat to ward off the biting wind. In early 1880, the managers sent him twenty dollars to aid him in completing the spring
term.[27]

It was considered a coup for the managers to have the support of
Armstrong and, later, Booker T. Washington. Equally important to
their existence was their ability to attract prominent white New Yorkers to their cause as managers, patrons, or advisers. Throughout the
years, the managers added to their number to replace those who resigned or died. One significant addition in December 1875 was Margaret Olivia Slocum Sage, the second wife of Russell Sage. A woman of
her means was a definite asset to the Colored Orphan Asylum, which
could count on her to provide a list of potential donors from the city's
philanthropic community. Years later, her establishment of the Russell
Sage Foundation in 1907 proclaimed the beginning of the era of the
modern philanthropic foundation. Ten million dollars from her husband's legacy of seventy million dollars were used to establish this
significant foundation.[28] Unfortunately, in the decade after the death
of James McCune Smith, the managers did not deem it important to

seek advisers from the black community. It would have helped to improve the relationship between the community and the institution had the latter reached out to prominent leaders such as the Rev. Henry Highland Garnet or Theophilus Gould Steward, the pastor of Brooklyn's Bridge Street Church, or Susan Smith McKinney, the Empire State's first African American female physician, to advise them on matters of race.

Death, too, had a significant effect on the COA during the last quarter of the nineteenth century. A major blow to the orphanage occurred in 1881, when Mrs. James Stokes (Caroline Phelps Stokes), the daughter of Anson G. Phelps, an adviser to the managers, died. Caroline had a deep interest in Liberia, which her father helped to establish through the American Colonization Society. A financial supporter of the orphanage following the Draft Riots, she left them three thousand dollars in her will. The *New York Times* reported that "the colored people were special objects of her solicitude." Her daughter, also named Caroline, wrote that during her mother's final illness, Dinah, the black cook, exclaimed, "O, Lord, take old Dinah, and spare her!" More deaths followed. In 1882, Lucy J. Eno, a manager since 1858 and the daughter of Elisha Phelps, a distinguished lawyer and Connecticut congressman, died. Lucy Eno's will enriched her beloved orphanage with a grant of five thousand dollars. Her husband, Amos R. Eno, was a dry-goods businessman who became a real estate millionaire. He died in 1898 with an estate valued at twenty to forty million dollars but willed only three thousand dollars to the Colored Orphan Asylum. The advisers William F. Mott and William F. Onderdonk and former Superintendent William E. Davis also died in 1882. These deaths were followed by that of Adviser Samuel Willets in early 1883. Willets had supported the asylum from its inception. A wealthy man from various business interests, Willets gave generously to the needy. The *New York Times* noted that "the widows and orphans and the deserving poor of the city, to whom he had been a friend in deeds as well as words" would mourn his passing. As a member of the Society for Promoting the Manumission of Slaves, he helped to secure passage of a law providing trial by jury for those accused of being fugitives from slavery.[29]

The last two decades of the century would result in the end of the nineteenth-century orphanage. Within in a few years, child welfare reformers would challenge vigorously the wisdom of indenturing and eventually even the importance of orphanages themselves. It would be during this period that institutions sought to have college-trained administrators rather than superintendents who were basically farmer-mechanic types. The shift toward a modern institution would be gradual, but its arrival would alter forever the concept of child care.

Meanwhile, the COA, now in existence for forty-five years, needed to expand at its Harlem location or build elsewhere. The annual report for 1882 called for a new building to provide space for infants under the age of two. "A child in its mother's arms renders her unable to labor for the support of her family," noted the secretary. A rejected mother stated poignantly, "only the grave, then." The managers appealed to women for funds. "Mothers in happy, prosperous homes, who know nothing of privation . . . we are willing to be your almoners. Rich women, we are willing to conscientiously spend your money for these helpless babies." Their appeal apparently moved some to give, for they received $1,397 in subscriptions and donations in 1883, compared to $1,195 the previous year. They also received $147.21 in 1882 from an exhibition with, as the secretary reported, "an unusually large number of respectable colored people present." Work was begun in 1883 to enlarge the building to provide three nurseries for twenty children each, at a cost of forty thousand dollars. It was hoped (and expected) that friends would come to their aid. Circumstances in 1883 led to the hiring in February of Mary M. Everett as matron, but an illness soon led to her resignation. Mrs. Hutchinson, the superintendent's wife, became acting matron for three months.[30]

The first half of 1884 was a busy period in the life of the institution. Despite its early intent to care specifically for orphans, the institution now had more half-orphans and destitute or neglected children than orphans. To better reflect the mission of an institution that also admitted children sent by magistrates for delinquency, a new name was in order. Consequently, the Association for the Benefit of Colored Orphans in the City of New York became, effective July 1, 1884, the Colored Orphan Asylum and Association for the Benefit of Colored Children. The task of finishing the building, a duty that had eluded the managers for nearly two decades, was greatly aided by the $10,225 legacy of Samuel Willets and the sale of railroad bonds. Available funds paid for the construction of three nurseries, playrooms, bathrooms, a kindergarten school, a visitors' reception room, and apartments for the institution's officers. The declining health of Superintendent Hutchinson necessitated the hiring of an assistant while Hutchinson took a six-month vacation in the South, which commenced on December 1, 1884. The principal's report for the year proudly proclaimed that "the school is supplied with the latest and most approved textbooks, reading charts used in teaching color, form, etc." Religious instruction was provided by a Mr. Angell, who informed the board of managers, "my interest in your institution grows stronger and my labors more delightful when I see the attention of the children at our pleasant Sabbath morning service. As I look back to the dark days of slavery [and see how it] made the condition of the colored people so lamentable, and see how much good by your institution and collateral effort for the despised race it makes my heart glad and I feel that it is impossible to do too much for such a cause."[1]

As of December 1, 1885, the institution had just under two thousand dollars in the treasury. Food remained their single highest expense item, at $11,606.47. It cost 32 cents per day—$2.23 per week or $116.27 per annum—to feed each of the 323 children.[2]

Death was always a constant in an institution with children susceptible to illnesses that vaccinations had not yet been developed to prevent. These deaths, while sad events, were expected and planned for. Worse were the deaths that came silently, like an animal pouncing on unsuspecting prey. Tragedy struck the institution in November 1885, when Dr. William Frothingham accidentally shot himself through the eye while cleaning his pistol. Frothingham, a Civil War surgeon, was described by the *New York Times* as the friend of the poor, whom he never charged, because "he never thought of presenting a bill for services to persons who would be pinched by paying." The Rev. Dr. Charles A. Stoddard eulogized him with these words: "How many here who can attest the skill and unwearied patience with which he brought them back almost from death to life; how he changed pain to health." Suicide was dismissed, as gun-cleaning material was nearby and the physician had been planning to shoot his daughter's dog, which had mange. Despite the dismissal of suicide rumors, some remained doubtful. His will, written ten days before his passing, provided three hundred dollars each to the Children's Aid Society and the Society for the Suppression of Vice of New York—but five hundred dollars to both organizations if his life ended by an accident. Although Dr. Frothingham had worked in the COA for twenty years, he left it nothing in his will. He was replaced by Dr. W. T. Alexander as resident physician.[3]

Industrial Education

The institution reached a milestone at the end of 1885. Since June 9, 1837, 924 children had come under its care, with 101 placed out as indentures. A few fortunate ones were sent to Hampton Normal Institute in Virginia, five became teachers, two were employed in the Chicago post office (one a registry clerk and the other a letter carrier), and one had become a journeyman cabinet maker. Another former resident was an engineer on the West Shore Railroad. According to Second Directress Mrs. William H. Onderdonk, the managers were "desirous to establish a thorough foundation for complete practical instruction in industrial arts and household work [to prepare the children for life's work]." To help accomplish this, they established a sewing school and stressed "knowledge of the arts of the household industry." They admitted that indenturing boys to farms left them basically ignorant, but their goal was to train children to be well qualified "to make good servants of the old sort." Modern critics must question why they wanted to keep them as "good servants of the old sort" when such servitude implied slavery. Onderdonk was a product of the prejudices of her era; few viewed the Negro escaping the alleged biblical curse of carrying water and hewing wood. It would be decades before the managers recognized the bankruptcy of this policy, which kept African Americans in a servant class, except for the few who were lighter in complexion and considered by common belief to be brighter in intelligence. Their belief system informed them that they were "saving" children from the perils of urban life, and they were pleased that their moral guidance seemed to them to be having a positive effect. Not since 1877 had a child been enticed to run away, and not since 1880 had a child left the premises without permission.[4]

Boys were instructed in simple carpentry on Saturdays. The managers lamented that those who showed aptitude for mechanics could not expect a white man to tutor them for life's work. Again, the managers made absolutely no effort to publicize this discrimination, nor did they attempt to influence donors or friends who might be in a position to train and hire some of the boys or seek out potential employers from the black graduates of Hampton Institute. They could have sought an alliance with the city's black intellectuals and activists. In 1890, Henry F. Downing, a prominent African American and former diplomat, informed the *New York Age* that, after years of struggle to integrate the counting houses and other businesses, "the great house of Weschler and Abraham of Brooklyn are taking steps which forecast the removal of these barriers of which we so bitterly complain, initiating their policy by employing me in a position which accords most happily with my deserving and capacity." Certainly, these women, who were themselves among the city's elite, could have quietly sought to aid the integration effort. Instead, they hoped that someday someone might endow a school for teaching colored boys trades so that "their talent no longer be hidden." Booker T. Washington established the Tuskegee Normal and Industrial Institute in 1881 for such a purpose, and that institution became an outlet for several of the boys who enrolled in the Alabama school during the next few decades. Secretary Murray offered a theme that became widely associated with Booker T. Washington: "Let us all remember that to be a good house servant, is to be a most valuable person, and one most difficult to find; and let us apply ourselves diligently to forming this desirable character in our little ones." The managers sought funds to establish a "cottage of industry" to house and train about twelve girls in domestic science until age thirteen, which would be "of the greatest possible use to these children in after-life." Murray and the other women felt this way because they believed that heredity determined one's fate. They were amazed that so many children came from a background of poverty and feeblemindedness yet somehow managed to "make a good people as they do."[5] They were unable to comprehend that poor individuals often strive to overcome their background en route to a life of success. This should not have been hard to realize, given that contemporaries such as Andrew Carnegie had risen from the depths of poverty to become successful and wealthy captains of industry.

One of the "good people" was William H. Gardner, who became the second recipient, after Ezra Wright, to attend Hampton Normal and Agricultural Institute on funds provided by the late Caroline Phelps Stokes. A half-orphan who was "almost a white child," William entered the institution in 1878 and left in 1882, at age ten. He informed Superintendent Hutchinson on October 19, 1886, three weeks after his arrival at Hampton, that he was to study grammar, math, European and Asian geography, English history, spelling, the Revolutionary War, and carpentry. His rigorous schedule began at 5:15 in the morning, followed by a 6:00 march to breakfast, study from 7:15 to 8:15, and time to shine his shoes and brush his clothes before class started at 8:50. After lunch, classes resumed at 1:40 until 4:00, followed by dinner at

6:15. The students were in bed by 9:30. William turned out to be a poor student, and in 1886 it was decided that the sixteen-year-old should have a place where he could earn a salary. Hampton had declined to hire him as a waiter.[6]

The concept of domestic science for girls received a boost in late 1887, when Grace Dodge, a member of New York City's Board of Education, social worker, and philanthropist, spoke to the managers about industrial education for the children. In September, the institution hired Miss E. Anna Buchanan to teach boys how to make beds, a function that Superintendent Hutchinson did not think practical for boys. The domestic-economy lessons started with table service and ended with a three-course meal. Boys and girls were both taught sewing, with boys performing as well as the girls. In October, the managers decided to let boys in the first and second grade participate in cooking classes. The managers wanted the industrial program ultimately to help children to love and respect labor as well as learn "the secret of being awake to the pleasure and profit of self education through life, in all things needful, wise and good." In 1890, a three-month trial period was initiated, with two classes weekly in washing and ironing, chores that would aid the children in their indenturing assignments. The baker was instructed to teach the children how to bake bread, set a table, and serve guests. To make sure that the indentures were treated fairly, Mrs. James B. Wright visited the homes of six indentures in early 1889. She found "all giving satisfactory services, showing the good results of our industrial training." The employers, she reported, were satisfied with the children's housekeeping skills. "This speaks volumes for our industrial teacher (Mrs. Gillette) as the complaints used to be that the children were so helpless, from not having an idea of work." The institution's intent was to train generations of female domestics. Two published letters from indentures emphasized domestic assignments. Twelve-year-old John Jamieson wrote the superintendent, "I hope you will come down and see how nicely I make beds. I broke three dishes,—I felt bad about it. I iron yet, but I don't wash [clothes]. I wash dishes Mondays and Tuesdays." Twelve-year-old Fred Dumpson's letter indicated that he lived with a large family of whites. He proudly reported that "I wash the dishes, set the table and wait on the table, scrub and wash my own clothes and make my own bed." What contemporary twelve-year-old American today would boast about his domestic skills? In the fashion of Booker T. Washington, the children were taught to find dignity in their work, regardless how menial or degrading it might seem to others. Besides industrial training, the children received instruction based on New York City's Board of Education requirements. The teachers' report by Mary E. Fresne for 1896 was full of praise for the children's progress. The kindergarten teachers stressed manners and morals; the industrial students were taught carpentry, cooking, washing and ironing, house cleaning, cane seating, and sewing. The students wrote to friends twice a month, which allowed them to practice their lessons in word usage, punctuation, capitalization, spelling, and sentence structure. These compositions helped the teacher to gain "valuable insight into [the student's] characters." The students had supplementary reading in U.S. history, natural history, science, and health. It was reported that "for children so young they have a very good idea of the history of their own country."[7]

The managers were convinced that industrial training was the best (and only) option for their charges, and they eagerly awaited the remarks of an avid supporter in early 1892. A Miss Austin, formerly of Knoxville, Tennessee, addressed the managers about her twenty-two years of experience among southern Negroes. The minutes reflected that she "gave valuable counsel in reply to questions about the intellectual and industrial capability of colored children and youth and the best method of fitting them for usefulness in such positions as they may be called to occupy." Austin recommended that 80 percent of the instruction be industrial training. This recommendation elicited very little debate, as the main advocate of regular school instruction, Mrs. Grace Van Dusen, a board member since 1866, was ill and died a few months later.[8]

Again, the industrial classes only prepared the children to live in a society that expected no more than menial labor from them. Ironically, the inside back cover of the annual report for 1886 contained a selection written by James Montgomery. The first two stanzas of the eight stanzas read as follows:

I know the scorn the colored child,
the gay, the selfish, and the proud;
I know his sorrowing accents mild
are mockery left by thieves half dead;
nor see an infant Lazarus lie to the thoughtless crowd.

I cannot coldly pass one by—
stripp'd hounded,
at rich men's gates, imploring bread.

To really aid the children to have a life far superior to that known by their ancestors, the white ladies should have sought alliances with other reformers to demand the inclusion of black workers into unions. This they were unable or unwilling to attempt. Fortunately for the institution, black New Yorkers maintained an interest in the managers' work despite their condescending attitude toward them. The minutes for January 8, 1886, reported that a large number of African Americans came for the Christmas entertainment. A black woman left the institution one thousand dollars in 1886. Her home in Oyster Bay, New York, was sold, with the proceeds divided between her church and the asylum. An act of generosity was inexplicably rejected in 1888 when black New Yorkers offered to provide entertainment to benefit the institution. The terse sentence in the minutes noted simply that "it is not considered advisable to accept."[9]

The asylum suffered two losses in 1887, beginning with the death of former Superintendent Orville K. Hutchinson on February 9. He had served the institution since June 8, 1869, shortly after the move to 143rd Street, and was credited with putting the house in order with his energy and business acumen. In 1885, the poor health of Superintendent Hutchinson and the absence of his wife, who was vacationing with him, led the managers to replace her with a Mrs. Morse, the acting matron. Second Directress Harriet S. Onderdonk (Mrs. William Onderdonk) wrote, "he was a man of thorough principle, [whose] integrity was of the highest and purest order; he was eminently free from any taint of guile, and remembered for an almost unerring justice in deciding between either adults or children, or in cases where both were involved." The asylum children attended his funeral, and their "singing was very touching, drawing tears from many eyes." Even the indentures felt the loss of their mentor. Ruth Williams wrote that "we mourn him as we would a father, for he tended us with the patience of a shepherd. No one knew his feelings when one of us went astray." Hutchinson was replaced by his assistant, Martin K. Sherwin, at eight hundred dollars per year. Mrs. Hutchinson decided to remain as matron.[10] A few months later, death claimed Sarah U. Underhill, one of the pioneer managers, at age eighty-nine. She was eulogized for "the sweetness and quietness of her disposition, her simplicity and dignity were only equaled by her integrity, upon which we could always rely in the needed hour."[11]

The Colored Orphan Asylum received a huge financial windfall in 1893, when Maria Stuart (Mrs. Robert L. Stuart) left them a legacy of $59,230.77, to be paid in installments until 1899. Her husband, Robert Stuart, had made a fortune using steam to refine sugar. Mrs. Stuart's generosity was received with bewilderment. Mrs. James B. Wright "secured [her] subscription for over 30 years and could never get her to give more than five dollars." The managers estimated that Mrs. Stuart had given them over the years (including the legacy) about $91,000, the largest amount then to date.[12]

The diversity of children in the institution reflected all the pathologies of society. For example, Eugene Blaines, age five, was admitted after his father deserted the family. Eugene's mother was a lewd woman who sat him on a hot stove, which resulted in a "severe burn on his right leg." Mrs. Frances Greenwood beat her child with "a stick with three leather thongs and a strap with a heavy iron buckle on the end; also a cord with loops . . . placed about her wrists while she was suspended from a door and whipped. Sometimes [the woman tied her] up by the thumbs and whipped" the traumatized child. The report for 1894 noted that the children needed to have self-reliance. It was the contention of the managers that proper conduct and the acquisition of a strong moral base would aid the children in overcoming the influence of heredity and early associations. They believed that results would come once "much time, much thought, much labor is required of all who give themselves to it, even to following the children out of the institution to their different homes, not only to shield them from the ill usage of neglect but to encourage their best effort in the service of employers." This strong belief explained their disappointment with an unmarried eighteen-year-old who lost her baby. Visits to her revealed that she was "indifferent about her manner of life." It was noted that "she is of the lowest parentage and it has proved impossible to awaken her higher instincts."[13]

More pleasing was the progress of thirty-year-old George F. Douglas, a Howard Law School graduate who was admitted to the bar in the District of Columbia. Douglas wanted to practice law in Kansas, because the state had low levels of prejudice and offered opportunities. He had planned to his move in early 1895 but was delayed by the nation's dismal financial situation. Meanwhile, he was admitted to practice in the D.C. Court of Appeals. Douglas wrote on November 24, 1894, "this is of the utmost importance, for it will give me an excellent standing in whatever jurisdiction I may desire to practice." Douglas moved to Kansas in the spring of 1895, but circumstances led him to return to Washington. In 1896, he was reading and studying law in Newark, New Jersey, where he was admitted to the bar. Compared to clergymen or physicians, African American lawyers had difficulty succeeding in their profession. Unlike the former two professions, which catered to their own race, black attorneys practiced "before a white judge often against a white lawyer and generally with a white jury." A study of professional Negroes in 1900 in Pennsylvania noted that there were only twenty-four African American attorneys, compared to 411 clergymen and sixty physicians and surgeons. Lack of steady work led Douglas to request and receive a three-year loan for three hundred dollars from the managers, which he volunteered to pay back at 6 percent interest. However, the managers, pleased with his success, which reflected their nurturing, generously settled for 3.5 percent. Douglas was an activist Republican who worked for William McKinley's presidential victory in 1896.[14]

George Douglas represented to the managers proof that the asylum's teachings could uplift Negro youth whose background destined them to failure. This assessment, however, was inaccurate in several respects. Children were not merely putty to be molded into carbon copies of Anglo-Saxon achievement. While some, like Douglas, rose to eminence (compared to all those trained to be merely competent and contented domestic workers), uncounted others left the institution unable or unwilling to till the land or clear the tables and became derelicts, thieves, prostitutes, or unmarried mothers. Were they all destined by heredity to be failures, or did a racist environment contribute to the lack of opportunities that persuaded them to seek release in illicit activities? Those who chose the latter lifestyle were deemed by the managers as simply responding to hereditary instincts, whereas the successes were the result of proper moral training and guidance from the staff and managers.

The managers considered themselves the guardians of their charges. However, some parents resented that the managers kept the whereabouts of their children a secret. In late 1893, a father who had brought two sons to the institution in 1885 came and demanded to know their location. The superintendent refused to enlighten him, as the man owed the asylum $1,384 for their board. The enraged father returned with an attorney, and, after negotiations, Superintendent Sherwin returned the younger boy—upon receipt of fifty dollars immediately and the payment of six dollars monthly. Eugene Lyons was returned to his father, but the location of his brother Louis, then indentured in Glen Cove, New York, was kept secret until a writ of habeas corpus forced Sherwin to identify his location. Louis soon ran away to his father's home. Justice Charles L. Guy of the New York Supreme Court ruled in 1907 "that children cannot be held by institutions as collateral security for the amount due for their support and maintenance."[15]

Throughout its history, the Colored Orphan Asylum faced the perils of fire. While none compared to the catastrophic 1863 Draft Riots, a fire on New Year's Day, 1895, caused extreme anxiety. Charlotte Yorke discovered a fire in the basement of the west wing under the dining room and notified the matron, who ordered the girls out to the lawn, where they marched in the bitter cold to the hospital building. Fortunately, the fire had broken out shortly before noon, before the dining room was crowded. Sherwin's prompt action in closing the heavy sheet-iron doors kept smoke from the main building. The damages amounted to twelve hundred dollars, of which one thousand dollars was covered by insurance. It was noted in the annual report for 1895 that the fire "was allowed to come to show us what our building requires; and now, with the new fire escapes, strengthened walls, stairs and fire proof ceilings, we feel we have done what we could for the safety of the lives placed in our care."[16]

Corporal Punishment

Corporal punishment in the asylum became an issue of contention for the managers and staff. This issue had been raised several decades earlier, but it warranted more attention near the end of the nineteenth century, as the use of corporal punishment was beginning to be challenged by children's rights organizations. However, orphanages were not all in agreement about the need to eliminate corporal punishment. Kenneth Cmiel noted that at no time in the nineteenth century did the Chicago Nursery and Half-Orphan Asylum considered doing away with corporal punishment. In contrast, the New York Juvenile Asylum prohibited its use in 1896, but the resulting discipline problems led them four years later to declare that it provided "great advantages" if "administered by a just and responsible official." They decided the following year that alternating the daily activities between work and play would "remove almost wholly temptations to mischievous and rebellious outburst, or sullen defiance of authority." In June 1894, the COA managers gave the principal the right to punish for minor offenses. There were only two cases in July, but the number increased to twenty-seven in December. First Directress Mrs. Willard Parker suggested that good children be treated to a trip to the American Museum of Natural History. However, in their estimation, some children's behavior warranted more physical force. The State Board of Charities had ruled in 1890 against corporal punishment, noting that its use could not "be divorced from an inevitable tendency to abuse." The managers voted in January 1896 to end corporal punishment. Throughout 1896, the managers and staff experimented with different forms of punishment, none of which were particularly effective. Some older children were given extra chores for two or three days, lost their play time, or were forced to miss trips outside of the asylum. Some misbehaving girls were prohibited from wearing their Sunday clothes; others were given just bread and milk for a meal. Some teachers were severely reprimanded for coercing children or not allowing them to leave their seats for a long period of time. Previously, the superintendent had struck some of their hands no more than six times. In 1897, the managers checked with the Juvenile Asylum, the Catholic Protectory, and the House of Refuge, and they all agreed that the law prohibiting corporal punishment needed to be more flexible. They all wanted a return to some slight form of corporal punishment as "a final resource." The managers discussed the use of solitary cells, lighted on all sides, as punishment areas. They even considered converting the girls' closet into a punishment room and using food as punishment, not in the usual sense of deprivation but instead feeding the children "more than usual [to make] them more restless and anxious for release." The children began to realize that they could misbehave and not be physically punished, which prompted them to act in a more destructive manner. It was noted in the 1897 minutes that "an unusual number of aprons, dresses and other clothing was reported mended [by Manager] Mrs. Onderdonk [who] explained that the children amuse themselves by tearing their clothes." Either the children's behavior was out of resentment of working without salary or it was a clear statement that they did not care for their unfashionable clothing. The managers used a "disgraced class" from 1898 to early 1902 to shame students into good behavior. Misbehaving students were placed in a special class, which the children found humiliating. The abolishment of the disgraced class was followed by the establishment of the disgrace table or closet or by being sent to bed early. In February 1898, the matron, Miss Elizabeth Jones (who was hired in 1897), "instituted a sort of reception for the girls as a reward for good behavior. She [had] different girls three times in a week [and] sometimes [had] special treats [for them]." Earlier, in May 1897, 250 children went to Grant's Tomb, where they sat "on one of the grand stands and [sang] twice to the interested crowds." Despite the carrot-and-stick approach, discipline would remain a sensitive topic for years. Manager Wood's request for clarification on corporal punishment to Mr. Hill of the State Board of Charities resulted in a vague response to the asylum's inquiry: "There were other forms of punishment otherwise than corporal," he noted in 1907.[17]

Also, discipline was lax because the staff was underpaid and overworked. Proper care was not given to the children, a situation that would remain a problem for years. Living conditions in the building were not always impeccable. Manager Mrs. Leonard D. White reported that babies slept in the same undershirt for a week at a time. She suggested the making of flannel and cribbing flannel drawers. The baby bathroom was in poor condition; separate bathrooms were substituted for large circular tubs in the girls' bathroom. The tablecloths in the children's dining room were soiled and ragged. It was noted on a different visit that the girls' bedspreads were very soiled, as they were washed only once a year. It was decided to wash all of them immediately and for twelve spreads to be washed weekly throughout the year. These unsanitary conditions would be a harbinger of problems that would plague the institution over the next half century, until they could no longer be kept from the press.[18]

The Colored Orphan Asylum sought to present a positive view to the public through their annual reports and occasional favorable newspaper article. This was done to gain good publicity and elicit donations. They would often highlight the progress of a former inmate as a means to inform the public of the great service that they were providing to a race of people in desperate need of help. Young people saved from depraved relatives or from a life of vice and crime appreciated the asylum's assistance. The annual reports included letters from indentured children or those who remembered their old homes years after leaving. These selected letters informed supporters and potential donors of the good things the asylum was doing to uplift the less fortunate Negro orphan or neglected child. The half-orphans Marcelino and Aurelio Sanchez were admitted on December 11, 1880, and returned to their father on August 30, 1895. Soon thereafter, Marcelino wrote Superintendent Sherwin that the asylum boys "don't know exactly now that they are in a nice place. What a blessing it is to go to school,

and try not to waste a minute of their time. I have had many temptations such as I never had [in the institution] but I try to overcome
them all. Every time I am tempted I think of the phrase 'yield not to
temptation.'" Twelve-year-old Sarah E. Thompson wrote after leaving
the asylum that she realized it was "very dear to me and should be to
every child who enters its doors." Marcelino Sanchez's resistance to
temptation was shared by others. Fifteen-year-old Howard Price informed Sherwin that God had rescued him from his enemies. He had
returned to his mother when he was fourteen and, now working in his
first job, he earned four dollars monthly cooking, tending to the fur-
nace, and caring for horses in the absence of the barn man. Howard
gave half of his salary to his mother and wanted to send some to
Sherwin but had none to spare. Most rewarding to the managers was
Henry Wentworth's letter to "Miss B." (possibly Ellen Bunting), which
reflected their fervent hopes for their young charges and justified their
commitment to uplifting a race. Wentworth was nearly thirty years
old, married, a member of the YMCA, and self-employed. He wrote, "I
am in truth self-respecting, self reliant and quite practical in all my
views. The foundation of all was laid at the colored orphan asylum. I
think if all the boys in that home would carry the teaching they received there all through their asylum life, they would never stray from
the path of honesty."[19]

African American Employees

The orphanage's ambivalent relationship with the African American
community carried over to its hiring policy. The black employees in
the institution were poorly paid and rarely employed in positions of
high salary or decision making, with the exception of a few teachers
or a nurse, but usually not if there was a qualified white one available.
The trained nurse (presumably a white woman) resigned at the beginning of 1885. Secretary Sarah Murray wrote in the minutes that "a
respectable middle aged colored woman" had been hired at twenty-five
dollars per month. But in February, Murray wrote that a trained nurse
had been hired to replace the African American woman. The white

nurse received thirty dollars per month, because she was trained and recommended by Dr. Frothingham. A Miss Fletcher was hired as a colored teacher for School No. 6 in December 1896 and was cited in the January 1897 minutes: "and although she had been there only since the holidays promises well." Several managers considered the presence of African American teachers desirable, but the majority questioned whether colored teachers would affect the institution unfavorably. In 1897, the resignation of a teacher led to the hiring of a black woman, a Miss Reid, who began "with good promise." It was reported in May that Miss Reid kept excellent order. The managers discussed in June the possibility of hiring more black teachers but decided to check with the principal, Gertrude Smith, for her view. This would be an important issue, because of its relationship to the discipline issue. Many of the children "acted out" against authority, which disturbed the white teachers and the matron, who did not know how to handle their misbehavior. In contrast, a black teacher might have recognized the cues that caused frustration on the part of the children and thus intervene before discipline was necessary. Despite the promising nature of black teachers, the asylum remained ambivalent about hiring them. A vacancy in the teaching staff in 1904 elicited from Superintendent Sherwin an opinion that "a white teacher was preferred for colored children." This ambivalence carried over to other African American professionals. It was reported in the July 1906 minutes that the dentist, Dr. Frederick R. Smith, had left. Smith recommended that a Dr. Reed, a colored dentist, be his replacement, but the hospital committee was asked to decide if they wished to "procure a colored dentist if possible." They eventually did hire a black dentist, Dr. Charles H. Roberts. An Englishwoman was hired as nurse for the asylum's hospital, even though a black nurse was available. The reluctance to hire blacks for professional positions showed that the managers were comfortable in keeping people of color in subservient roles. All twenty-one of the servants in 1900 were of color, but the nurse, four seamstresses, an engineer, a gardener, the matron, the assistant matron, and the superintendent were all white. On the other hand, the managers were extremely loyal to Charlotte Yorke, a longtime housekeeper who became physically unfit after an accident. She was given fifty dollars and a leave of absence, and a white woman was hired to replace her, not as a housekeeper but to be an assistant to the matron. Miss Yorke was essentially the matron's assistant without the title, but a white woman who assumed her duties was too good to have as lowly a title as housekeeper.[20]

Asylum Education or Public Education?

The decision of whether to educate the children in the asylum or send them to nearby public schools was an issue that concerned the managers in 1898. The Board of Education advised Superintendent Sherwin not to send the children to nearby public schools "both for their own good and as a way of reducing [the asylum's] expenses." The managers decided to wait a year before applying to send the children to neighborhood schools. Implied but not explicitly stated in the Board of Education's advice was that the neighborhood schools in West Harlem catered to white children. Harlem was over a decade away from beginning to change into an African American community, and it would be over four decades later before the area around the asylum at 143rd Street would turn "black." New York's schools had been legally integrated since the 1870s, but residential patterns kept many of the schools de facto segregated. The industrial curriculum suffered a setback in late 1897, with the death of the industrial teacher on December 23. It was difficult to find a replacement until they decided to experiment with a student teacher from nearby Teachers College to instruct the children in sewing one hour per day. A white laundress on staff was hired to teach laundry work and simple cooking. The managers saved a few dollars by paying the two a combined salary of nine to ten dollars weekly instead of fourteen dollars for a regular industrial teacher. Even though the asylum's curriculum was the same as the one that the Board of Education offered throughout New York City, the managers' emphasis on industrial education was reinforced when Booker T. Washington visited on February 13, 1899. The minutes indicated that thirty visitors were in attendance. The "children were quiet

[and] attentive." Washington lectured on "the gospel of the tooth-brush," a lecture that was also given to Tuskegee students. "No student is permitted to remain who does not keep and use a toothbrush." The use of a toothbrush and attention to cleanliness brought out "a higher degree of civilization," argued the educator. The managers believed that their emphasis on industrial education had been vindicated when the associate superintendent of the Board of Education visited in 1902 and "reported our work better in comparison to many of the [primary departments] of the public schools," as the teacher's report noted. It was emphasized that the asylum's students displayed better discipline and a higher standard of work than many of their counterparts in the city's public schools. This was attributed to the smallness of classes, the eleven-month school year, and the presence of the children contin-uously in the building. Employers were pleased to have indentures that had learned self-sufficiency before leaving the institution. Employers' accounts verified that "in some respects we are successful," reported Lillie Skiddy Parker, the chair of the education committee and daugh-ter-in-law of First Directress Mrs. Willard Parker Sr.[21]

Washington's lecture resonated with the managers on several lev-els. It pleased them that their emphasis on industrial training was shared by Booker T. Washington, arguably the nation's most recog-nized advocate of industrial training. It also reinforced their commit-ment to reform those Negro children who came to them products of poverty, licentiousness, and apathy. The annual report for 1899 re-corded their "aim . . . to understand the children" who came from backgrounds so alien from that of the middle- and upper-class white women, with their fine homes, servants, and, for many, summer homes in the mountains or at the shore. The report continued: "inside [this building] is the life of a race of people whose lives will be free of problems that will be hard to face, and whose environment before coming to us has not been all that would naturally make good men and women." Their stated objective had not wavered for decades. They wanted to produce children who would become "industrious, sober minded" adults. "There is to-day six millions of our negroes living in one room cabins, and five millions of these can neither read nor write. Is not their ignorance and degradation a danger to our whole country?"

Industrial education was the black person's salvation, argued the managers, who believed that it made children "self-respecting and competent" workers once they left the security of their asylum home. Some of the managers shared the belief that black adults did not possess the ability to train children properly. The March minutes indicated that "Mrs. Chapin spoke of a girl returned from a trial in a colored family as unsatisfactory although her work in the inst[itution] is good. Mrs. Chapin questions whether the colored people can train girls carefully or strictly." This biased opinion, of course, overlooked and ignored all those individuals who trained their children to obey the laws and to strive to be good citizens even while others denied them the rights of citizenship. This white supremacist sentiment existed in the asylum even among the staff. There was racial tension in early 1900, when the managers postponed a decision on whether it was wise to have white and black servants eat at the same table. Some managers had contact only with servile African Americans or were so used to semiliterate or illiterate parents or guardians that they could not see that within this group there were those who were properly training and guiding the youth. A letter from Maggie Winston reinforced the image of an ignorant person. Her letter of November 15, 1894 or 1899 (the last numeral is blurred), to Superintendent Sherwin was as follows:

> Mr. Chorwin
> Dear Ser
>   I write to you sorry to say I have no home or no way of taking care of Robert Robert my nepheu. I will be compel to leave him to you to put him whir ever you thind is best as I am alone woman and just making out at presen myself.[22]

Here was an uneducated woman who obviously had love for her nephew and wanted him to have the comfort and security of a home, albeit one that was an institution.

Despite the efforts of the managers to make good Christians and useful citizens of their charges, setbacks were not infrequent. Twelve-year-old Mabel Ballard was indentured to Mrs. O. E. Haskins on March 20, 1902. Soon after her arrival at Haskins' Rutherford, New Jersey, home, Mabel wrote a Mrs. Duval that she thought of God and read the Bible twice a day. Homesick, she added, "I felt as though I didn't have one friend around me." Something happened to cause Mabel's behavior to become obnoxious and detrimental to her relationship with Mrs. Haskins. It may have been depression resulting from homesickness, or perhaps she had a personality disorder. In an undated letter to the asylum, Mrs. Haskins wrote, "I regret to say that her work is not to be dependent upon but I believe she is perfectly honest and moral in her conduct." Mabel returned to the asylum on July 8, 1907, eight months before the expiration of her indenture. The managers tried to keep her in the asylum as a salaried employee, but two weeks after her arrival, the police took her to court, which sent her to the Magdalen Home, in New York City. From there, she was transferred to the Institute for Feebleminded Women. Upon leaving that institution, Mabel's bad behavior and temper cost her several positions. Mabel wrote in November 1917 with a request that the asylum "get some good Quaker to visit her" at the Frederick Douglass Hospital in Philadelphia. There was no record that a Mabel Ballard had been in the Frederick Douglass Hospital; therefore, her case was turned over to that city's Urban League for further investigation.[23]

Rachel Hardy was another girl whose behavior confounded the managers and staff. When she was nineteen, she wrote Superintendent Sherwin, on November 2, 1902, that her stay in the asylum was "the happiest days I ever spent and I don't expect ever to have such grand times as I had at the home[;] if only the boys and girls only knew what they had to be thankful for[.] I only wish I could tell them, because I have been out in the world and I know that the world gives some hard knocks and hard lessons. I hope the home will stand long and open its sheltering arms to many poor orphans as it did to me and all I can say is God bless the Colored Orphan Asylum." On May 5, 1903, Rachel wrote to Sherwin that she could cane chairs, make beds, sew, cook, read, and write and that she had been studying singing and the piano for two years. She stressed that her letter was lavish praise, of which she could not give enough for what they had done for her. She wrote Sherwin on March 3, 1904, that she wanted to visit after a seven-year absence. "I shall feel something like the prodigal son must have felt, to be once again in the home that sheltered me when a child." She was thankful that she had escaped the poverty, ignorance, and misery that surrounded her in Chester, Pennsylvania. Her letters were a remarkable tribute to the Colored Orphan Asylum and one that made the managers feel that their work was justified. It was all the more remarkable because seven years earlier on December 3, 1897, the indenturing committee noted that the then fourteen-year-old Rachel "was one of the worst girls we have ever had." She was returned by an employer, but the managers sent her to the Juvenile Asylum out of fear that "she would probably contaminate our children" if kept in the building.[24]

Search for a New Home

The building that had housed Rachel Hardy was now inadequate for the needs of the institution. It was decided to relocate to a less congested area, where the children would be surrounded by nature. In 1903, the managers considered and then rejected the possibility of buying the Roman Catholic orphanage, with its two buildings that housed 1,400 children. The property on 143rd Street had benefited from Harlem's development and was estimated to be worth $544,000, without the building. A year later, the completion of two nearby subway lines increased the value of their property to $850,000. Manager Mrs. William H. Lee argued that they should purchase land near a railroad line. Although their charter originally required that they reside in New York City (then Manhattan), the 1898 merger with southern Westchester County (the Bronx), Staten Island, Queens, and Brooklyn to form the five boroughs of New York City broadened their search area. Funds were available after the sale of U.S. bonds, and they possessed an additional fifteen thousand dollars in bonds and mortgages that could be liquidated easily. Thirty sites were visited throughout the year before a decision was reached to buy the estate of the late Robert Johnson, a dry-goods businessman, for eighty-five thousand dollars. This prime real estate included eight hundred feet along the Hudson River and was just five hundred feet south of the Mt. St. Vincent station on the New York Central Railroad. The managers improved their financial situation by selling their least valued securities and railroad stocks and by calling in a fourteen-thousand-dollar mortgage they held on property at 153 West Seventy-third Street in Manhattan.[25]

Robertson and Potter were selected as architects for the new building, which they estimated would cost about $350,000 once moving expenses, construction, and equipment was added. Initially, they wanted to have a main building, eight cottages, a house for the superintendent, and a central lighting and heating plant. Eventually they changed the plans to have six cottages and to spend up to $375,000.[26]

A cottage system was something the managers had wanted since 1888, after Sheltering Arms had adopted one. (Out of 972 orphan asylums listed in the 1910 census, 125 were cottage institutions.) Elise Gignoux, the corresponding secretary, declared in the annual report for 1905 that the cottage life would aid in the children's future industrial pursuits. "Great leaders of the colored race seem to agree in thinking that industrial training is the training best adapted to the present needs." This ignored the debate over industrial education versus classical studies then raging between the supporters of Booker T. Washington and W. E. B. Du Bois. "It is most urgently hoped that friends of the race will come forward at this time and will make possible the erection of the four remaining cottages," concluded Gignoux. Friends were not receptive to the plea, as only $492 was received in subscriptions/donations for 1905. However, the cottage fund received support in 1907, when Mary Clark Thompson, the daughter of Myron H. Clark, the former governor, gave the asylum fifteen thousand dollars. Clark Cottage was named in honor of her family. Eventually, $406,270 was spent on building the new home in Riverdale, in the Bronx. The cornerstone was laid on May 12, 1906, with moving day set for June 26, 1907. Four plans were examined for space and cost before the managers agreed to plan B's designs for a central building two stories high on each end with three stories in the middle. The main building would house 120 children, and the proposed ten disconnected two-story cottages would accommodate twenty-five children each. The cottage system was planned to make the children less susceptible to contagious diseases and decrease loss of life in event of a fire. "The children can more easily and practically be taught the requirement of the life for which they are most fitted namely domestic servants, trades, etc." It was believed that their participation in cooking and cleaning in the cottages would "nearly approach the family standard," which would make them attractive to future employers.[27]

The construction of the new building, with demands on funds for furnishings, grading of land, moving expenses, and other costs, put the asylum in the familiar position of appealing for public funds. The appeal committee sent letters in November 1906 to "all the colored pastors in [New York City] asking them to raise funds with which to build another cottage on our new site and suggesting that the children of the neighborhoods raise money with which to buy a large bell called "the Roosevelt bell."[28]

The public appeal to the black community was poorly timed. On August 13, 1906, a white customs official in Brownsville, Texas, assaulted a black soldier for "disrespecting" a white woman. Random shooting that evening killed a white bartender and wounded the chief

The Riverdale building, c. 1907. (Courtesy of Harlem Dowling–West Side Center for Children and Family Services.)

of police. Although all the soldiers were accounted for and no ammunition was missing, twelve soldiers of the Twenty-fifth U.S. Colored Infantry were charged with murder and conspiracy to commit murder. President Theodore Roosevelt, angry that no one would name the guilty party or parties, dishonorably discharged 167 men even though there had been no confession, indictment, or trial. The black press and black churches soundly criticized Roosevelt for his callous action. There is no record of the outcome of the managers' appeal, but it was unlikely that the black community was currently interested in honoring the president with a bell. Roosevelt's callous decision was only overturned by the secretary of the army in 1972.[29]

Nor can it be expected that the black community would be in a giving mood had they read Lillie Skiddy Parker's education report in the 1906 annual report, which called for funds from "the kind friends who are interested in the teaching and training of these little black waifs."[30] A waif, or homeless child, while an accurate description of the orphans in the institution, inaccurately described the majority of children, who were half-orphans or had been sent to the asylum by the courts. Parker might have considered her reference to "little black waifs" as a term of endearment, but probably many African Americans considered the words pejorative. In addition, "black" as a racial term would not have appealed to many, despite its use in the title of Du Bois's famous 1903 book *The Souls of Black Folk*. Despite the occasional contemporary use of "black," it would take six decades before it enjoyed widespread currency as a racial designation. At that time, those who chose integration or assimilation favored the nomenclature "colored"; more militant individuals advocated for the adoption of a capitalized "Negro" as the proper race term.

Parker's belief that the institution indeed helped the unfortunate "waif" was certainly strengthened by the message sent by a former "old boy," Thomas H. Barnes, who had retained strong feelings for his "home." Barnes entered the asylum in 1860 as a nine-year-old and had witnessed the building's destruction during the Draft Riots. He requested from Superintendent Sherwin a photograph of the Fifth Avenue building to use in a lecture about growing up in the institution. Even after departing forty-two years earlier, he felt "a keen interest and cherish[ed his] memory of the grand old institution."[31]

6

New Start in Riverdale, 1907-22

The Cottage System and Punishment

The trustees were determined that their new home in Riverdale would be modeled on the cottage system, which was then in vogue. The New York Juvenile Asylum had embraced the cottage system in 1897 as a way to enforce discipline and "to stimulate the intimacy of family life." The imitation of home life consisted of using knives and forks instead of spoons, china instead of enamel dishes, and chairs instead of backless benches. Some well-behaved children lived in "honor" cottages with their own rooms; misbehaving ones slept in "correctional" cottages under the eyes of a night watchman. The Hebrew Sheltering Guardian Orphan Asylum in nearby Westchester County, New York, preferred young cottage mothers who had "pedagogical training or . . . kindergarten training." The Carson and Ellis College in Philadelphia provided white girls with "a complete unit of family life, with kitchen, dining room, and common room."[1]

A few months before their move in March 1907, the trustees decided that "the housemothers are to be colored" and that they would perform their duties at a salary of twenty-five dollars monthly, without the assistance of caretakers. However, not all agreed that the housemothers should be African Americans. Mrs. J. L. Chapin questioned the advisability of employing black housemothers. It is not clear why Chapin expressed this sentiment. Perhaps she believed that black women did not know how to properly discipline children. Six colored women were hired, but one white woman, Charlotte C. Stoutenburgh, was retained as a housemother until an opportunity arose to transfer her to the main building. Four of the cottages were named after former managers: Founders Cottage was named in memory of Anna Shotwell and Mary Murray, Van Dusen Cottage was named to honor the late manager Mrs. Samuel B. Van Dusen, Caroline Cottage honored the financial contributions of Caroline Stokes (Mrs. James Stokes), and Onderdonk Cottage was named in memory of the longtime manager Harriet S. Onderdonk (Mrs. William H. Onderdonk). The women also decided to install a drinking fountain in honor of the unnamed eight-year-old girl who had saved the asylum's Bible during the Draft Riots. The cottage system got off to an inauspicious start. An early visit in September 1907 revealed dirty bathtubs in all the cottages and unattractive dining-room tables in the boys' cottages. The third floor of the main building was very untidy. Caroline Cottage passed inspection, but the boys' lavatories in Founders Cottage had a very unpleasant smell. For several years, the lack of sanitation persisted in the cottages' bathrooms. To alleviate the problem, the managers decided at the end of 1910 to pay the cottage children to clean the facilities, realizing that money was more motivating than a pleasant environment. This reward system was not approved of by those who believed in the power of the stick or hand. However, First Directress Mrs. Willard Parker Sr. spoke strongly against the use of corporal punishment after learning that the matron, Elizabeth Jones, had spanked a child for slapping others and that the second directress had observed three nurses holding sticks "in attitudes of a disciplined nature." The question of what types of punishment were acceptable remained a topic of debate. In January 1910, the committee on punishment arranged for new penalties and called for teachers and housekeepers to cooperate to maintain proper discipline. The trustees decided "that a closet be built for the punishment of the children and that the First Directress [Carolena M. Wood] shall obtain information about corporal punishment."[2]

Despite the initial inconveniences, at the end of 1907 the ladies were pleased with the cottage system, which represented a return to the early days of the asylum and its emphasis on a closely knit home environment. It was reported in the annual report that "the cottage or home life is to be the life for the little ones instructed to our keeping," even though it was more expensive than the previous system. The

fireproof building, with concrete floors, iron stairs, six large classrooms, an officers' dining room, carpenter shop, children's library, assembly room, storeroom, bake shop, kitchen, managers' room, boot-
repair room, large sewing room, quarantine department, and eight
apartments for male employees was aesthetically pleasing. Children
had to share a room, except for those who received a prize room as a
reward for being the best boy or girl.[3]

Lillie Skiddy Parker, the chair of the educational committee, recommended ending the industrial class, because the children were doing
housework in the cottages. Sewing, however, continued for the girls,
with the older ones cutting, basting (sewing loose, temporary stitches),
and making plain garments for personal use. The older boys worked
on the grounds, graded the roads, and tended to the garden. The workload raised the issue of keeping the children out of school for two
months during the summer, to which the educational committee ob-
jected. Principal Gertrude Smith wanted those kept out of school for
housework to study one hour each day under her direction. The executive committee suggested that children attend school regularly and perform duties before or after school hours. This debate would continue
for decades, as some managers believed that the household chores and
field work better prepared the boys and girls for their life's work than
did classroom instruction. Lillie Skiddy Parker indicated that "our children enjoy their studies, and in most cases really try to do their best,
and they should go out into the world a little better for the love, peace,
and beauty which surround them."[4]

The breakage of china was representative of problems in the cottage system. The minutes for the October 1908 executive committee
meeting noted "a lack of management of housemothers in cottage No.
2." For punishment, it was suggested that the guilty children be made
to use the disgraced cup and plate. It got worse in December, when it
was reported that there had been a great deal of glass broken in Cottage No. 3. It was reported in January 1909 that "the cottages are in
good order, but excessive breaking of china continues." The following
month's minutes reported less breakage but also that "the children lack
knowledge and care in setting the table." To offset the breakage, the

Hotel Belmont, which had opened in 1906, donated in May large quantities of china. The trustees hoped to eliminate the breakage in August with the announcement that every three months money to purchase something for the house would be given to the cottage that had little or no breakage. Unfortunately, the breakage did not subside; the Hotel Belmont generously sent another large donation of dishes to the asylum in 1910. The breakage problem was partly a result of poor supervision on the part of the housemothers, but, more significantly, some of the children were malicious, having been sent by the courts. Others may have broken dishes, angry at being compelled to do housework. The superintendent sought in 1913 to curb mischievous behavior and to grant the children a sense of ownership by introducing the use of institutional currency for all over the age of eight. Later, children ages twelve to fourteen were placed on a pay scale for good conduct. They were paid by the hour for work done but were made financially responsible for their board and clothes. This practice was initiated to make them more conscientious about their clothes and give them practice dealing with money. Other institutions adopted a similar currency policy, in the hopes that it would "soften" the routine of institutional life. Previously, unlike outside children, those in the asylum did not carry pocket change to purchase candy or an inexpensive toy. They did not understand how to use money in ordinary transactions, which other children took for granted. Twelve children, responsible for the bookkeeping, banking, and clerking, handled between fifteen hundred and two thousand dollars monthly and maintained 175 individual bank accounts.[5]

In light of the breakage problem, the 1908 annual report's description of the cottage system was disingenuous. Corresponding Secretary Mrs. J. Tufton Mason wrote that the cottage system gave children "a sense of ownership and of importance that instills self-respect, and with self-respect comes improvement in deportment and appearance." She added that Southern Negro migrants "know very little about sanitation, ventilation, filtered water, or the use of the bath tub." This made it more imperative that the Colored Orphan Asylum educate the individual and not the race. Mrs. Mason was stating what apologists for slavery had pronounced for centuries: Negroes would not amount to much in a group, but individual Negroes, particularly those with "white" blood or, at least, exposure to white culture, could be saved from the helplessness and depravity of their race's destiny.[6]

Mrs. Mason and others considered this a truism, especially as the staff witnessed every day some form of depravity committed by the children. Raised in vicious homes where survival meant quick instincts to ward off parental blows, these children, despite their age or youthful "cuteness," were often sadistic in their behavior toward weaker or less violent children. Ten-year-old Marin William Cumbo heated a can of water, which was against the rules. Alfred Mills, angry that Marin would not give it to him, "dished the water into Marin's face, burning him badly on the right side of his forehead and upper part of his right cheek but did not touch the eye." (Later, Marin, without any scars, became Marion Cumbo, a celebrated cellist who performed in "Shuffle Along," an epoch-making Broadway musical comedy that brought fame to Florence Mills.) On New Year's Day, 1909, nine-year-old Annie Caroy threw a pail of boiling water on the legs of Bertha Holt while she was in bed. The Institute for Feeblemindedness at Ellwyn, Pennsylvania, strongly recommended that in three years Annie should not be placed in a position where there were young children. Annie was "placed out" to work on October 7, 1913.[7]

Problems with the cottage system continued throughout the fall and winter of 1909, which coincided with the supposedly smarter and more mature children leaving the premises for outside schooling. It appears that those left behind resented their condition and purposely acted out in disobedient or destructive ways. Langdon Cottage was reported to be "filthy from top to bottom"; the house mother, Margaret Booth, was deemed incompetent. Clark and Willets cottages were considered to be in bad order. A fire in the winter caused $307 in damages to Clark Cottage. Only Van Dusen Cottage received excellent evaluations. The conditions were so bad that Anna Alexander, the chair of the cottage committee, requested that "the supervising house mother be a white woman."[8] Instead of replacing the incompetent house mother with a qualified African American, the conclusion was that only a white woman had the skills to provide excellent work.

Readers of the annual report for 1909 were not informed about the poor conditions of the cottages. Instead, looking for donations, the trustees presented them with a glowing and completely misleading evaluation. Recording Secretary Florence Taylor wrote, "the cottage life continues to bring forth many pleasing results in our new home, and we find the children take great pleasure and pride in helping the house mothers make their cottage an example of orderliness and cleanliness." She indicated that there was a friendly rivalry between the cottages. Those with a perfect inspection were permitted to display a flag. Taylor added that the boys assisted in improving the grounds by grading, building a new drive, and laying out a playground with a baseball diamond and a running track. A stone grandstand overlooking the baseball field added to the amenities. In an unrelated manner, the executive committee minutes but not the annual report noted a potential problem with the indenturing system. The State Charities Aid Association questioned the "amount of work imposed on children placed in private situations." Miss Wood was to investigate "to ascertain the method of treatment of indentured children and the best method of visiting them."[9]

The chaotic cottage system represented in microcosm the problems with institutional life, and it helped stimulate a national debate among child welfare reformers, who were pondering the merits of home care over institutional care. They wanted to know to what extent should the public supervise the practices of private child welfare agencies and what standards were necessary to achieve uniformity among institutional and foster home care.

White House Conference of 1909

Although by 1908 the majority of the children in the asylum were not orphans, it was becoming apparent that adoptions would provide the love and security that many of the children so earnestly needed. Meanwhile, the managers were looking for the best homes, "trusting that under true Christian influences [the children] may become worthy men and women." Despite this lofty prose, for inexplicable reasons, the indenturing committee rejected the application of a black family, Mr. and Mrs. Abram Hollenbeck, to adopt Leonie Carter. They decided to indenture her for one year "without the usual payment." It was not clear why they rejected the application, which was submitted through the New York State Charities Aid Association, and there is no record of the fate of the child. In January, the indenturing committee referred to the board of managers the feasibility of having young children placed for adoption "if suitable and responsible parents should apply." In March, they agreed that colored families could adopt orphans. The first approval came in December, when a family in Trenton, New Jersey, James and Emma Rose, took an eighteen-month-old child who otherwise would have been sent to the House of Refuge on Randall's Island. In March 1910, the indenturing committee was reluctant to approve two applications that "showed illiteracy." In April 1911, Hastings Hart, the superintendent of the Department of Child Agencies with the Russell Sage Foundation, advised that colored ministers should be consulted about homes for children but not to accept their word unsupported. Hart's suggestion probably was attributed to an incident earlier in 1911, when the placement of eight-year-old Ruby Clark on trial for adoption with a Mrs. Strumpf of 312 West 119th Street ended in failure. The child was returned because she lacked "a congenial temperament." An unusual adoption occurred in 1920, involving four-and-a-half-year-old Gladys Yeager, who had lived with the Simmons couple for four years. Mrs. Simmons died, and her husband, now a single parent, was given permission to adopt her, "as he is very fond of Gladys and able to bring her up properly," as the aftercare committee (the former indenturing committee) noted. Equally interesting was a request from a Mr. Johnson, an orphan in the asylum in 1879, "to adopt a little girl of six or seven years [of age]." The disposition of his request is unknown. Children too old for adoption were no longer sent out as indentures. It was decided in May 1908 to indenture children to work in the asylum. Charles Alston was assigned as a helper in the boiler room. Robert Murray became a carpenter. They were paid an undisclosed amount of money to purchase certain items of clothing.[10]

The aforementioned information occurred in the context of a national concern over the fate of children in institutions. The mood was that children would be better off in a home situation, whether that be adoption or foster care. The White House Conference on Care of Dependent Children on January 25, 1909, brought together two hundred delegates, and one of its themes was that inefficiency or immorality, not poverty, was the cause of family disintegration. The conference was a landmark in child welfare history, "in many ways marking the discovery of children in America," declared the sociologists Andrew Billingsley and Jeanne M. Giovannoni. The conference concluded that families should be kept together by "diminishing or removing altogether the causes of orphanages, of child destitution, and child delinquency." There were several immediate responses to the conference. Booker T. Washington spoke at the gathering and declared that a child was better off in a foster home "than he is in the average orphan asylum." Washington noted that it would be more productive to provide funds to keep a child "in the natural environment, until he gets the strength and experience which has made [whites] great and strong and useful." He added that Tuskegee Institute was suspicious of applicants from orphanages. Catholics argued that their institutions, rather than the home, did a better job of developing character. The historian Matthew A. Crenson argues that "the White House Conference started nothing and settled nothing." Other scholars countered that institutions dulled children with their regimentation of uniforms, marching to and from meals, silent meals, and dependence upon the institution and that it was essential to get children into homes. As important as the conference suggestions were, and even though the Colored Orphan Asylum would, within a few years, adopt many of the measures, they were remarkably silent in 1909. There are no references to the White House Conference in the board of managers' minutes, the executive committee minutes, or the annual report.[11]

Verbank Farm

The institution's finances received a major boost in 1910 with an unexpected receipt of funds from two disparate sources. On February 1,

1910, the asylum held $296,500 worth of railroad mortgage bonds. The following month, Smith Ely, a former mayor of New York and a former congressman, gave the orphanage twenty-five thousand dollars for the endowment, provided that they raise matching funds. Five hundred dollars was used as seed money for that purpose. Appeals were sent out in June to twelve hundred individuals, in the hopes of raising three thousand dollars. Carolena M. Wood took a temporary leave in November to raise funds for the Smith Ely Fund. Meanwhile, Smith Ely died on July 1, but his will matched the twenty thousand raised by the institution. Mrs. Daniel Willis James, a manager since 1858, provided twenty-five thousand dollars to "buy and equip a farm." On October 17, the asylum purchased the Tobin Farm at Verbank, in Dutchess County, New York. The 144-acre farm comprised well-watered fertile land with a house and barns. Based on Booker T. Washington's recommendation, the Tuskegee graduate H. B. Norton and his wife were hired as farmer and matron to operate the farm. Four boys and one girl were in the first group sent to Verbank to learn farming.[12]

The women were so pleased with the operation at Verbank Farm that they decided in late 1912 that it would be a farm school "for the older boys . . . whose decided tendency was for country life." (Unfortunately, many boys had no tendency to learn farming skills.) It showed a profit in 1912 of $251.95, but for a number of years, until it closed in 1920, farm fires and discipline problems would cause headaches for the institution. Harry or Harvey Cook was sent to Verbank Farm by the district attorney of Dutchess County after being arrested for assault. He was expected to be transferred to the asylum, which concerned the superintendent. The superintendent wanted the courts to send him to another institution, "unless some suitable home could be found to receive him." Cook came to the asylum, where he was not permitted to sleep in the same room with other children. The trustees had earlier worked with the Committee on Urban Conditions Among Negroes to assist with young girls returned to the asylum for unsatisfactory conduct. They hoped to do the same with young Cook.[13]

Problems persisted at Verbank Farm, where, on August 26, 1913, the investigator J. R. Fugett reported that Wilbur Raddick was refused lodging and food and was beaten with a club by Mr. Barnett, the farm supervisor. The hungry and frightened boy spent the night in a neighbor's haystack. E. Ferris stated that Raddick had informed him that Barnett told him to seek employment in Peekskill or somewhere else. Ferris employed the young boy in exchange for room and board. Raddick had previously worked for a Mr. Collins, who was abusive when intemperate, an account confirmed by others. Barnett initiated a vagrancy warrant against Raddick to get him to leave Verbank. Barnett came to Ferris's residence, removed Raddick, and took him to work for Peter Matthews, a Dutchman. Neighbors complained that the Verbank boys were undisciplined, noisy, kept late hours, and were a potential threat to young white girls who visited neighbors in the evening. This version of the out-of-control-teenager story had two other interpretations. Barnett stated that Raddick had left Collins for unknown reasons but that he wanted to stay at Verbank Farm, in violation of the policy of letting placed-out boys return. Barnett sent Raddick back to Collins, who returned him the following day. Barnett then sent Raddick back to the asylum in New York, where Miss Scheurman refused to keep him. Raddick returned to Barnett, who "took up something in his hand to scare him" but did not strike him. According to Barnett, the boy started a vicious rumor that he had been abused by the supervisor to gain sympathy from the neighbors. Barnett explained to the neighbors that he had fed Raddick and locked him up the first night in the feed room because he was not allowed to return to the house. A third version had Raddick leaving an abusive Collins. Barnett chased and beat the boy on his arm, which left a partially healed wound near the elbow. Neighbors assisted Raddick and denied that he stole food. Peter Matthews took the boy for a week's trial upon Barnett's request. The convoluted story ended when Raddick promised to work hard and be obedient. This saga reflected the difficulty the ladies had trying to run a farm a great distance from New York City.[14]

By 1914, Verbank Farm was developing into a liability for the asylum. The farm was run now by James Aiken, a Hampton graduate who was undecided if he would stay another year, a typical reaction shared by his predecessors. His wife, a trained nurse, tended to the health of the boys, who ranged from ages fourteen to sixteen. The farm produced various vegetables and dairy products. The local school district refused to accept the Verbank boys, probably because the farm committee chairwoman did not want to pay the school tax. Verbank's problems were symptomatic of the institution's financial condition and compounded by a lack of direction. The COA faced, as of November 1, 1914, a $10,274.78 deficit. Beginning in early 1915, boys committed by the courts for "truancy and improper guardianship" from age twelve to fifteen and who had completed the fifth grade were accepted at Verbank Farm. Mr. Aiken was "fitting 4 boys for Hampton [Institute]." A series of fires plagued the farm. On November 2, 1916, the cow barn was destroyed. Wagons, crops, and a horse that refused to leave its stall were lost. All the cattle except one were sold, as there was no place to keep them. A brief period of euphoria over the farm's productivity, the construction of new barns, and the acquisition of a new herd of cows was curtailed when another fire, on August 15, 1919, destroyed the cow barn, silos, milk house, hay, feed, fertilizer, and wagon. The cows were spared, but it was decided to sell the herd "at once." The farm was sold seven months later for five thousand dollars.[15]

Education

The asylum school situation presented a problem for the COA. In October 1903, a committee composed of Ellen M. Wood, Mrs. Joseph W. Tilton, and Florence Warner met to find out if the Hebrew Orphan Asylum had spent less when the Board of Education had run their school. The Hebrew Orphan Asylum advised against having the board run the school, because it would cause a "lack of harmony between managers and teachers, the selection of the poorest teachers from the public schools for its positions, the absence of individual training in the education of the children among other reasons, besides it being cheaper to run it themselves." Nevertheless, a resolution was adopted in February 1911 to have the New York City Board of Education take over the asylum school. The trustees formally agreed to do so in April. The educational committee suggested in September 1911 that the children remain in the institution longer and engage in more industrial training. It was decided to keep some girls of school age for an extra year in the asylum "to receive special industrial training and assist the house mothers." In August, the board of managers decided "to plan for . . . a graduating class of say 12 of the oldest girls, to be . . . trained not only in domestic science but in consideration for others in manners and thoughtfulness." In October, the after-care committee discussed training girls as nurses to assist in the nurseries and kindergarten classes but then decided that "we part with our girls at too early an age to accomplish this." However, conditions were so bad that it was reported in October that all but two classes "were demoralized owing to the inexperience of the teachers." This observation contrasted with that of Lillie Skiddy Parker, the chair of the educational committee, who wrote in the annual report for 1908 that she was gratified with the school's improvement since a visit several years earlier at the Harlem location. "I was first impressed with the order and discipline, there seemed to be no particular effort required by the teachers, and the children acted in a respectful and obedient manner as a matter of course." She added that their progress was in advance of those in the city's public school. (Again, we have an exaggeration of progress in the annual report that was contradicted by the minutes, which the public did not read.) Parker was especially pleased that the children were contented with the housework in the cottages, which they all shared equally in doing. She even praised their attempts at cooking tasty dishes for the trustees' lunch. An appeal for books and magazines yielded contributions from six donors of one hundred volumes of children's books, nine volumes of Booker T. Washington's autobiography *Up from Slavery*, and magazines.[16]

It was decided for social and academic reasons that the older children should attend public schools outside of the institution. In June 1909, the board of managers approved the educational committee's recommendation that older children attend public schools in the nearby Kingsbridge section of the Bronx. By November, twenty-five residents attended an outside public school; the "backward" children were kept in the asylum. Mrs. Tilton asked if this procedure "was a proper form of punishment." Lillie Skiddy Parker, the chair of the educational committee, considered it "a great incentive . . . as each child hopes by good conduct and high marks to be chosen as one of the favored." She added that having fewer children in the asylum school allowed for greater individual attention for the slower ones. The education report for 1910 was promising. The asylum school educated 235 children, with thirty-seven attending neighborhood schools. The departmental system was employed, whereby a teacher would teach a subject to all the children. "The child comes into contact with each teacher during the day which seems to add interest and enthusiasm to the work of both teacher and pupil, and often prevents friction," noted the principal. Miss Rodman, a teacher at Wadleigh High School in Manhattan, observed that some of the asylum children were "more intelligent than any she had received." Carpentry classes were offered by a student from Columbia's Teachers College. The chair and secretary of the educational committee visited Tuskegee in March "to study methods in school with a view to improving our school work." The emphasis on industrial education had not changed, as it was still believed that farming or household work was the lot of black youth. In fact, even exceptional children were steered to Hampton Institute or Tuskegee Institute, both proponents of industrial education. There was no interest in enrolling a promising young person into Fisk, Howard, Lincoln, or Spelman, which were black liberal arts colleges. Principal Alice F. Halpin noted in the annual report for 1918 that the seventh and eighth grades were discontinued because of a lack of pupils. The few children eligible for those classes attended Public School 7, in Kingsbridge. In mid-March 1919, Secretary Ruth S. Murray notified the Board of Education that "against their better judgment" and only because they were ordered to would they send seventh graders to Public School 7. She was insistent that the Board of Education be responsible for their safety once they left the asylum. It appears that the concern was less for safety than it was for children getting into trouble. This issue became paramount in 1921, when the Board of Education wanted nine children above the sixth grade to attend an outside school instead of learning in a mixed-grade class in the institution. The trustees did not want the children off the premises unescorted. The Board of Education ordered them to do so, even though the asylum complained that a caretaker accompanying them would take up half of his workday and that the traveling time would prohibit them from interacting with the outside children in school sports or other events. Despite the disagreement, the superintendent of schools, Dr. William L. Ettenger, and Dr. Frank D. Wilsey, vice president of the board, were generally pleased with the work of the asylum school, especially the children's performance in oral and written languages.[17]

New Leadership

The inability to attract a quality staff was blamed on Superintendent Martin Sherwin, whose personal management style irritated both the staff and the managers. The trustees had to cope with an increasingly older and weaker Sherwin. By 1900, his duties had become too much for one person. He managed the asylum, supervised the staff, visited indentures, handled minor repairs, and did what other superintendents had done for the past six decades. However, the dying days of the nineteenth century and the arriving new century called for a superintendent who was less of a farmer/mechanic and more of a sociologist/psychologist—someone who could make the institution more efficient while addressing the rapidly changing society that was providing them with the children. For years, Sherwin had resisted having an assistant, but now it was time to hire one. "It was understood that he should be a white man." Certainly the trustees did not understand or care how the children received this message. Why bother having black men of competence around as a role models when the children were merely being trained to become domestic servants or farmhands? The women wanted this assistant, as noted by C. T. Gilman, the chair of the search committee, to be "a man of strong [and] sterling Christian character who would bring a high missionary zeal to his work. He must too have a love for children and power in discipline. Such a man would be of great help in supplementing the work of the chaplain." They wanted a man with a college degree to help guide the asylum's school curriculum as well as someone versed in business philosophy. They sent inquiries to Oberlin, Earlham, Northfield, and some Methodist colleges to assist them in their search but ultimately decided in the spring of 1900 not to hire an assistant for Sherwin. They relented on this matter in 1908 and hired one. A more serious problem confronted them that same year. An investigation began over Superintendent Sherwin's intemperance and general lack of competence. This resulted in no immediate action, but the sparks were reignited in 1911, when the house mothers signed a letter accusing the superintendent of alcoholism and rudeness. They claimed that he had tried to make them feel that they belonged to "an inferior race" and that he had no interest "in the future welfare of the [children] of the colored race." They threatened to resign if he continued as superintendent. Since the accusations were serious, it was decided that the "charges . . . should be dealt with in a prompt impartial and decisive manner." Sherwin's resignation was accepted effective August 1, 1911, with salary paid until December 1, 1911. In light of his twenty-seven years of service, the trustees provided a recommendation noting that "he was earnest in his work for the welfare of the children, and had good judgment in selecting homes for them when they left the institution. We especially commend his business ability [which] has kept our expenses at a minimum to produce satisfactory results."[18]

Frank W. Barber was hired in 1911 to replace Sherwin. Corresponding Secretary Helena L. Knox described him as one who brought "training in the modern theories of education [from Teachers College] which we hope may help us to a more intelligent training of the children." She added that "the Board longs for better things, physically, mentally and moral improvement, in a word for the uplift of a race whose latent possibilities the white man but dimly apprehends." Barber had only been in the superintendent's position since August 1, but he quickly assessed that an improvement in the buildings and grounds would affect positively the morale of the children and staff. He presented an extensive report to the executive committee in November. Barber recommended repairs or improvements including installing hedges, grading walkways and roads, painting all the buildings, removing dead trees, improving the drainage system, sprucing up rooms and offices to make them more attractive, upgrading or replacing furniture, and removing unsightly fixtures such as an old barn. Barber's estimate of $2,250 was not granted for all items, but many of his recommendations met with board approval.[19]

Superintendent Barber brought to his position a scientific perspective in running an institution that, as of December 1, 1911, housed 295 children. His leadership led to the executive committee discussing the future of the Colored Orphan Asylum at their January 1912 meeting. They considered the following seven areas for discussion: (1) conditions of admission, (2) provision for training, (3) conditions of discharge, (4) number to be admitted, (5) whether the asylum was dedicated to the good of individual children or for the uplift of the Negro race, (6) the quality of the workers, and (7) investigation of the condition of the applicants for admission. These areas were serious issues that needed resolution if the asylum was to continue to serve the African American community. The Colored Orphan Asylum had, over the years, admitted more nonorphans than orphans. Of the 295 children in the asylum as of December 1, 1911, forty had both parents living, and 169 were half-orphans. The courts were sending more delinquent and troubled children to the institution. These seven items would occupy the energy and finances of the asylum for years to come. The after-care committee decided a week after the executive committee meeting that placed-out children be sent only if they received a monthly wage and pocket money based on age and "capacity of the child, and the circumstances of the family which it is placed." They also required that a monthly report on the child be forwarded to the asylum. The few children still in indentures were to be visited, with the date of each visit recorded. The managers also looked to have some of the younger children adopted by families. To facilitate this, they allowed some children to board with families, hoping that the close relationship between the child and a couple would lead to an adoption.[20]

The trustees were so pleased with the superintendent's first year of leadership that they raised his salary, in October 1912, to three thousand dollars, from $1,999.92. They wanted him to make a stronger advancement in the educational spirit of the institution and see quicker progress in the children's development. They cautioned that "opportunities to do something worthwhile will depend on his financial management and his work in making the institution known and valued in the community." The "community," of course, was Harlem, whose leadership would question Barber's and the institution's racial arrogance. Fred Moore, the editor of the *New York Age*, an African American weekly, demanded to know why the asylum replaced removed colored people with whites. Barber was given "authority to discharge Charlotte Yorke when he considers it better for the institution that she should go and give her $300 [a year's salary] in appreciation of her long [forty years] service." An engineer died in December 1912, and the majority of the executive committee preferred that the replacement be a white engineer. In the spring of 1913, "the question of mixing white and colored people in the dining room" was addressed by the COA. Superintendent Barber changed policy and had "the new colored employee eating at a separate table in the children's dining room." Paradoxically, the ladies thought it appropriate to invite "a group of the high class colored people in to visit." An invitation to Harlem's black elite was a display of racial tolerance, but, simultaneously, working-class blacks were relegated to a Jim Crow dining room. One must question if they ever thought about the effects that this prejudice had on the children, who daily witnessed such discrimination. The ambivalence of the COA about race led them to ask Barber if it would be acceptable for them to "hire a colored man to work our grounds." Barber replied that the children could handle repairs to the walk areas around the cottages, "under a colored man engaged to take charge of the work."[21]

While there were a few children working as indentures, the trustees were now, in 1910, seeking to board them out to willing families. On November 2, the indenturing committee decided at a special meeting to request information about their methods of boarding out children from the Philadelphia Home for Destitute Children. The reply noted that "colored children were often successfully boarded out with relatives." The committee recommended to the Board of Managers that the institution try to board out twenty children and to request that the State Charities Aid Association find good homes, which would provide space for the asylum to admit more deserving children. Before boarding out children, the COA had the immediate responsibility to look out for the fate of the children who left the institution. Carolena M. Wood, who became first directress upon the resignation of Mrs. Willard Parker Sr. in 1908, was authorized to investigate the homes of children who had left the institution. She also was to investigate the homes of those children who were recently committed to enter the institution. Wood's duties were to contact the State Charities Aid Association about children eligible for adoption "and place them in homes through that association." In December 1909, Wood recommended that the management maintain an interest in those that had left the institution and help them acquire an education useful for a vocation. Educating children for a vocation instead of for a profession referenced the management's opinion that the children should not aspire for a higher calling but be contented with the possibility of a "good" job.[22]

The indenturing committee (the minutes still reflected this name) reported in December 1911 that since January 1909 many children had been discharged to relatives "of whom no further record appears to have been kept." They decided to see if the School of Philanthropy could provide a student to study 219 children "and prepare a thesis containing their history after leaving the asylum, also the cost of such an investigation." There was no student available, but the School of Philanthropy provided the names of two investigators who would charge ten to twelve dollars weekly for three weeks. Ann L. London was hired through the State Charities Aid Association to begin, in mid-February 1912, to investigate "applications for children, the cases where complaints have been made, the other children placed out, and finally, those placed with parents, except when it served best to do all the work in one neighborhood, before proceeding to others." The indenturing committee decided on January 22, 1912, to visit all children where there was dissatisfaction, all children placed out, and those discharged to parents and relatives during the past six months. The executive committee adopted in April the report of the committee on records that declared that complete records should consist of family history, the child's history, admissions sheet, physical record, weekly record, reward of merit, correction record, semiannual digest of progress, follow-up record, index card, discharge card, and investigation card. The records were to be retroactive to either October 1, 1911, or

January 1, 1912. In July, a Miss Wood and Mrs. Barton formed a committee to organize an alumni association to keep in touch with former
indentures currently living in New York City.[23]

In the spring of 1912, the Committee on Urban Conditions Among
Negroes (known later as the National Urban League) asked the COA to
assist them. Subsequently, a Mrs. Jackson was employed to work with
the after-care committee to find suitable homes for girls. If the finance
committee could handle the cost, the trustees wanted to hire "two colored students from the School of Philanthropy for practical training in
institutional work for the school year." In November, they decided that
under favorable conditions girls could be placed in homes in New York
City. This decision was made despite the city's temptations, because it
was more difficult to protect innocent, lonely, and naïve girls from
sexual predators in the country areas. The after-care committee had
difficulty in deciding whether a black or white woman would be a
competent investigator "to investigate applications, visit regularly all
children placed out, keep records and take charge of correspondence
in regard to the children." After some deliberation, they concluded that
a white woman would be a more acceptable investigator. Perhaps they
reached this conclusion based on the belief that a white investigator
would have more credibility as an authority figure with black families.
The after-care committee also decided that a black woman should be
located to visit those who had left the asylum, to help them adjust to
their new social life. In February 1914, Mrs. Adelaide Norwood of 119
West 103rd Street in Manhattan volunteered to handle that responsibility. A list of seven volunteers was provided to the executive committee, which planned to explain to them "the need that we desire them
to fill and arrange the best means of carrying out our purpose."[24]

In November 1915, the superintendent asked the executive committee for permission to place children in Catholic homes. The executive committee gave its approval if no law prohibited the practice. Soon
after, the trustees decided against placing them in Catholic homes. The
topic became irrelevant when the after-care committee ruled in December that it was against the law to place Protestant children in Catholic
homes. The effort to place them in Catholic homes underscored the

need to lower the number of children in institutional living. The annual report for 1915 stated that there were 267 in the house on November 30. Only thirteen children were orphans; the other 254 were public charges who came from homes lacking in discipline and affection. Despite the asylum's struggle with the issue of corporal punishment, it was administered to children who lacked respect for authority. The annual report frankly noted that "while nothing military is attempted, a wise and firm management is insisted upon, not such as will crush the will, but such as will generate a frank, natural and open manner, the same as would be expected from a child in a normal home." Nonetheless, institutional living was not normal. Nor was dormitory-style living, albeit in cottages, conducive to privacy during the crucial years of puberty. Problems also persisted with children placed out. Complaints continued that the children were irresponsible. The trustees thought that a gymnasium on the premises would assist children to learn proper character traits through vigorous physical activity and games that called for teamwork and cooperation. The trustees decided in May 1918 to board children in homes near New York City. The boarding-out committee recommended that this method was more practical than building new buildings for housing. The experiment was to last six months, with the city paying for the children's board. The experiment was successful and became a staple of the institution's policy.[25]

The boarding concerns increased in 1919. Children were boarded out in Brooklyn, the Jamaica and Corona sections of Queens, and Mt. Vernon in nearby Westchester County. These areas were preferred for their suburban atmosphere, away from the crowded tenements susceptible to crime. Approved households received $3.50 weekly plus the child's clothing and medical and dental care. Nineteen children were boarded out on November 30, 1919, at a cost of $1.22 more per day than the cost of keeping them in the asylum. The trustees thought the extra cost was worth it, because the children had a "good home, proper training and a happy life." Homes were difficult to find; the asylum had strict standards. Too many African Americans, in the boarding-out committee's opinion, lacked knowledge of children or were "too fussy and expect too much from a child of eight years or younger." The asylum believed that too many individuals did not take "a real deep interest in [the child's] character building." Whether the foster parent was "too fussy" or too strict, eight of twenty-eight placements ran away. Again, young children felt lost away from the asylum, the only home some had ever known, and they had difficulty in adjusting to strangers who neither had the time for nor interest in coddling them.[26]

The boarding-out situation still presented obstacles for proper placements. The increased payment led to some more desirable homes but "the scarcity of proper homes, the restlessness of some of the boarding mothers, and the lack of child knowledge" remained drawbacks to boarding out children. There were 150 written applications for children, but most failed to meet the asylum's standards. The physical environment was undesirable, some children were left alone, people were transient, some lacked "mother love," and some were looking for cheap labor. It was interesting that the principals of schools attended by boarding children considered them "the best dressed and the best behaved children in the school and [they] show[ed] a scholarship second to none." While this credit reflected on the asylum, it also revealed that many boarding parents were conscientious and supportive of these children's appearance and study habits. A problem of theft by boarding children worried the after-care committee. The executive committee decided in March 1920 to give each child five cents weekly "to promote honesty" and to stop them from stealing from their boarding parents. Harold Thompson stole school library books, but his action was dismissed by the trustees: "He is not a good inheritance as he was born in Auburn prison." Two sixteen-year-old boys, Harold Mower and William Larkin, were sent to the House of Refuge at Randall's Island for petit larceny. After this criminal activity, the after-care committee decided in December 1922 to teach the children about stealing, "so that when they are placed out in homes where they meet temptations" they would have strength to resist taking the property of others. The problem, as certainly the committee members realized, was that the children had nothing, and now they were exposed to those who, in contrast, appeared to have plenty. A young girl might not realize that a woman with ten pairs of earrings would notice a missing pair. The annual report for 1921 revealed that five children had been sent to reformatories; two were entered into institutions for feebleminded-ness. Ten left their employment without permission.[27]

Better health records were established in 1911, when Dr. Edward Cussler instituted a card system. He examined 235 children and noted that twenty-six had pulmonary tuberculosis and twenty-five had tuber-culosis of lymph nodes, with another eighteen showing indications of a tuberculosis taint. Cussler determined that the older children should sleep outdoors and should receive extra nourishment and tonic treat-ment as preventive care. After he found that the children were inade-quately fed, the matron and superintendent were told to "prepare a more generous dish for the children." Seventeen children were af-flicted with congenital syphilis. Some suffered from chronic diseases such as Pott's disease (tuberculosis of the spine) or syphilis in active stages. He recommended that these types should not be admitted in the future. Dr. Cussler strongly urged that some regulations be adopted "regarding admissions of cases of chronic diseases or deformities to an institution that is not equipped for their treatment." Concurring was the hospital committee, which decided that children with diseases should not be admitted, with their cases being returned to the court that originally assigned them to the Colored Orphan Asylum.[28]

Internal Problems and Du Bois's Criticism

Despite their racial chauvinism, the COA took seriously its role as a benefactor to colored children. Early in 1912, as mentioned earlier, they questioned whether they were striving for the advancement of the individual or the uplifting of the Negro race. The annual report for that year addressed that concern. In an appeal for prospective mem-bers to join, First Directress Carolena M. Wood noted that many of the city's seven hundred thousand Negroes were Southern migrants who lacked parental skills. "The ever increasing standard of efficiency," she wrote, "demands [that we] shall make men and women who are worth while." Wood viewed herself and her colleagues as surrogate mothers to the children and not to the race they came from. This point was punctuated by Wood's conclusion that they were more than an orphan asylum; they were *The* Association for the Benefit of New York City's Colored Children.[29] In effect, they were saying that the Negro race is lost but that the children could and deserved to be saved. That assessment would haunt them three decades later, when they needed the help of the black community to save them from the embarrassment of closing.

In 1913, the COA altered the school curriculum and restructured the staff to introduce industrial classes in cooking, sewing, agriculture, and carpentry for seventy-five students. A chorus of fifty-four was established, with thirty-one taking music lessons. They decided in February to reorganize the staff, to increase efficiency. The first assistant was a woman whose responsibilities were to supervise the institution under the direction of the superintendent. The second female assistant was responsible for the cottages, nurseries, records, and bank; she approved requisitions and was in charge of bills of goods. Additionally, she was available for minor social work. The third female assistant was responsible for cutting material in the sewing room and was in charge of the store supplies; she also supervised the kitchen, bakery, and cold storage. The fourth assistant's task was to visit children's homes as an investigator. The fifth assistant was an office girl who handled bookkeeping and general office duties.[30]

The restructuring could not mask the reality that the asylum was, in 1913, plagued with problems, which were symptomatic of ineffective leadership. Frank W. Barber caused chaos when he offered his resignation, effective January 1, 1914, after just over two years in the superintendent's position. He left to do educational work in Connecticut at a time when the institution sorely needed someone who could apply more scientific and progressive measures in making and keeping the asylum relevant. Carolena M. Wood wrote the committee on superintendent on October 7, 1913, that the institution "needs only a competent staff to make it a thoroughly successful means for the public welfare." She cited as her qualifications growing up on a farm, supervision of servants since childhood, study and travel abroad, and deep sympathy for other races. Her education consisted of studying at the New York City Mission Training School, New York University Law

School, the Union Theological Seminary, and the School of Philanthropy. A trustee since 1895, she served as first directress from 1909 to 1913, as acting superintendent for six months in 1914, and as treasurer from 1915 to 1919. (Later, she went to Germany in 1918 to aid stricken children. She traveled to Nicaragua in a daring attempt to settle the uprising led by General Augusto Sandino against American occupation from 1927 to 1933.) The trustees gave her the position until they could find someone who had more extensive training and experience in institutional work. Despite her hard work, she was unable to achieve results, and she resigned in April 1914. Wood died on March 12, 1936. She was replaced by Dr. Mason Pitman, a graduate of McGill University in Montreal, who had organized a hospital in South Africa during the Boer War. He began working on June 25, 1914, and served as superintendent until mid-1938, when charges of mismanagement and fiscal deficits forced him to resign.[31]

More damaging from a public relations viewpoint was W. E. B. Du Bois's scathing criticism of the Colored Orphan Asylum's management. Du Bois, editor of *The Crisis*, the organ of the NAACP, had visited the institution in 1910. He wrote in the August 1913 issue: "this institution is not well run, the children and their guardians are not happy, the teaching force certainly lacks efficiency and the governing board seems helpless." He faulted the unnamed white teachers for lacking love and sympathy for the children; they are aloof, he added, because they shun social equality. In turn, the children were resentful, stubborn, and, he could have added, in light of past events, destructive. The black teachers, he opined, were qualified but humble and submissive. Du Bois blamed the management for wanting black teachers to "accept the very caste system which his training and ambition justly lead him to rebel against." He noted that this resulted in timid teachers, for to behave otherwise meant insubordination and impudence. The civil rights activist stated that it was wrong to have a board overseeing an institution for colored youth without a race representative aboard. Du Bois's attack was not a condemnation of white control over a "black" institution. This he could not do, because he himself was the only African American with a position of responsibility in the National Association for the Advancement of Colored People, a civil rights group founded by white socialists and philanthropists. The trustees did not respond in print to the accusations. Instead, they held a special meeting on September 18, 1913, and weakly claimed that they treated the children as they would whites "of the same class," that they had no color line, and that their objective was "to train the children to be good citizens and to earn their living in the station of life to which they have been called." They did not even broach the issue of a black board member until 1918; one was not approved until 1939.[32] They clearly missed the tone of Du Bois's complaint, which was that the COA's patronizing and condescending philosophy was to keep the youth in their place instead of working to make American society, with all its possibilities, a reality for them.

Du Bois's outburst was precipitated, in part, by summer disturbances within the asylum. An article in an unidentified black newspaper, "Things Rotten at Riverdale," accused the management of condoning "brutality to the children." The parents of Frank Edwards sued the institution for twenty-five thousand dollars, claiming that a blow from the house mother, a Miss Baylor, had caused deafness. The parties eventually settled for one thousand dollars. Then Frank's brother, Arthur, made a similar claim against another house mother, Emily Moore, for twenty thousand dollars. In 1915, Arthur's attorney lost interest, and the case remained dormant until 1923, when the court decided to clear the calendar. Judge Edward G. Whitaker ruled that a "charitable institution is not liable for the negligence of its servants." To be on the safe side, the COA then purchased liability insurance of fifteen thousand to twenty-five thousand dollars. Meanwhile, in 1913, older boys, resentful of their treatment, initiated a strike at the asylum.[33]

The annual report for 1913 made no reference to Du Bois's criticism or to the charges of brutality. Outgoing Superintendent Barber declared that "an effort has been made . . . to develop a happy home spirit among workers and children, believing that the strongest power in shaping the life of any people is the true home." He added that the institution had developed this "spirit" by holding "several special events . . . to bind us together and to gain for us friends in the big city." Pitman was pleased that the asylum's orchestra had performed on the grounds at one of the lawn festivals and that the children had sung at the Emancipation Day celebration. Barber considered it imperative that they equip the children with the means "to win their inheritance." He noted that "dignity of labor, firmness of purpose, lofty ideals, deepened spirituality are the legacies we should provide which will burst the doors of opportunity, conquer all difficulties, and crown noble effort for the true advancement of future generations with real success."[34]

These noble words overlooked the decline in control within the institution. Conditions were more chaotic than ever, but this information remained within the minutes of the board or the executive committee. The annual reports offered a glowing depiction of harmony and progress. The general public, which lacked access to the minutes, were inclined to accept unquestioningly the positive but misleading annual reports. Alice F. Halpin, principal of Public School 49 (the asylum's school), presented a glowing report in the annual report for 1913. She proudly noted that on April 21, Dr. Joseph S. Taylor, the district superintendent, found on his visit that in some subjects the asylum children were not surpassed by any other district school. Taylor gave an "A" rating for "the assembly discipline, fire-drill and general tone of the school."[35]

Despite Barber's desire "to develop a happy home spirit," the trustees in early 1914 granted the superintendent "power to administer corporal punishment under conditions prescribed by law." These powers were also extended to the farmer James Aiken at Verbank Farm and to the farm's matron. Dr. Pitman recorded thirty-one cases of punishment between July 1, 1914, and April 9, 1915. Most of the offenders were guilty of stealing or disobedience. Two damaging articles appeared in the *New York Times* in 1916. Second Deputy Commissioner of Charities William J. Doherty found the institution lacking in cleanliness. "One of the cottages used its shower bath for punishing the boys. When they were good they escaped bathing." Most of the children spent time in the kitchen studying. The matron said, "that's the proper place for them; that's where most of them will have to spend their lives when they go from here." Carolena M. Wood echoed this sentiment, adding that they might as well learn cooking, since few would ever become clerks or stenographers. Pitman admitted to using a strap because moral suasion had failed. A nurse admitted that she used a strap on children as young as five years of age. She confessed that she hit four or five daily. The adverse publicity resulted in her returning to Scotland after being replaced by a black woman, a Miss Henderson.[36]

If Du Bois's blunt and harsh criticism had any effect, it was probably that it caused the trustees to seek out more black employees. In August 1914, they noted a preference for a colored man to be a custodian for the boys; earlier, they had employed an African American dentist, Dr. Gertrude E. Curtis, who was popular with the children. A black nurse, Miss Hardman, was hired in January 1917. While this change in hiring practice showed a recognition of the city's growing black professionals, the management was still ambivalent about the ability of African Americans to perform well. They "question[ed] whether colored home mothers can ever maintain the standard of cleanliness and order." They even doubted if they were capable of properly disciplining the children. But were these women provided a decent salary that would encourage them to be more attentive to their duties? Were these white middle- and upper-class women guilty of class bias? The children needed as many positive black role models as were available, but on a deeper level, the white trustees needed guidance from Harlem's leadership, which would elude the management for another twenty-two years.[37]

The criticism of the house mothers appeared in the minutes for internal use. Helena Titus Emerson wrote in the 1914 annual report that "the house mothers and nurses . . . are serious, high minded women who regard their positions as opportunities for doing a great work for their people." She found it so gratifying that some of the trustees met weekly with one or more house mothers that it was recommended that all the trustees and workers follow suit. "It is such thorough understanding of each other by representatives groups of Colored and White people that will solve the 'problems' most quickly, and what could be of more 'benefit' to the Colored children . . . than the co-operation of the women of the two races?" This sentiment reeked of condescension, because no working-class black women who depended on the goodwill of upper- or middle-class white women would frankly offer criticism or disagree with their more "learned" viewpoints. The trustees needed to have frank discussions with their true equals: Harlem's professional black women who were members of the NAACP or other organizations. Riverdale's racial distance from Harlem was illustrated in late 1913, when thousands of New York's blacks met in a mass meeting to raise five thousand dollars for the Jenkins Orphanage in Charleston, South Carolina. In contrast, John E. Nail, a wealthy black realtor in Harlem, donated fruit to the COA.[38]

Helen Titus Emerson's excitement over the cooperation between trustees and staff was short lived. Just a few months after her report appeared in the 1914 annual report, the executive committee minutes for February 5, 1915, noted a problem with the "colored employees." The executive committee discussed "the treatment of [the] colored staff and what our difficulty with them is." The house mothers were blamed when employers severely criticized two girls for "negligence and inefficiency in the performance of their daily work." Problems with the black staff continued for years. The paucity of notes in the minutes for July 11, 1924, suggested tension if not insubordination from workers. The board voted to notify every worker by letter that "all directions given by the superintendent, his assistants and heads of departments come to them from the Board and must be implicitly obeyed. Failure to carry this out is equivalent to resignation." The rift, of course, went beyond this specific criticism. The black staff was not docile, like their nineteenth-century predecessors. The middle- and upper-class trustees, who were used to submissive servants in their personal households, did not easily accept the bolder behavior of these employees. They were accustomed to workers whose loyalty eschewed salary demands or verbal defenses of their rights. Such a worker was Charlotte Yorke, who had served the institution since 1871 as a nurse, assistant cook, head cook, girls' caretaker, and housekeeper. Her death on July 31, 1915, led to an executive committee's resolution printed in the annual report and forwarded to her friends, the African American press, and alumni. The executive committee's appeal to Yorke's friends for funds for a memorial yielded only eleven dollars by December. An appeal was sent to the alumni to meet and decide upon a memorial bell or clock. There is no record that either the executive committee or individual trustees saw fit to honor Charlotte Yorke's memory with a donation.[39] On September 14, 1917, 125 alumni returned to the institution and sang Charlotte Yorke's favorite hymn, "For All the Saints." A large brass bell was hung in the main hall inscribed "1871–1915, in memoriam Charlotte Yorke."[40]

The COA's troubled relationship with the African American community called for a bold move that, if enacted, would have altered the board's racial composition. For the first time in the asylum's history, the trustees considered having a black member. A Miss Wood recommended Mrs. E. P. Roberts, "an educated colored woman." Only nine were present at the meeting; therefore, the vote was scheduled for a fall special meeting, but the meeting was not held. A special meeting was held on January 17, 1919, with only eight in attendance. Absentee trustees mailed their votes on the motion "you are ready to admit colored women as members of the Board." The motion failed ten to six; it would take twenty more years to achieve an affirmative vote. In March, the trustees voted to destroy letters from trustees on the motion so that there would be no public record of the decision. Ironically, the racial ambivalence of the board was revealed a week before the Roberts decision, when the trustees agreed to the "engagement of a white trained nurse if no suitable colored [one] can be found."[41] In their estimation, it was more acceptable to hire a black subordinate, albeit a professional one, than to have an African American equal as a trustee.

Pitman's Scientific Leadership

Superintendent Pitman stressed in the 1914 annual report that he was the first superintendent in the COA to maintain accurate records, with an emphasis on social and medical diagnoses. In this respect, he was not alone; other institutions had also embraced using the social sciences to better serve their clients. Pitman introduced carpentry and domestic science into the curriculum to enhance the children's future employment prospects; this was recognition that neither labor unions nor the nation was ready to push for full employment integration of black Americans. It was crucial to Pitman that the institution did not have to apologize for the alumni's mental, moral, or physical conduct. Pitman wanted his charges not to end up paupers but to be equal to those raised in a normal family situation. Spiritual guidance was provided to the children by St. Andrews Episcopal Church, the Baptist Church of the Redeemer, and the South Yonkers Presbyterian Church, all in nearby Yonkers, New York. The children also attended Riverdale's Presbyterian Church and St. Philip's Episcopal Church, a black institution in Harlem.[42]

The annual report for 1915 provided statistics on the family background of the children in the institution and under care.

Category	Number
Children whose fathers were deserted by mother	23
Children of unmarried parents	38
Children of unknown parentage	43
Children of widowers	86
Children of separated parents	49
Children who are full orphans	62
Children whose mothers were deserted by fathers	108
Children of widows	142
Children having both parents living and married without separation (includes cases of physical, mental or moral unfitness of one or both parents)	88
Total	639

This information was vital in helping the managers make placements. While it provided families or at least investigators with significant insights into children's backgrounds, only four hundred dollars was budgeted for the after-care committee for 1916, out of a total institutional budget of sixty-five thousand dollars.[43]

A close analysis of the children's background by an investigator, Dana Humphrey, indicated in late 1916 that only eighteen were orphans. Seventy-four had fathers who had deserted the family, compared to seven mothers who had deserted. The parents of sixty-four children were unmarried. Six children had at least one parent who was insane; thirty children had a parent in an institution. In one case, both parents were in prison.[44]

With so many children from troubled backgrounds, the issue of corporal punishment dominated the board's meetings in April and May 1917. A teacher, Alice F. Halpin, wanted to administer corporal punishment out of Superintendent Pitman's presence. The trustees informed her of their disapproval and advised her that "discipline should be maintained without its use." The Board of Education, in response to the asylum's inquiry, stated that "while the[y] realize that teachers do whip at times, nevertheless if it becomes known, it would mean instant dismissal." Miss Halpin was informed of the policy and was warned of the consequences if violated. The house mothers met in April and discussed corporal punishment, which suggests that they were not guided by the Board of Education's policy or its jurisdiction. A determined Miss Halpin asked if the trustees would permit corporal punishment if the city and state gave permission. First Directress Lillie Skiddy Parker replied that "the matter would be reopened for discussion."[45]

A Tentative Reach out to Harlem

The discipline problem was symptomatic of the need of the trustees to have better rapport with the children both in and outside of the Riverdale building. On March 23, 1917, the after-care committee made the first tentative outreach to the Harlem elite community. On that date, they met with the women's auxiliary committee of St. Philip's Episcopal Church in the parish house, on 213 West 133rd Street. The church offered its facility as a social center for the Colored Orphan Asylum's use. Dr. Pitman suggested that black ministers visit the children who left the asylum, because their community standing gave them easy entrée into homes. The discussion between the two groups opened up the possibility of children coming to St. Philip's for classes and club activities. The after-care committee agreed to inform the Harlem YMCA and YWCA whenever a child was returned to the care of a relative; thus an effort could be made to keep the youngster off the streets. The following month, the after-care committee provided the women's auxiliary committee with the names of fifty children to visit. In 1920, Zion African Methodist Episcopal in Yonkers and that city's Colored Club feted the asylum with a late summer picnic.[46]

These tentative efforts to develop a relationship with the African American community, while showing a growing awareness on the part of the institution to improve their public relations, lacked a degree of sensitivity that is crucial to good relationships. An example was the trustees' pride in the children's musical abilities, which they stereotypically attributed to the Negro's innate gift for rhythm. In November 1922, First Directress Lillie Skiddy Parker appealed for a piano. The institution had "organized a most successful choral class and are singing all the old plantation melodies. Is there not some admirer of these old melodies who could give us a piano?" she pleaded in the *New York Times*. Parker would probably never reference "old plantation melodies" had there been an African American trustee. Many whites loved the old songs such as "Old Black Joe," "Dixie," and "My Old Kentucky Home," but middle-class blacks held them in disdain, considering them unwelcome reminders of slavery. Even though the Fisk Jubilee Singers and Jenkins Orphanage had successfully played plantation music for appreciative white American and European audiences, blacks in New York had, as early as 1913, protested against plantation minstrelsy as undignified. On March 16, 1935, twenty-four boys sang unaccompanied spirituals at a children's concert, which suggests that either the trustees were ignorant of the elite Negro's distaste for spirituals or arrogant in their dismissal of that concern.[47]

World War I and the Colored Orphan Asylum

After America's entry into World War I in April 1917, twenty-two of its alumni were in the army and four in the navy by December 1 of that year. The army recruits were members of the Fifteenth Infantry Regiment New York National Guard, which became the 369th Infantry

Regiment, nicknamed the Hell Fighters for their exploits on the battle-field. President Woodrow Wilson's declaration that America was fighting to make the world "safe for democracy" rang hollow with blacks in and outside of the military and inspired some dissenting voices to denounce black patriots for supporting the war efforts of a nation that could not provide them democracy in the South. A riot occurred in the San Juan Hill section of Manhattan after black national guardsmen refused police orders to move from the corner of Sixty-first Street and Amsterdam Avenue. Col. William Hayward of the Fifteenth Infantry New York National Guard filed a complaint on July 5, 1917, against police officers Fletcher and Hensen, for falsely arresting Pvt. Lawrence Joaquin, who was sentenced to ten days in jail.[48]

Black soldiers were victims of blatant discrimination and violence from Southern civilians and elected officials. Mayor Floyd of Spartan-burg, South Carolina, protested the War Department's decision to send the Fifteenth Infantry New York National Guard to nearby Camp Wadsworth. He complained that the soldiers would not accept "the limited liberties accorded to the city's colored population." The sentiment in the town was that any black Northerner who expected service in a soda shop would "be knocked down." The spokesman for the Chamber of Commerce bluntly stated, "we don't allow negroes to use the same glass that a white man may later have to drink out of; we have our own customs down here, and we aren't going to alter them." The threat was not idle; some soldiers were beaten in Spartanburg. Ironically, prior to their departure, the YMCA secretary at Camp Whit-man requested from the asylum "a letter of good cheer to the [Colored Orphan Asylum] boys . . . soon to leave for Spartanburg."[49]

The asylum children aided the war effort by providing supper en-tertainment for recruits at nearby Camp Whitman, in Suffolk County. The trustees sent twenty-six alumni in the military a 1918 Christmas message and gifts but declined to include cigarettes. The children, con-cerned about the war's effect on civilians, arranged to send to Europe assorted clothing items. In early 1921, they contributed ten dollars to Herbert Hoover's relief fund, which they saved by skipping butter for one day.[50]

The racial prejudice shown men in uniform, disgraceful as it was, had its counterparts in New York. In October 1917, Dr. G. A. Carstensen, the rector of Christ Episcopal Church in Riverdale, resigned over opposition to "some of his policies and to the presence of children from [the asylum] at the church services."[51]

Financial Troubles

The Colored Orphan Asylum faced financial problems during 1918 and 1919, as the nation's war priorities caused a nationwide check on institutional building and as private funding was diverted to the war effort. It was noted in April 1918 that the asylum's property on Bradhurst Avenue in Harlem was sold for $6,823, but the operating budget's deficit was still $6,500. The purchase of $17,900 of securities in July prompted the executive committee to authorize the finance committee to borrow up to five thousand dollars by October 11 to meet expenses. At the end of 1918, unpaid bills amounted to $7,944.84. The deficit rose throughout 1919. The trustees thought about but rejected a fundraising appeal "to establish a house for boarding out children, or for a new cottage on the grounds." In April, they decided to build a school and a playhouse at cost of seventeen thousand dollars. The following month, the finance committee was authorized to invest two thousand dollars in 4.75 percent Liberty notes. The spiraling deficit reached $16,980.78 by December 12, 1919. By 1921, the financial situation had not improved. Unpaid bills amounted to $12,157.23 in May, which prompted the trustees to sell twenty thousand dollars' worth of Northern Pacific, Great Northern, and Chicago, Burlington, and Quincy railroad joint 4 percent bonds. The funds received were not used to pay bills; they reinvested three thousand dollars in Northern Pacific and Great Northern joint 6.5 percent bonds. Although they had received nearly $101,000 in capital accounts for the period from 1914 to 1921, the trustees preferred to operate throughout much of their existence with deficits, periodically selling securities or calling in mortgages to meet emergencies.[52]

Some questioned the trustees' decision to invest while burdened with a growing deficit. Obviously, they wanted to plan for the future and were unable to depend consistently upon contributions, which had declined over the decades. They had the financial advice of business-savvy advisers who provided sound investment tips. The trustees made it clear in the annual report for 1918 that nothing would be spared for the welfare of their charges. "It has been our aim to put the children in the best of physical condition as well as to improve them mentally and morally. . . . The sleeping quarters are well ventilated, work and play regulated and supervised, wholesome and nourishing food in ample quantities, properly prepared, and served at regular intervals, result[ing] in enviable health." While the words were sincere, it would be only in a few years that the institution's care of children would be severely attacked in the New York press.[53]

The developing adverse financial situation affected the COA's potential merger with its counterpart in Brooklyn. Throughout the first half of 1918, the trustees began a relationship with the Brooklyn Howard Colored Orphanage, which had suffered financial scandals and charges of mismanagement a dozen years earlier. In January, 126 children came to the Colored Orphan Asylum from Howard Colored Orphanage. Howard wanted to send an additional four hundred children, but the COA was unable to accommodate them. In February, the two institutions discussed a possible merger. This was a mixed bag for Riverdale. Howard's debt was fifty-five thousand dollars, and their farm, Kings Park, was mortgaged for ten thousand dollars. The farm was attractive because Verbank Farm was remote and, even before the fire and sale, had become too expensive to run. However, in March, the trustees for Riverdale decided that it would prove too difficult to reestablish Howard, which, after the merger, they would have to run.[54]

Part of the financial problem stemmed from the large enrollment. The trustees sought to lessen its enrollment figure in 1922 by offering funds to any institution willing to accept Protestant colored girls over the age of twelve. The offer came with the proviso that "money is given to erect a wing for that purpose on the building they are now constructing." If this was achieved, the Colored Orphan Asylum required representation on that institution's board. This matter was referred to the mental development committee for consideration, but there is no evidence of any offers. The problem was less one of crowding (there were 275 in the building on October 31, 1922) and more of the type of children in the institution. Seventy-six were admitted between November 1, 1921, and October 31, 1922. Of this number, two were returnees: one from the hospital and the other from his employer. Thirty-nine were sent by the department of public welfare, eighteen were admitted by the courts of New York City, five came from poor-law officers outside of New York City, and three were transferred from other institutions.[55]

The large number of children from troubled backgrounds caused problems with discipline, although the trustees were pleased that in 1918 there was a marked improvement in the children's behavior. This was, according to the annual report, attributed to a "spirit existing between the workers and the children [which] has been a source of much pleasure and affords abundant material for future favorable conclusion." The change occurred after the trustees initiated group responsibilities that led the children to think of themselves as "part and parcel of society." The management was pleased that, outside of the asylum, strangers were always surprised to learn that they came from an institution, so well mannered were they. Again, the trustees were masking the discipline problem by not telling the truth in the annual reports, which were sent to friends and potential donors. The issue of discipline remained unsolvable. The annual report for 1920 noted that discipline was good, thanks to the merit/demerit system that had been in effect for several years. Sports, shopping excursions, outside attractions such as the circus and a chartered boat to Bear Mountain, and a scenic picnic area near the U.S. Military Academy at West Point kept the children in check. One had to read the executive committee minutes (which were not available to the public) for more ominous reports of disobedience. It was recorded in the executive minutes for March 1, 1921, that the "boys in cottage No. 2 [are] to wear overalls till they see fit to not destroy their suits."[56] Why would young boys show rebellion or disobedience by destroying their suits? It never occurred to the trustees that the children resented wearing uniforms, which were unlike the fashionable clothing worn by their peers outside the asylum.

As the trustees and staff struggled to find a proper method of punishment, discipline problems increased over the next two years. The
boys' behavior was so bad that, with the exception of Cottage No. 7,
they were relocated to the main building for better supervision. An
earlier move in January 1921 to punish them by putting them in the
nurseries failed. It was rumored that teachers were applying corporal
punishment. A storekeeper and a nursery mother were dismissed for
whipping the children. Discipline improved in April 1922, when the
trustees decided that the chairs of the after-care, executive, and educational committees should develop a plan to "take into careful consideration the mental report" on both the normal and subnormal children
admitted to Riverdale. The mental development committee decided in
May to board out normal children, to send children of low mental
scores to other institutions, and to keep slightly subnormal children in
the asylum. This decision lessened tensions between the normal and
mentally deficient children; Dr. Mason Pitman noted in his annual
superintendent's message for 1923 that discipline was better than it
had ever been since his appointment nine years earlier. This he attributed to "the removal of a number of marked mental cases" and the
children's interest in their clubs and sports. He was particularly
pleased that a YMCA leader, after watching the boys play, commented
on their teamwork, a trait that Pitman observed bode well "for their
future welfare."[57]

These troubled youths were not only hard to place; it was feared
that they would have a negative influence on others in the institution.
A girl with dishonest traits entered the asylum in 1904. According to
Marguerite A. Bradshaw, "she was handicapped from the start by a
mother who had a record of being a pickpocket and a prostitute and
by a father who was serving a sentence in Sing Sing [penitentiary] for
murder." A sixteen-year-old entered the institution in 1918, sent from
a reformatory where he was incarcerated for theft. He was so easily
influenced that the after-care committee recommended that he be sent
somewhere for permanent institutional care. A third child's mother
was an epileptic who had several illegitimate children and was considered feebleminded. All three were believed doomed by their heredity.
It was the hope of the trustees to send these and other troubled and

older children to other institutions. The trustees thought that those who needed such close supervision would benefit from a vocational department within the institution, which would make them self-supporting after leaving the asylum. While the feebleminded group represented a burden, the trustees were proud of all the former boys and girls who had gone on to productive lives as nurses, doctors, lawyers, undertakers, and postal employees. One of the more popular young men was Bertie Fields, who was born in 1890. He had been employed at the asylum for several years before his death in 1921. Friends contributed $144 to install at Riverdale a memorial plaque in his memory.[58]

All the problems the institution faced called out for them to seek allies in the black community, not only for financial reasons but as a base to aid them in solving the social issues that faced so many youth in postwar America. Regrettably, it would be nearly a decade before the trustees would seriously reach out to the citizens of Harlem to be partners in the endeavor to serve black youth. Unfortunately, it would be in a manner of a person stuck in quicksand who suddenly notices the person he had consistently ignored when both were on solid ground.

7 Riverdale: Trials and Tribulations, 1923-36

The beginning of 1923 found the asylum in a financial crunch, an all-too-familiar situation. Three thousand dollars were needed for the boarding-out department. Even though there were unpaid bills totaling $10,327.32 and the finance committee had sent out appeal letters, the trustees had their legal adviser, Wilson M. Powell, invest twenty-two thousand dollars. The large sum for investment appeared unwise in light of an August visit to the asylum by the trustee Mrs. Garrett du Bois. She indicated that "everything was in splendid condition except the children's underwear. They were rags." It was amazing that investments took priority over proper clothing for the children. The trustees evidently supported their adviser's recommendation that investing in bonds and mortgages would provide them with funds for several rainy days. Unexpected funds, fortunately, came from several wills. Hannah Heyman contributed ten thousand dollars, Louis T. Lehmeyer willed one thousand dollars in late 1923, and Thomas D. Hurst and Anthony F. Troescher gave ten thousand and three thousand dollars, respectively, in 1924. These legacies were added to Heyman's gift to invest twenty thousand in bonds and mortgages. However, the financial situation did not ease up. The February 1927 financial report indicated that while the institution had $38,069.88 invested in the U.S. Trust Company, their account in the Fifth Avenue Bank held a paltry $64.68. This pattern of investing while bills remained unpaid or were paid late, coupled with occasionally selling bonds or stocks to pay bills, would continue for years.[1]

The school report for 1923 reflected the results of mental testing of the students. The asylum's school at Riverdale, known as Public School

49, had 170 pupils in grades 1A to 6B. In May, the Board of Education's Bureau of Reference, Research, and Statistics found that 55 percent of the children were mentally and educationally fit for grades beyond the ones they were in, 25 percent were in the correct grade, and another 25 percent were in grades beyond their mental and educational ability. (The calculation may have been wrong, as the total comes out to 105 percent.) Beginning on November 23, 1923, students were placed in grades based on mental capacity rather than appropriate age. The trustees were elated with the 1926 graduating class of nine students: six girls and three boys. Their school was first in the district in the city-wide sixth- and eighth-grade spelling test. Tremendous favorable publicity was received from Anne K. Walker's letter to the *New York Times*, in which she wrote that everyone at the commencement exercise recognized that the Negro has the capacity "for absorbing and assimilating the same educational opportunities that are provided for the white race." "One came away," she noted, "with a feeling that from such an epitome of Negro talent and Negro development can be derived a finer sympathy and understanding of Negro life and its influence upon our advancing civilization." Still, many of the children in the school were, in the vernacular of the day, labeled "retarded." In 1927, the asylum listed for the first time the ages and grades of children. There were 431 children in school for kindergarten through grade 8B. The slowness of some of the children is revealed by the discrepancy between the grade in which they were enrolled and their age. For example, a typical sixth grader is twelve years old. Of the sixteen sixth graders, four were fourteen years old; one was fifteen years old. There were even greater differences in the lower grades. Only three children in the fourth grade were age nine, typical for that grade, whereas sixty-four were older than age nine. The students were hard workers, and their efforts were publicly acknowledged. On commencement day, June 25, 1928, the thirteen graduates heard Michael Williams, editor of *The Commonwealth*, say, "as I have listened to your beautiful voices, the songs of your race, I have realized as never before your racial gift to the world." He urged the attentive group to become leaders, not followers. In November, the educational committee requested three thousand dollars for 1929 to hire an "Inspirational Leader" to perhaps live at Riverdale, "to be a scout leader if possible, and to advise the boys about vocational training, etc." A month earlier, the children started a monthly school paper, *The Fortyniner*, which made them "youthful pioneers seeking the 'gold of education' in [public school] 49."[2] It was telling that Michael Williams encouraged the children to become leaders, whereas the asylum still considered vocational training the best opportunity for Negro youngsters to make it in society.

Boarding Out

The boarding-out report for 1923 acknowledged both progress and problems. The boarding-out program had commenced in 1918, in Jamaica, Queens, with African American families who lived in frame houses with six rooms and a bath. Now, five years later, there were forty-four boarding homes on tree-lined suburban streets in South Jamaica and six others scattered between neighborhoods in Brooklyn and in the Maspeth and Richmond Hill sections of Queens. All the locations were in the western Long Island portion of New York City, close enough to be monitored by the asylum yet far enough from the crowded tenements of Harlem and its crime and temptations. Most of the foster fathers were porters, messengers, or chefs with railroad or steamship companies. The boarding-out committee was happy that seventeen homes had no other children living there. This prevented jealousies forming between the boarding children and the foster parents' biological children. Five of the boarding children were adopted by their foster parents, and one child who had boarded with his uncle and aunt were adopted by them. Girls were in demand, as "only one home welcomed a boy!" The after-care committee decided in December 1924 that children on trial for adoption "may take the name of the prospective adoption parent at the time of placement." Previously, the child kept his or her name for a year, until the one-year trial period had concluded, which could lead to some awkwardness. The boarding-out children were expected to live normal lives, like any other child; they ran errands and performed light housework. The children learned to live with different people, to adjust to a schedule unlike the one that they knew previously, and to be economical in dress and behavior, as the "foster parents [did not] tolerate dirty faces, soiled or rumpled clothing or unshined shoes." Not all of the children were respectful of their new surroundings. Five boys were returned for lying or stealing, and two girls were returned for poor home reports and school failure. Louise H. Abbott, a psychiatrist from the New York School of Social Work, was hired to administer the National Intelligence Test and the Thorndike-McCall Reading Scale to help in placements.[3]

The asylum's strict standards for suitable homes made the task so difficult that the after-care committee "asked for a ruling [in 1925] for placing children from [age] 15 to 16 in Jewish Homes." The board, in a display of religious chauvinism, "voted that when it is possible we place our children in Christian homes." Left unsaid was the sentiment that "Christian" meant Protestant only.[4]

Another issue of concern was the inexperience and immaturity of the young teenage girls. A number of older girls at Riverdale needed care until they were mature enough to deal with the world. The trustees decided in February 1924 to place the approximately eighty girls in cottages with three women, who would instruct them in domestic science. Despite the five-thousand-dollar cost, "it is the policy of the Board to have every child stay through the school term in which they enter," the secretary recorded. In November, the court was asked for cooperation in permitting the trustees to keep these girls for at least a year.[5]

These girls, who were considered to be "slow" or mentally "retarded," may have suffered from the as yet undiagnosed attention deficit disorder. Children of this type needed diversions to avoid boredom. The institution requested donations of a gymnasium, a swimming pool, a chapel, and a radio or movie projector. Harry M. Warner of Warner Brothers presented the institution with a movie booth and two professional machines and arranged for weekly showings, commencing May 21, 1926. In June, jungle gyms, ladders, slides, and swinging rings were installed for the children's enjoyment. A good friend of the asylum, Mr. Warner, also donated in 1935 a new "talkie" motion-picture projector for weekly movies. It was obsolete by 1939, and First Directress Lillie Skiddy Parker, distressed that the children were watching old, uninteresting movies, appealed to readers of the *New York Times* for a new one.[6]

The trustees had to search for more ways to educate and entertain their charges, as they kept admitting more neglected and dependent children. They were the first institution that the courts or the State Board of Charities called upon to admit African American children. It was suggested by judges and the State Board of Charities in the spring of 1925 that the asylum admit children up to the age of sixteen. The asylum's committee on delinquent and dependent colored children recommended that the admitting age for girls and boys be raised to twelve and fourteen, respectively. (Many delinquent children were admitted by the COA as "dependent" children because the institution was reluctant to have delinquent children on their premises.) The trustees decided in December 1926 to accept boys only up to age twelve, because accepting older boys could lead to potential behavioral problems. They accepted more by boarding out eighty-seven mentally normal children instead of adding more buildings. This led to the admission of 175, with eighty-four sent by the Department of Public Welfare and the New York City courts sending seventy-two. Although the trustees were willing to accept more admissions by freeing space via boarding out more children, they declined the State Board of Charities' 1926 request that they admit children from counties outside of New York City. They were "taxed to capacity with New York [City and] it [was] impossible to take more outside children." Racism played a large part in these admissions. In 1925, 8 percent of the cases in the city's children's courts were Negro boys who were school truants, engaged in disorderly conduct, or had run away from home. Often, the police brought them to court but would overlook the same misbehavior on the part of white youngsters.[7]

With the shifting of more children into the boarding situation, minor problems developed for both the institution and the children. The boarding-out report for 1925 recognized that supervision was easier when homes were in a group but that that arrangement led to "a weakness, due to occasional upheavals among groups, which should be guarded against by a reserve of homes in other localities." Being labeled "a home child" stigmatized the children to others, who teased them unmercifully. Circumstances, however, made it impossible to avoid completely the group-home concept, as the Board of Health disallowed placing more than three siblings in the same home. In this case, they were placed in homes near one another, to facilitate them attending the same school and church and to ease visiting opportunities. This latter concession was a vast improvement over the old indenturing system, whereby siblings were often separated by hundreds of miles without knowledge of their siblings' location and, in some instances, losing touch for years, if not forever. The children adjusted fairly easily to boarding homes, where the living arrangement was similar to that of cottage life. It was more difficult, however, for the children to adjust to the difference in meal times, the host family's food preferences, and, most importantly, personality differences. It soon became apparent that many of the boarding-out children, especially girls, felt uncomfortable outside of the asylum. The executive committee decided that the institution would make dresses resembling the current fashions of public school children. Textile High School in Manhattan agreed to make dresses and hats from fabric provided by the asylum. Dr. Pitman provided gingham, three different kinds of blue baize, and bindings for skirts. He bought ready-to-wear middy blouses, which were cheaper and more attractive than any made at the asylum. The boarding-out children's homes were visited twice a month, at "irregular and unexpected times during the day," a procedure that verified that host families were deserving of their charges. Recipients of excellent health care, the children had dental evaluations every six months, and their weight and height was recorded quarterly.[8]

The increased number of children from Harlem led Pitman and the trustees to call for better cooperation with that community. In 1926, they agreed to give twenty-five dollars "for the survey on the needs of the colored girls in Harlem." Ironically, their attention to Harlem left them in the embarrassing position of overlooking the needs of the children in the institution. Their own internal observations informed them that running away was a problem that needed attention. One runaway boy drowned while swimming in the Hudson River. While loneliness caused some of the boarding children to run back to the asylum or to family members, others had a history of running away before they entered the asylum. To their credit, Pitman and the trustees understood that they needed to provide "a more active and possibly exciting environment." This was discussed in August 1927, but no action was taken. Like parents of young teenagers, the management was leery of letting children explore their neighborhood, let alone the Bronx or Manhattan. The following year, however, they allowed some children in small groups to attend outside movies or concerts, to picnic, and to watch the Babe Ruth–led Yankees.[9]

The asylum had to curtail its intake of unwanted cases. The COA, with the exception of the Katy Ferguson Home for Unmarried Mothers and the Salvation Army, was the only Protestant agency receiving delinquent African American children. In April 1927, the Big Sisters, Incorporated, expressed a willingness to assist the Colored Orphan Asylum "in preventing unsuitable cases from being sent to the institution." The trustees decided to request funds "to make investigations of certain cases to see if they can be returned to their homes, because of overcrowding at the asylum." This request was both necessary and urgent, as numerous repairs were needed at Riverdale. The toilets in the boys' cottage were in bad condition. A new bake oven was needed, five hundred dollars was needed for plumbing work, and a broken radiator caused damage to two rooms in Pitman's house. All the buildings needed repairs. In short, the place was in shambles: the cost of all repairs and maintenance projects was estimated at $25,945.24. The trustees discussed but took no action on suggestions to cut expenses by closing cottages and reduce the school schedule "and the corresponding increase in boarding out expense." In October, Pitman consulted with the advisers "to discuss how[,] for the Board was acting wisely in going beyond their income in trying to provide for the needy colored children of New York." By December 9, 1927, unpaid bills amounted to $19,938.77, with a deficit of $14,469. The financial situation changed somewhat at the year's end, when Olivia Eggleston Phelps Stokes, a manager/trustee since 1882, died on December 14 and left five thousand dollars to the COA.[10]

The Colored Orphan Asylum shared with other child welfare agencies a bloated budget, inefficient management, and a shaky future. For these reasons, twenty-five child agencies decided to combine in November 1927 to form a section of the Welfare Council of New York. The agencies, public and private, included the Hebrew Sheltering Guardian Society, the Hebrew Orphan Asylum, the Catholic Guardian Society of Brooklyn, the Children's Aid Society, the Brooklyn Home for Children, and the State Charities Aid Association. Their objective was to pool "ideas, experiences and information" to avoid "needless duplication of effort that may exist and insure more adequate use of the existing resources for the care of homeless or dependent children."[11]

Propaganda or Sincerity?

The financial situation led the asylum to appeal to the public for funds. Their campaign for 1927 relied on three photos included in the annual report. The caption beneath the photo of a young black boy eating an apple stated: "not 'swiped' from a corner fruit stand, this apple! Fresh fruit, and fresh air, and good food—a chance to live, and learn—and learn to live; these things are part of the program at Riverdale-on-Hudson." The second photo suggested the alternative to benevolence. The caption beneath a second photo of a boy reads: "Here is raw material for—what? Harlem gangster, or—good citizen? The Colored Orphan asylum offers the environment to produce citizenship, education, health, and moral guidance may go far in determining the 'finished product.'" The third photo is of a girl in the dentist's chair. The caption reads: "Whether the tooth comes out or not she is acquiring habits of physical well-being. She is learning to cook and sew and to face on more equal terms the life she will live 'afterward.' There will be problems for her race to solve. The background of life in an efficient social group, under careful training, will aid her in their solution." The appeal's subtext was very clever. The first two were meant to appeal to white guilt over racial bigotry and white fear of vicious black youth indiscriminately harming them or their property. The third was an appeal for white benevolence to aid more Negro children, not unlike contemporary appeals for pennies a day to feed starving children in El

Salvador or the Philippines. All three captions strongly suggested that
black children needed institutional care under white supervision.
Money from white New Yorkers was needed now—or their tax dollars
would support them in prison later. Readers of the 1928 annual report
viewed a photograph of the main building at Riverdale with a catchy
caption. "How much better a stately, well proportioned building, surrounded by trees and spacious lawns, than the crowded tenements and
streets of Harlem! Here are formed strong bodies and high ideals." The
caption suggested that only middle-class white women in an institutional setting could produce decent, law-abiding, and productive children of color. Yet some of the "black" boarding homes in Queens were
also amid trees and lawns. To verify that they were achieving results
and would accomplish more with extra funding, the trustees proudly
quoted an unidentified but "well-known" visiting physician who testi-
fied: "of all the institutions I have visited, I find the children here the
best behaved, cleanest, healthiest, and best nourished." In under two
decades, this observation would be severely challenged by the State
Board of Charities.[12]

The institution's financial distress resulted in nineteen fewer admissions in 1927 compared to the previous year. Typically, the majority of the 195 admitted children came from troubled backgrounds. One
hundred and eighty-two children, with boys accounting for 123, came
from the Department of Welfare, New York City courts, county poor-
law officers, and county courts. Recognizing that many disturbed girls
needed professional help, the trustees admitted in the 1927 annual
report their desire to hire a female physician "who is also a trained
psychiatrist." For years, the majority of the children in the Colored
Orphan Asylum were not actually orphans. There were 487 children
under care in 1927, but only 34 were orphans; 183 were half-orphans,
and 237 had both parents living. The status of thirty-three children's
parents was unknown. These figures led Superintendent Pitman to
utter, "we are really an orphan asylum in name only. I have often
asked myself . . . should this be?" Pitman added that a foundation
needed to conduct "a careful and painstaking survey of the situation."
In 1931, he asked, "what is an orphan asylum?" He again thought that
"an interesting survey might solve the problem."[13]

Home Placement

The after-care report for 1927 delineated the status of those who had no homes after leaving the asylum. Seven were working in homes, another seven were on trial for adoption, and thirty-six were in "free homes." One boy was attending Howard University; one girl and one boy had run away. Interestingly, in the free homes, thirteen children resided with white families, "whose homes required supervision and the help of the institution's influence in controlling the child." Two years later, the asylum advertised in the *Rural New Yorker* "for suitable homes for the children within 100 miles of New York." Presumably, these would be "white" homes. Children were placed in white homes because the asylum had difficulty finding black homes that met their standards; they were unwilling to place children in Manhattan's apartments. But white families were clueless about a number of cultural differences between the races. Did they know, for example, that black children used Vaseline on their legs and arms to avoid an ashy look? Or that their scalps had to be periodically greased to make their hair more manageable?[14]

Many of the children came from backgrounds not associated with life in New York City. This was a fact that parallels the asylum's growth since the late 1830s, when it began to accept the children of runaway slaves or recently emancipated ones. While there were references in the minutes of the early 1900s to "problems" associated with children of Southern migrants to New York City, it was not until 1928 that the asylum compiled a list of the states and countries where the children and their parents were born.

The diversity of the children's backgrounds created problems for the superintendent and staff, as they expected to have all the children conform to institutional life. This may explain some of the disciplinary problems that confounded the institution during this period. The survey revealed that while 339 children had been born in New York (city or state), 192 of the fathers and 210 of the mothers were born in the South (including Washington, D.C.), which suggests that they were suspicious of whites and had probably instructed their children to be so too.[15]

State or Country	Child	Father	Mother
Alabama	0	0	1
Arkansas	0	0	1
California	0	3	3
Canada/England	0	3	4
Connecticut	2	0	6
Delaware	0	0	1
Florida	2	11	7
Georgia	18	36	31
Louisiana	1	5	2
Maryland	1	1	4
Massachusetts	5	6	1
Mississippi	0	0	3
Missouri	0	1	0
New Jersey	13	8	2
New York	339	56	82
North Carolina	10	32	34
Panama	4	2	0
Pennsylvania	6	1	4
Porto Rico (Puerto Rico)	2	0	1
Rhode Island	0	0	2
South Carolina	17	53	55
Tennessee	0	1	0
Texas	1	0	1
United States (unknown states)	24	32	25
Unknown	18	65	51
Virginia	27	51	65
Washington, D.C.	0	2	5
West Indies (Dutch, British, Danish)	17	138	116

Boarding out had increased to 281 for the year 1929, compared to a mere twelve in 1920. Ninety-eight of the 281 were permanent guests of the foster families. The after-care committee regretfully reported that little success was achieved with children placed with relatives.

"Little interest has been shown the children when they were small and the delayed offer of a home [is] apt to indicate a deeper interest in the children's economic value than in their need of education and training," lamented the chair.[16]

The number of children received by the after-care committee for placement increased during the early years of the Great Depression, averaging nearly seventy-four for the years 1928 through 1930, compared to nearly fifty-one for the years 1925 through 1927. This was attributed to "the extended supervision to children placed with relatives of second degree, whereas, before 1924, (when there were 38 under care) they were discharged outright."[17]

The needs of the boarding-out department increased as the economic condition worsened during the prolonged Great Depression. Boarding homes extended from Poughkeepsie in upstate New York to western Long Island, across the East River from Manhattan. An influx in applications led to an increase in staff and larger offices. There now was a need (and funds) for a medical and dental clinic, "a temporary shelter, and a department for the distribution of clothing." The institution now required the addition of a psychologist, for regular mental testing to determine suitable homes to meet children's special needs and to insure minimum problems at school. By October 31, 1931, there were 701 children under care, which elicited from a beleaguered Pitman that, unlike the past, he no longer knew the names of all the children. "I hope," he stated, "the day may come . . . when we can go back to a normal number . . . and be able to give more personal care." The trustees discussed hiring a psychologist at two thousand dollars per annum to administer mental tests and to "advise on behavior problems both at the institution and in the boarding homes, and also if possible on vocational guidance." Beatrice Taylor, a graduate of the University of Denver and Columbia University, was hired. She conducted a psychological survey of the children in the institution and those boarding out in August 1932. The following year, she advocated having the boarding-out mothers receive parental education and the opportunity "to talk over their problems." It soon became clear that many children had difficult psychological problems because of the pathologies in their lives, but funds were not available for intensive psychological testing.[18]

The boarding-out report for 1931 reported that 149 foster mothers cared for 472 children. The committee wanted to establish a vocational school for older children, which meant the establishment of "specially selected urban boarding homes." The after-care committee noted that there were homes where adopted children lived, free homes where children were still in school, and working homes where the young adults worked as maids, mothers' helpers, elevator girls, house boys, gardeners, garage workers, farmers' helpers, checking clerks, factory workers, grocery clerks, and truck drivers' helpers. These were the jobs that Negroes in adult society were relegated to accept, as few had the education or opportunity to be professionals. The asylum's curriculum insured that the children would have little or no aspiration for professional careers. The boys learned to make bookcases, clothing closets for classrooms, tables, smoking stands, and magazine racks. The annual report proudly declared that "both boys and girls show their natural aptitude for cooking and delight in preparing some part of the menu for the trustees' luncheon when they meet here."[19]

In early 1932, the after-care committee decided to give the children monthly wages "to do away with the evil of giving them a large sum of money at one time when they are encouraged to make their own deposits." However, this must have led to some problems or misunderstandings, because in 1933 the committee stated, "the children are to be allowed to have the money they have earned when they demand it."[20]

The institution continued to grow as the economic situation caused the dissolution of families and as unskilled Harlem workers faced destitution. By September 1932, there were 822 under care: 275 at Riverdale and 506 in boarding homes. The board of trustees gave Dr. Pitman power to increase enrollment "after serious and careful consideration of the needs." The adverse economy made it difficult for the after-care committee to find homes that would provide employment to those who reached the age of sixteen. Secretary Ruth S. Shoup stated in the 1932 annual report that "the boarding out department has become the backbone of the organization. . . . We can now envision a time when all the children will be in real homes except the few who are definitely maladjusted." She could make this statement confidently: the board-ing-out department had been reorganized and given a new center in Queens, additional staff, and a dental office. Homes were now located in Westchester County, north of New York City, and in both Nassau and Suffolk Counties on Long Island. It was becoming clearer that the lack of practical industrial training and the closing of professions and trades to those between the ages of sixteen to twenty-four thwarted ambition. These untrained and underskilled children were competing for jobs with unemployed but skilled workers. The only solution was to provide them with vocational training if resources could be located in the community. In June 1933, the after-care committee reported the existence of three possible schools for trade training. The Dowington Industrial and Agricultural School in Pennsylvania offered "good me-chanical training and required tuition" but had "poor living condi-tions." Manhattan Trade School had "high standards [and was] competitive." The Harlem YMCA was a subway ride away, and stu-dents could board there or commute there daily. Six boys out of nine graduates from the asylum school were sent to Dowington in Septem-ber, but four performed poorly, with low scores in arithmetic. In Janu-ary 1934, the trustees wanted to send two or three girls to Dowington but decided "that the right type of girl would not be available." The following month, the children's committee asked the trustees to con-sider sending two girls, "if the right type were available."[21]

Institutional problems developed in 1933, when New York City re-duced by fifty-five cents weekly the amount they contributed for the expense of boarding out children. This led to the asylum reducing by fifty cents weekly—twenty-four dollars monthly—the pay to boarding mothers, which ended up costing the trustees five cents weekly per child. New York State law held the institution responsible for girls up to age twenty-one, instead of eighteen, as previously observed. Now, restless girls with few skills and interests had to remain in the institu-tion longer. A third problem involved Public School 49, the asylum's school, which was forced to teach a ninth-grade class, as there was no nearby high school for its graduates to attend. The first-year high school class at Riverdale cost an extra fifteen dollars per student, be-cause the Board of Education would not provide books or equipment.[22]

In 1934, for the first time in its existence, the institution admitted foundlings, eight in total, which increased Riverdale's population to 229. The 558 in boarding homes far outnumbered the thirty-one in after care. A dilemma confronted the after-care committee, which was inundated with applications for girls for domestic work and for boys for farm work, at a time when the institution was still searching for extra vocational training, to help prepare the children to be wage earners. The trustees agreed that they needed to do a careful study of domestic, farm, and industrial fields, but in early 1935 they purchased bonds with a book value of $29,353.07, which led to a deficit in June of $8,376.65.[23]

The after-care committee's report in 1935 indicated that children had difficulty in going from a dependent status to that of a wage earner. "Their childhood experiences have often made them irresponsible and unable to give sustained effort." "We hope," confessed the chair, "to be able to give the children more intensive training before placement in these [wage] homes." Much of the problem stemmed from the children's low intelligence, as the brighter students were in boarding situations. Some of the more fortunate children, eleven in all, from both the institution and from boarding out, were employed by the Citizens' Conservation Corps (later, known as Civilian Conservation Corps).[24]

The low average intelligence was confirmed by the school report for 1935. The average IQ was 89, which represented the dull-to-normal group, with a range in IQ from 55 to 135. Fifteen children participated in the June 25 commencement exercises, providing a special unit on Negro history, with displays of their original notebooks and posters. After forty years in public school teaching, including organizing the asylum's school in 1911, Alice F. Halpin retired. "There could have been no one whose going could have caused greater sadness to the children for they were all aware of her great love for them." Many openly wept at her farewell party, reported her replacement, Principal Alice S. Bracken. Finally, in 1936, the trustees were able to introduce an experimental program, with an emphasis on vocational training and academic work. The children not academically suited for high school were to be "fitted for trade school." At the end of the year, the trustees found that "this new venture is proving very satisfactory."[25]

For the first time in many decades, the asylum faced a major health crisis, by admitting children with communicable diseases. The Great Depression, with its side effects of food shortage, improper housing, and poor public health, led to a rise in tuberculosis. There was an increase of tuberculosis among children admitted from Harlem and other congested urban areas. In May 1935, the trustees' appeal for funds appeared in New York's daily papers. First Directress Lillie Skiddy Parker informed the *New York Times* about the challenge dealing with "the marked increase in incipient tuberculosis among Negro children." The appeal resulted in the receipt of $56.30 by June. This money was used to examine regularly the boarding-out children. In 1937, there were thirty-five positive tuberculosis cases among the children.[26]

The COA and Harlem

The white trustees' growing interest in Harlem's problems was not met with indifference. The Harlem Renaissance writer Gwendolyn Bennett wrote a brief history of the Colored Orphan Asylum for *The Crisis*, the organ of the NAACP, which emphasized that "prominent doctors, dentists, nurses and morticians [and postal workers and police men] throughout the country were at one time wards of the [institution]." Harlem was taking more notice of the asylum, because its glee club entertained listeners every second and fourth Sunday morning on radio station WJZ. They also appeared at 9:30 A.M. on WBNX. The young singers traveled throughout the city to perform before enthusiastic audiences at schools, churches, and fraternal organizations. The highlight was performing at Carnegie Hall, in a young people's philharmonic program in 1935. The children's musical talent was rewarded: an alumnus, Harold Thompson, was a soloist with the Utica, New York, Jubilee Singers, and another "old boy" performed in "Porgy and Bess" on Broadway.[27]

George Conliffe (*with dark neckerchief, right of center*) and other boys in glee club uniforms, c. 1940. (Courtesy of George Conliffe.)

A bizarre episode in the orphanage's history involved the trustees' encounter with George Baker, a black man better known as Father Divine. His interracial followers believed him to be God incarnate. Divine was one of the early twentieth century's most controversial and enigmatic individuals. The charismatic Divine established a Peace Mission movement in Harlem and sought to assist Negroes adversely affected by the Great Depression. Madeline Green deserted her husband and seven children on July 2, 1932, to join Father Divine. Samuel N. Green, Madeline's husband, had a housekeeper who left his employ in mid-1935, which caused the beleaguered postal clerk to ask Judge Jacob Panken to send his seven children, ages three to fourteen, to the Colored Orphan Asylum. The court subpoenaed Madeline, but she was "lost in the anonymity of a cult name." Mr. Green was willing to pay sixty-five dollars per month for all seven if placed in the asylum. The judge argued that the financial burden would be on the city because the true cost of boarding the seven children would range from $160 to two hundred dollars monthly. The children probably were not admitted, as this information appeared in the *New York Times*, and there are no references to this saga in the minutes of the trustees or the executive committee. The asylum kept Father Divine at arm's length. In late 1936, the executive committee declined his request "to put on a sacred concert at the asylum." They informed him that there was no date available in early 1937. They again encountered Father Divine in 1943, when Executive Director Henry R. Murphy (Pitman's successor) informed him that Daniel Gill had mailed to the institution $27.25 as a response to Father Divine's teaching. Father Divine responded that it was unusual for one of his followers to support an organization that was for the exclusive benefit of one group "or so-called race, color or creed, as we respect the entire human race and not any limited portion of it."[28]

Centennial Celebration

The year 1936 was the centennial for the Colored Orphan Asylum. Certainly no one associated with the institution in 1836 believed that it would last one hundred years or that by then 9,244 deserving young people would enter its doors with hopes of being loved and cared for and spared the cruel uncertainties of a hostile environment. Ruth S. Schoup took time to reflect upon the institution's history since its founding. Her sentiments, expressed, four years earlier, in the annual report for 1932, were apposite for the centennial celebration. Stroup noted that the founders would have been shocked by the changes. Instead of heating irons on coal stoves, workers now had the ease of electric irons. The automatic potato peeler removed the drudgery of peeling potatoes, and the use of "an electric clothes marker tags the eighteen thousand articles of clothing." The vast majority of children were no longer orphans, as the first enrollees had been. In 1931, only thirty-nine of 701 children under care were orphans. Nearly half, 338 children, had both parents living, while 264 were half-orphans. The children in 1837 had few games to play, certainly no organized sports, and few amusements to entertain them. Now, in 1936, they saw movies weekly; went to the circus, neighborhood theaters, rodeos, picnics in the parks, and baseball games at Yankee Stadium; listened to radio concerts; and had swimming, organized sports, and other fun-filled activities at Riverdale itself.[29]

A highlight of the centennial celebration was the visit of several "old boys" who had entered the asylum in slavery days. Thomas Barnes, eighty-eight, had visited the asylum several times from his home in Olean, New York, where he became a celebrity barber who had shaved the faces of dignitaries in Buffalo, including President Grover Cleveland, and had tended to Mrs. Cleveland's hair. Barnes entranced the crowd when he displayed the cotton shirt—now yellow with age—that he had worn on the night the asylum was destroyed in 1863. Randolph Bloome, ninety-one, the oldest living "old boy," gave the institution some shares of stock. A former "boy" over age eighty visited the institution at Christmas and recalled that the children at the Fifth Avenue residence had "had a happy time" even though they lacked the benefits of the children in 1936. The good works of the institution and its lifelong impact on impressionable alumni was indicated by a letter from Albert Swanson, who informed Dr. Pitman that he had listed the asylum as the beneficiary of his ten-thousand-dollar life insurance policy. Grateful, he wrote, "I figure this institution has done more for me than anyone or firm I can think of and I will be helping my race." The trustees probably took as much pleasure in the old boys' generosity as they did in the ten-thousand-dollar donations each from Samuel Stern, vice president of the Board of Education, and from the widow of Henry Parker Robbins, a wholesale meat and poultry dealer. Mary McLeod Bethune, president of the Daytona-Cookman Collegiate Institute in Florida, spoke, and entertainment was provided by the famous dancer Bill "Bojangles" Robinson, Cab Calloway, and Marian Anderson. The *New York Times* aptly summarized the Colored Orphan Asylum's one hundred years as a survivor of "three wars, two major financial panics, a devastating fire, the occupancy of five different homes, several epidemics, waves of race prejudice and a succession of the severest internal economies."[30]

Equally important to the trustees was a letter and a gift of ten dollars from a Mrs. Cobham, the mother of an alumnus. She wrote that her ten dollars for the anniversary fund was "in appreciation of what the . . . asylum had done for her boy who had left the institution" fifteen years earlier. Additionally, they were gratified with Dr. Godfrey Nurse's donated etchings for the library and the history of the institution in mural form, painted by Carol Hill, a Works Project Administration art teacher, assisted by several of the asylum boys. The gifts of these three individuals represented the community's interest in the betterment of the asylum.[31]

8 From the Colored Orphan Asylum to the Riverdale Children's Association, 1937–46

The glow from the centennial celebration quickly faded, and the COA faced growing internal concerns over their ability to care properly for children, amid continuing problems with finances and the developing external criticism of their leadership. The absence of trustees' and executive committee's minutes for the period of 1937 through November 1939 makes it difficult to accurately chronicle the history of the Colored Orphan Asylum at this critical period in its existence, during which they reached out to the African American community in a genuine effort to forge an alliance. The annual reports are the only primary sources for these years. Unlike the minutes of the trustees and the executive committee, the annual reports only summarize incidents or actions taken with an understanding that the general public was the reader. Much of the internal business, especially involving conflicts or controversial issues, was left out of the annual reports.

The educational report for 1937 was a mixed one. The declining population at Riverdale (211, with seventy admitted during the year but none after July) led to the termination of the kindergarten class. Children in grades 4A and higher were provided with prevocational classes in shop, cooking, sewing, and handicraft. There was a boys' and girls' class in cooking for low-intelligence students. The boys were instructed in cooking simple dishes: lima beans with tomato sauce, mock hamburgers, meat and rice loaf, black-eyed peas or "Hopping John," and scalloped salmon and peas. The girls learned to make well-balanced lunches and dinners and the proper way to serve scalloped eggs on toast, baked rice with cheese, scalloped potatoes, salmon cakes, and Creole shrimp. Two new classes in crocheting and knitting were introduced for girls in the fifth grade and up. They were taught how to make sweaters, caps, scarves, and small rugs. The boys made wooden crochet and knitting needles for the girls' use. Citywide tests placed those in the third grade and above "up to the norms in all subjects, with the exception of arithmetic in which, as a school, we are 10 months below the norm, to offset this however, they were a year and a half above the norm in literature." The continued emphasis on vocational training made little sense in an era when activists had taken to the streets to open up Harlem's workforce to all professions. One questions why they insisted on offering vocational classes when these skills offered limited marketable opportunities. (Certainly, they made the children more adaptable for home repairs and domestic chores, but this provided little relief in a competitive job market.)[1]

Raking leaves (*above*) and making beds (*next page*)—learning responsibilities and basic skills at an early age. (Courtesy of Harlem Dowling–West Side Center for Children and Family Services.)

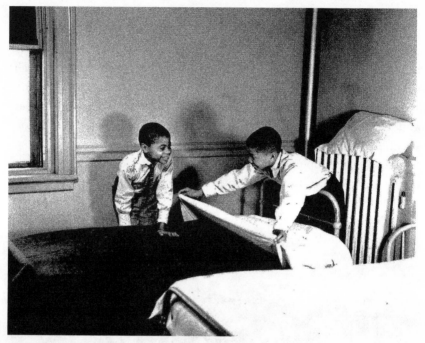

(Courtesy of Harlem Dowling–West Side Center for Children and Family Services.)

In 1938, Negro history was added to the curriculum of Public School 49. The children sold Christmas articles that they had made and used the earnings to do holiday shopping. They were so happy with the results that they immediately began to make items for the next year's sale. Principal Alice S. Bracken reported that five children were advanced in 1938, "when test results showed they were capable of doing higher work." Their formal education was supplemented with trips to the American Museum of Natural History, the Hayden Planetarium, the Museum of the City of New York, the Kingsbridge (Bronx) branch of the Telephone Exchange, and various parks.[2]

The skimpy record indicates that despite the institution's aloofness from Harlem, community leaders sought to make the children happy. Two of the community's most prestigious churches with progressive ministers reached out to Riverdale. Abyssinia Baptist Church in Harlem, led by the charismatic Adam Clayton Powell Jr., provided toys and gifts through Mrs. Helen Wadsworth. The Rev. John Johnson of Harlem's St. Martin Episcopal Church provided clothing for the children. Cab Calloway, the popular entertainer, visited the institution on November 5, 1937, and brought candy for the children. The talented dancer of Hollywood films, Bill "Bojangles" Robinson, personally gave each child ten cents, for a total of approximately twenty-one dollars. Two ecstatic boys took part in a television test with Robinson and "were simply thrilled with their experience."[3]

The COA's challenge was to provide adequate resources for children still at Riverdale and for those who were boarded out with families. Both challenges proved burdensome. The boarding home committee faced difficulty in finding adequate foster care homes, both because most blacks had low incomes and because the Negro sections in the greater New York City area offered "poor and inadequate housing condition." The committee hired a full-time home finder to counter competition from other agencies also in search of suitable foster families. Homes that were acceptable pleased the committee, because they believed that these homes provided the children with a "better financed, moral and physical environment than it will be possible for them to have at any other time in their lives." While this was true for those who came from neglected homes, it was an overgeneralization. The institution's financial condition became bleak at a time when the nation was struggling to recover from the effects of the economic downturn. The deficit for 1937 amounted to $16,908.69. The asylum's inability to maintain the facility and to provide proper care led to criticism from the New York State Department of Social Welfare. Investigation revealed that for several years the management had moved children into foster care instead of seeking additional resources to improve "both the quality of care and the [maintenance] of facilities."[4]

For reasons not entirely clear but perhaps because of rising criticism, Dr. Mason Pitman resigned as executive director in June 1938. His replacement, Henry Murphy, who was hired in July, made a considerable effort to increase Negro staffing and to work closely with Harlem's community leaders during his seven-year tenure. Just four months on the payroll, Murphy acknowledged that the institution had to seek cooperation with Harlem and not patronize its residents or its leaders. He expressed a desire to use Negroes "whose education, experience, willingness and judgment can help in the development of the program as determined by the Board." This was the first admission from anyone in management that the myth of white paternalism had failed and that it was imperative that the black community play not a dependent role but act as co-partner in the operation of the Colored Orphan Asylum. The hiring of Dr. Thomas H. Patrick Jr., a leading African American pediatrician, in 1939 to be the medical advisor for the foster home department was proof of Murphy's sincerity. Furthermore, the liberal executive director wanted to work with the community to find alternatives to sending boys "to correctional institutions because there is no other resource." He also expressed a keen interest in "first exhausting every means of maintaining the home" before placing children into foster care. More foster care, however, was needed, because the average length of stay for a child at Riverdale in 1938 was five years and six months, compared to only two years and nine months in 1930. This meant that it was imperative to double the casework staff if the institution was to seriously "undertake individualized and family case work." Murphy hoped to increase funding, as more people were paying attention to Harlem after a 1935 riot caused $200,000,000 in property damage. He admitted that the institution's continued operation on a deficit meant "eventual extinction."⁵

Under Murphy's direction, the asylum quickly moved to treat the children as individuals and not as statistics for reports. It was determined that testing, social casework, and clinical psychology "all play some part in our present program, but operate under many limitations because of crowded mental hygiene clinics, excessive case loads and limited funds." The trustees recognized that "greater efficiency will be realized when an intake staff and adequate psychiatric and foster home departments are organized." It still remained a challenge to find good homes and capable foster parents for adolescents, particularly if prospective foster parents had no experience in child rearing. As of October 31, 1937, there were 426 in boarding homes, with thirty-one in free homes and only two in wage homes. A year later, there were 402 in boarding homes, despite the placement of thirty-seven during 1938. Twelve children were placed in free homes and two in wage homes during 1938.[6]

In April 1939, Dr. Channing H. Tobias, chair of the committee on Negro child care of the Welfare Council of New York, noted that for ten years there lacked facilities for the care of dependent black children. Unlike the Colored Orphan Asylum, too many Protestant child care agencies' "charities or policies made it impossible to accept Negro children for care without extensive revisions that might affect their source of contributions," concluded Tobias. Only six of the thirty-four Protestant voluntary welfare agencies accepted African American children. He added that the merger of Protestant child care agencies, Negro groups, other denominational agencies, and the city would lead to more foster homes that would provide better care. Tobias admitted that part of the problem was the paucity of African American social workers. The asylum eagerly quoted Mayor Fiorello LaGuardia in the 1939 annual report: "Any move by private philanthropy to strengthen the quality of service which the Colored Orphan Asylum is now able to offer would mark the fulfillment of a basic community need. In terms of future welfare and relief taxes, it would be a wise financial and social investment." The combination of poverty, white fear of Negro youth violence, and lack of funding for child welfare resulted in a disproportionate number of black youth being labeled neglected or delinquent. For example, in 1939, 18 percent of children judged neglected by the courts in 1939 were Negroes, as were 23 percent of those adjudged delinquent by the courts, percentages disproportionate to their numbers in the city's population.[7]

The large migration of Southern blacks to Harlem rapidly changed the African American population in New York City, which rose to 320,000 in 1930 from 152,000 a decade earlier. Seventy percent of the city's black population resided in Harlem, mainly in overcrowded tenements, where they were susceptible to unemployment, disease, and crime. With a hostile police department and a citizenry concerned about potential racial uprising, black youth were more likely than their white counterparts to be judged as delinquent. Black youth, according

to the *New York Times*, made up 3.5 percent of the city's juvenile population but accounted for 10 percent of the court's juvenile cases in
1939. On November 1, 1939, the Children's Aid Society Service Bureau
for Negro Children and the Colored Orphan Asylum opened a joint
foster home application bureau at 154 East Fifty-fourth Street in Manhattan on a six-month, experimental basis. Seed money was donated
by the Davidson Fund established by John D. Rockefeller Jr., the
Greater New York Fund, the Federation of Protestant Welfare agencies,
and private donors. It was intended that more foster homes would be
an alternative to incarceration.[8]

Tremendous changes occurred in the foster home department. On
October 31, 1938, there was one supervisor, seven visitors, one doctor,
one nurse, one dentist, one clinical worker, one clothing worker, and
three clerical workers. A year later, under Murphy's reorganization
plan, there were still one doctor, one clothing worker, one dentist, and
a nurse with training in medical social service, in addition to two supervisors, one home finder, eleven case workers, one clinical worker,
and five full-time and one part-time clerical workers. The foster home
department's chair reported they had carefully investigated referrals,
used more scrutiny than before in studying applications from potential
foster care parents for placement, made better foster care home selec-
tions, and better supervised the children in foster care homes. A worker's case load was reduced to forty-five, compared to 110 to 120 the
previous year. It was hoped that in 1940 to have more vocational guidance and placement for older children. The chair acknowledged that
"there is a tremendous problem of care for the older Negro girl, which
no agency is touching at present." While social workers had accepted
as wisdom for the past thirty years the notion that foster home care
was the correct remedy for child care, the changing times demanded
that institutional care was needed for children not bright enough or
resourceful enough to negotiate the variables of community living.
Their lack of intelligence and/or social skills to co-exist outside the
institution put an extra burden on the asylum to care for more children
on site at Riverdale, which had $15,199.64 more in expenses than they
received in income for the year 1938. This deficit affected admission:

only seventy-nine were admitted between November 1, 1938, and October 31, 1939. Equally vexing was the institution's choice of deciding whom they should serve. It was financially impossible, Murphy emphasized, "to set up an adequate, comprehensive program for both boys and girls, from four to sixteen years of age, with mentality ratings ranging from 65 to 145." To Murphy's credit, he noted that the institution must collaborate with Harlem on that decision.[9]

The low number admitted to Riverdale by October 31, 1939, reflected the high cost of caring for children. It cost, on average, fifty-four cents more per day, or $198.38 more per year, to care for a child at Riverdale as compared to foster care. The extra cost was not justifiable and raised concern about the future mission of the institution. They could not continue to both care for children in an institution that was falling into disrepair and accommodate the growing need for foster care placement. The deficit for the year ending October 31, 1939, amounted to $13,541.68. A sense of urgency motivated the institution to "embark upon an interpretative program, looking toward increased community participation and financial support." To encourage more contributions from Harlem's small but growing middle class, the annual report for 1939 printed Judge Myles A. Paige's statement that there was a correlation between normal family life and a reduction in the number of neglected children. The African American judge called upon the community to take on the responsibility of supporting the asylum with their dollars, as most of the Colored Orphan Asylum's capital funds were tied up in real estate and mortgages. Lawrence G. Payson, the chair of the advisers, recommended that funds derived from sale of real estate or other properties be applied to loan repayments and that one-half of the monies from bequests or other sources be used to reduce loans, with the other half applied to investments. Payson made this recommendation because in 1938 the trustees had spent more than sixty thousand dollars of capital funds to improve the institution's heating, refrigerating, hot water, and electrical systems. A general public appeal printed in the inside cover of the 1939 annual report requested donors to provide $1,500 dollars to provide an adequate program of religious education, one thousand dollars to employ a trained cottage worker for a year, six hundred dollars to modernize the infirmary or renovate the auditorium, $350 to provide an older girl with enough training for self-support, and ten to one hundred dollars to clothe a child from three months to three years.[10]

Change in the Racial Composition of the COA

The most successful motivator to elicit funds, particularly from Harlem, was the institution's decision to make its membership interracial. Murphy noted in the annual report for 1939 that the asylum's future success was directly related to placing on the board representatives of different groups or "schools of thought." This was a clear signal that the trustees had to overrule their 1919 decision not to place a woman of color on the board. An opportunity to change the racial makeup of the board occurred following the deaths of Helena L. Knox and Mrs. Joseph W. Tilton. Helena T. Emerson, who was one of the members who voted in 1919 to have a colored woman elected a manager, resigned in 1939, with the request "that her place be filled by a Negro member." The election of Mrs. William H. Wortham led to the immediate resignations of Mrs. George F. Wagner and Mrs. Sidney D. Gamble, who had both joined in 1937. The absence of extant minutes for the trustees and executive committee for 1939 makes it impossible to determine if their resignations were in protest of the election of an African American member. However, that was indeed a possibility, because the secretary, Jane Johnson Garnjost, indicated that "regretfully we have accepted the resignations . . . with the hope that they may return to service at some future time." It was noted in the annual report that Wortham's election was "in keeping with the spirit of equality and brotherhood of our Quaker origin." Perhaps in a criticism of the resigned members, the secretary added that "inactive trustees and trustees with only a casual interest throw a heavy burden on the balance of a board. In a large and complex city . . . trustees should respect a variety of groups, interests and school of thought." The trustees, prompted by Executive Director Henry Murphy, realized that they needed members truly committed to racial progress and not merely those who wanted to help Negroes but were reluctant to associate with them as equals. In February 1940, the nominating committee requested the names of qualified Negroes and Jews to be added to the board of directors. This was a clear indication that the Colored Orphan Asylum, founded by Quakers and administered for one hundred years by white Protestants, realized that their salvation depended upon two historically oppressed groups. A black woman, Charlotte Anderson, the wife of Peyton F. Anderson, a physician and a Harlem civic leader, was elected in 1940 as a member and secretary. Jews had to wait another year for an election.[11]

The trustees wrestled with the budget issue throughout 1940, as they contemplated increased enrollment, fundraisers, and better after care. The end-of-year Christmas appeal brought in $485.96, after expenses. Quick cash was received in early 1940 when the trustees sold property at 446 West Forty-forth Street in midtown Manhattan for $7,500, of which $2,500 was in cash. The February board meeting centered on establishing "a central office in Harlem for case workers, space for clinical examinations and consultation, consolidation of all case and medical records." Funds obtained in July paid for a three-year lease on a Harlem office at 306 Lenox Avenue, near bustling 125th Street. The rising number of young delinquent black and white girls going to reform institutions highlighted the need for more foster care facilities. In May, the asylum received a four-thousand-dollar gift to place, for up to one year, twenty-five girls "to prove or disapprove the feasibility of this type of care as compared with institution care." Help was needed for girls who had to leave the institution after age eighteen. Fifty dollars was provided from the stipend fund to those who had job offers but no proper clothes. Girls who went to the Harlem YWCA for a machine-operating course received ten dollars. The board called upon trustees to make financial contributions for publicity purposes to aid in fundraising appeals. In March, a member pledged to "double any amount given by, or obtained through the Board members, up to $2,000." Amalia F. Morse, the widow of Charles H. Morse, a retired capitalist, left a bequest of $2,500 to the Colored Orphan Asylum.[12]

The trustees decided in June 1940 not to balance the budget by lowering standards but either to dip into capital funds or have a major fundraiser. The executive committee met on July 26 and agreed with the advisers' suggestion to sell railroad and electric shares to bring in $25,292, to cover the deficit for the budget period ending on June 30 and to meet the anticipated deficit for the next three months. The difference between per diem cost per child under care at Riverdale and in foster care amounted to $208 annually per child. Despite the monetary difference, the trustees decided in July to increase the population at Riverdale, but this would not include older delinquent children, because to include them would require amending their charter. Murphy found out in October that other agencies were admitting delinquents and classifying them as neglected, which they could do without amending their charter. They also offered "to care for Negro refugee children, who may come to the attention of the U.S. committee for the care of European children." It was not clear who "Negro refugee children" might be, unless they were North African subjects of the British or French displaced by the war in North Africa. In September, the trustees sold $20,677.50 worth of railroad and electric shares to meet the budget deficit for the period ending June 30. An extra $2,500 was added to the income for July, August, and September "to take care of the balance over and above [the] regular income." To avoid more money woes, the trustees decided in September to host a December event, either a musicale, dinner, or entertainment. They also wanted to find sponsors at fifty and one hundred dollars to support a child as well as to fund the formation of a biracial men's committee to handle vocational and placement problems, "which would gradually grow into a money raising unit." It was reported at the October trustees' meeting that Mr. Buch, a hired fundraiser, had brought in $2,260.40 via appeals but that he needed the assistance of a board member to increase donations. Two donors contributed a total of $38,000.35 for special purposes, foundations contributed $7,675, and the Greater New York Fund accepted the request to put the Colored Orphan Asylum's name on Coca-Cola dispensers in exchange for a percentage of the proceeds. Still, funds were desperately needed. The foster home caseworkers carried forty-seven cases each; this load needed to be reduced by hiring additional workers. Riverdale lost their Works Project Administration librarian, but keeping the library open without one led to book theft. The closing of other child care agencies placed a burden on the Colored

Orphan Asylum to take them, as children were "piling up at the Department of Welfare."[13]

The secretary reported in the November 1940 meeting that there was gang activity in Jamaica, Queens. The trustees vowed to look into the matter to determine how best they could serve the community. They decided to place only younger children in Jamaica when vacancies occurred, both to prevent older children from joining gangs and from becoming victims of random gang violence. At the December meeting, the trustees wanted to get clear of financial deficits. "Our financial secretary can plan ways and means for a campaign, can prepare publicity and carry out details, but the actual contracting of large groups of individuals remains essentially a Board function." The foster home department was hampered by high turnovers and low salaries. It was recommended that a superintendent be hired to assist Murphy, who was both the superintendent and executive director. Funds were needed for a large indoor space and gymnasium. The trustees vowed to emulate the founders of the asylum, who used "each reversal as a stepping stone to greater service in the community. If we are going to carry the standard they bore so bravely, we must arouse public sentiment to our support," the secretary noted. "Then it will be possible to carry out a program, not only for ameliorative and palliative measures, but a program of real preventive work." It had helped that the *New York Times* had earlier provided favorable publicity with an article about Alice Beasley, a former "old girl," who displayed at a hobby show a miniature Colored Orphan Asylum.[14]

The year 1941 began with the trustees selling ten thousand dollars of railroad bonds to have funds for the general purpose account. The publicity committee, formed in 1940, raised $949.37 after expenses since December 1, 1940. Four thousand leaflets were mailed for further fundraising. A special meeting on January 17 scrutinized the financial portfolio. (See table on the next page.)

A 4 percent return on gross investment was reported, four mortgages had foreclosed during the past five years, and investments had decreased $270,000 in the past ten years. There was, to their further embarrassment, a $106,000 loss on the sale of an investment originally worth $164,000. The sale of securities added another ten thousand

Approximate Book Value	Approximate Market Value
Bonds $162,000	$124,000
Stocks $108,000	$90,000
Mortgages/Certificates $311,000	no market quotation
Real Estate $16,000	no market quotation

dollars in losses. They decided to study "to determine if there [was] an increase in salaries with fewer children at the institution." They also wanted to determine "if [an] increased budget justifies budget deficit" and whether "the finance committee [should] advise [the] Board of loss of income whenever securities are sold." These were important questions, and answers were quickly needed: the deficit at the end of 1940 amounted to $29,164.32.[15]

The publicity committee recommended in February 1941 that a development committee be organized to assist in fundraising and to cooperate with community agencies to form a unified and coordinated community program of foster care and training for neglected and dependent African American children. On May 22, supporters attended the Broadway showing of *Native Son*, starring Canada Lee and Ann Burr. The production cleared $250 and the publicity from the fundraiser yielded a hundred-dollar contribution from the Utility Club. An additional $5,988.73 was raised by November from foundations, individuals, and the proceeds of a football game at the Polo Grounds between the Colored All Stars and the black New York Yankees football team. It was expected that Mrs. John D. Rockefeller would donate one thousand dollars. The Japanese attack at Pearl Harbor on December 7, 1941, followed by the United States' declaration of war against Japan and Germany caused Laurence G. Payson, the chair of the advisory committee, to express fear that hostilities might impede fundraising efforts. He added that "a much closer cooperation between all people now exists," which brightened the picture for the asylum's future.[16]

The deterioration of the facilities, staff turnover, and the influx of more African Americans as staff members and trustees would dominate the business of the Colored Orphan Asylum for the next few years, as the trustees struggled to find the means to remain a vital institution. The trustees acknowledged that "a great deal of furniture and equipment is badly needed at the institution." However, a more pressing concern was the inadequate salary of foster home workers. It was anticipated in July 1941 that six or seven foster home workers would leave by October 1. The low pay caused nine staff members to resign by November 14, a 40 percent turnover in the caseworker staff. The turnovers, the lack of funds, and the general chaos adversely affected upon the asylum. Forty percent of new admissions were adolescents, with the median age of children being older than those admitted two years earlier. Mrs. William H. Wortham, the chair of the children's committee, noted an "unrest among children after visitors" left. Even the school, recently a source of pride, was experiencing difficulty with the children's conduct, which was described "as being very bad."[17]

Although the trustees had from the beginning hired black workers to be laundresses, child care providers, house mothers, and the occasional physician or dentist, they now made a concerted effort to employ more African American workers and professionals, which served a dual purpose. It made it easier for the children to relate to the staff, which shared their cultural heritage, and it gave the Harlem community a greater connection to an institution that was providing care for its children. In February 1941, Hazel Jones Hardy, a graduate of Howard University, became the asylum's dietician. She replaced Rosa E. Paige, who was promoted to the matron's position after serving as dietician since 1940. John W. Poe, also a Howard graduate and a supervisor at the Department of Public Assistance in Philadelphia for ten years, was hired initially as an institutional caseworker before being appointed assistant superintendent in September. By the end of 1941, the pediatrician, the nurse, the secretary, the dietician, the matron, the assistant superintendent, the head of the clothing department, and all the full-time positions with the exception of the executive director were held by African Americans. In just three years, Murphy placed forty-six African Americans on the payroll, which made them 80 percent of the institution's workforce. The election of black trustees would, during the next five years, follow a modest but similar pattern.

In late 1941, a Negro woman, Mrs. Melvin Proctor, the wife of a physician, was elected along with Mrs. Richard J. Bernhard, a Jew and the niece of New York Governor Herbert H. Lehman.[18]

Throughout the winter and spring of 1941, a number of prominent entertainers, dignitaries, and athletes visited Riverdale, bringing the beleaguered institution well-needed publicity. The heavyweight boxer Joe Louis refereed boxing matches between the boys, and Philippa Schuyler, a nine-year-old pianist, performed a benefit for the asylum in the home of Mr. and Mrs. Zabriskie, a direct descendant of Sarah Underhill, one of the original managers. Bill "Bojangles" Robinson, the black cartoonist E. Simms Campbell, the actress Fredi Washington, the educator and civil rights advocate Mary McLeod Bethune, and Yankee great Lou Gehrig all visited Riverdale in 1941. The most significant visitor, from a publicity standpoint, was Hattie McDaniel, the Oscar winner for best supporting actress in *Gone with the Wind*, who expressed interest in adopting a child.[19]

The Colored Orphan Asylum was one of the few institutions that provided for black children, which put them in the unenviable position of being inundated with requests for experimental or research projects. The children unknown to Pitman by name nearly became pawns to the medical profession, which was looking for human subjects for vaccine testing. In March 1931, Dr. S. W. Lambert of the Colored Orphan Asylum's board of advising physicians suggested that the trustees permit the Department of Health to use Calmette vaccine against tuberculosis on children ages four to ten. The vaccine had already been administered to children in Harlem and had proven successful overseas. The following month, the after-care committee, to their credit, vetoed the use of the experimental vaccine, because children in the asylum had received the Wasserman test. Again, to their credit, the executive committee in 1936 denied the Board of Health's request to use an experimental influenza vaccine on the children. In March 1941, the trustees approved a resolution in opposition "to the use of the children committed to its care for experimental studies of any kind, sponsored by any commercial concern." This policy, while unwritten, dates to March 1934, when Columbia University wanted to study twenty-five enuretic cases. The asylum did not have twenty-five bedwetters in the institution, but it was unlikely that they would have cooperated even if they could have supplied the children.[20]

Instead of aiding scientists interested in using the children as experimental specimens, the trustees wanted to provide their 166 charges in the Riverdale institution with the simple joys of childhood. In April 1941, the trustees requested that the Hayden fund underwrite a swimming pool and sponsor a summer program. The failure of that appeal led First Directress Lillie Skiddy Parker to ask readers of the *New York Times* in August to contribute $250 to cover the cost of sand, gravel, and cement. The Riverdale boys would dig a twenty-foot-by-forty-foot pool two to four feet in depth. A wading pool had been installed, but it was insufficient for older children. In September, after the concrete had proven too difficult for the boys to lay and spread, a generous couple, Mr. and Mrs. Eugene Harris, decided to honor their twenty-fifth wedding anniversary with a gift of $250 to hire a concrete worker to finish the job.[21]

The year 1942 was one of tension for the trustees as the money situation worsened. Throughout the year, the trustees sold shares in American Tobacco, Central Hanover Bank, and Eastman Kodak to have funds to avoid a deficit for the period ending June 30. An appeal letter written by Bill "Bojangles" Robinson and Canada Lee to five hundred Hollywood stars, a charitable boxing match by Henry Armstrong, various foundation grants, and a Harlem campaign eased but did not completely solve the money situation. A committee headed by Judge Hubert Delany was formed in October to foster closer relations with Harlem and to develop ways to approach the community about foster homes. Delaney came from an illustrious family. His father, Henry Delany, was the nation's first elected black Episcopal bishop. The judge's wife, Audre, was elected trustee in December, and in later years his two sisters, Sarah (Sadie) and Elizabeth (Bessie), would become famous for their 1993 book, *Having Our Say*, about their one hundred–plus years of life.[22]

The near closing of Wiltwyck School for Boys and the possible shutdown of the Services Bureau for Neglected Negro Children in 1942 convinced Executive Director Henry Murphy that it was time to make

Riverdale strictly a boy's institution. In March, the trustees decided to change their charter to accept delinquent as well as neglected and dependent children.[23]

Adding to his frustration over the increased costs of telephone service, insurance, clothing, medical and dental supplies, and food, Murphy was also confronted with the war taking away his workers. Some were drafted, but others opted for the better wages and benefits provided by war industries. It became more taxing to find reliable women or couples for the cottages' supervision, and many cottages were left empty. While the preference was for married couples who were even tempered, affectionate, adequate cooks and tolerant of shifting adolescent moods, the trustees were willing to compromise and accept unrelated persons to be "parents" in the cottages.[24]

Admittance of Whites and a Name Change

Although the money situation was a growing problem, of more immediate concern was a state law prohibiting segregation in publicly funded residential child care facilities. Ironically, an institution that was founded because white institutions prohibited the admission of black children now found itself in jeopardy if it did not admit white children. This measure confronted the Colored Orphan Asylum with a difficult choice. A first option was to close the facilities and go out of business to avoid integration, but that was neither feasible nor considered. A second option, to stay in the child care business, would mean that the Colored Orphan Asylum would have to change the name that had identified it for the past 106 years, because "colored" in their incorporated name automatically implied the exclusion of white children. Their third option was whether to admit neglected, dependent, or delinquent white children at the expense of African American children, who had fewer resources. While the name change was easy (but expensive) to accomplish, it by itself would not address the issue of integration. However, a name change was something the trustees had considered for years. It had suited the asylum's early period, but for decades the majority of the children had not been orphans, and the nomenclature "colored" was losing acceptance among more militant individuals, who preferred "Negro." The August 10, 1928, minutes noted that Miss Wood had spoke of renaming the institution and requested names. No action was taken until July 12, 1940, when it was decided that the board would consider operating in the fall under the name of Association for the Benefit of Negro Children, instead of its incorporated name, the Colored Orphan Asylum and the Association for the Benefit of Colored Children in the City of New York. In October, the trustees suggested a name change to Negro Children's Association, with an option to consider other names. In November, the trustees considered Negro Children's Association, Murray Shotwell Center, and Association for Negro Children; in December, Murray Shotwell received six votes, one more than any other choice, and in February 1941, they decided to legally change their name to Murray Shotwell Association. However, they did not file a name change with the secretary of state in Albany, probably because of the $25,000 filing fee. On September 11, 1942 (after the passage of the Race Discrimination bill), the trustees discussed the name Riverdale Children's Association. On March 12, 1943, they considered Riverdale Children's Association and New York Children's Bureau as fitting names.[25]

A contest was held for a new name. Henry Murphy, who was unable, according to Fitz Harvey, to participate in the contest, privately suggested to the teenaged Fitz that he should include "Riverdale Children's Association" along with the other names that he intended to submit in the contest. On February 11, 1944, fifteen-year-old Fitz Harvey's entry, Riverdale Children's Association, was "picked" by the judges as the winning entry. Tremendous publicity resulted from young Fitz's "lucky" selection: Paul Robeson, the singer, actor, and human rights advocate, donated a twenty-five-dollar war bond, which Mayor Fiorello LaGuardia presented to Fitz in a ceremony on April 6. The name change was officially approved by the trustees on December 11, 1944, and filed a week later with Secretary of State Thomas J. Curran.[26]

The admission of white children would be more problematic. Throughout their history, the institution had never admitted white youngsters. The trustees had in the past admitted American Indians, dark-complexioned Latinos, and even those who looked "nearly white," but now they were reluctant to admit whites over African Americans who were still uncared for. On occasion, a youngster who could easily pass for white would be admitted, but it was clear that all or part of the child's ancestry was non-European. In early 1937, the trustees, operating on the principle that they served only youth of color, denied admission to a twelve-year-old white follower of Father Divine. They also cited a lack of experience in finding white foster homes for white children, which seems implausible, considering their earlier experience of housing indentures with white families and that some boarded-out black children had gone to Caucasian homes. In March 1943, Judge Jane M. Bolin inquired as to the delay in admitting white children. A reluctant board decided in April that they would accept any Protestant child regardless of race or color. At a spring meeting, Dr. Channing Tobias "expressed the feeling that it would be wiser to take time and get ourselves in readiness to do a good job, rather than rush in unprepared." Meanwhile, ten places for white children were reserved. They would be accommodated either by placing five black girls from the main building into foster homes, placing five boys from Cottage 6 in foster homes, or transferring five boys from Cottage 6 to other cottages. By October, they expected to have in place a biracial program that would help the staff and children to adjust to the new racial dynamics. It was decided to limit admission to whites only until vacancies were filled but to continue to place both races in foster homes. The trustees hoped that the sacrificing of a few Negro children to accommodate the admission of whites would "be a stimulus to white agencies to accelerate the placement of Negro children."[27]

At the beginning of 1945, there were two white children and 540 black children under the care of Riverdale Children's Association, with four white children under study for foster care. In March, a bigoted judge refused to send a neglected white child to the institution. But by 1948, 18 percent of the children in Riverdale Children's Association were Caucasians.[28]

Amid the budget crisis, the name change, and the reluctant admission of white children, the institution, like the rest of the nation, was praying for the safety of their "boys" fighting overseas. Letters from alumni informed the children of geographical areas previously un-known to them. At least 180 former residents served in the segregated military after the declaration of war in December 1941. The children supported the war effort in early 1943 by selling scrap newspaper for three dollars and collecting old rubber, tin, rags, and scrap metal. In February 1943, the management purchased a twenty-five-dollar war bond, the second one secured from money raised by the children.[29]

The trustees remembered the alumni serving in the armed forces and aided their morale with letters and gifts. Several unidentified "old boys" in service informed them that they had appreciated their guidance during their formative years. Elvin Bell, who was adopted while in the Colored Orphan Asylum, was a war hero. He rescued three sailors from a raging fire on the deck of the USS *Lexington* in a battle in the Coral Sea. The Navy and Marine Corps medal was awarded to the brave sailor and a promotion in rank "for conspicuous bravery and devotion to duty." To honor all the former residents in the military, the trustees decided in 1943 "to develop a service flag or honor roll, with the names of all the boys in service."[30] By September 1944, the trustees had gathered the addresses of ninety-one former boys still in the military. The children raised sixty dollars for gifts to send to happy recipients overseas. Undoubtedly, many former residents were wounded and some even killed during the conflict. The institution's records revealed that a former boy who was wounded in the South Pacific expressed thanks for his Christmas gift. It was noted in the spring of 1945 that Tyron Marshall, a former boy in the institution, had been killed in action.[31]

The trustees' concern for those in the military did not lessen their attention to the pressing problems with both Riverdale and the foster care system. The increased pressure on the institution to provide care, the high staff turnover resulting from low salaries and poor living quarters at the institution, and the increased workload on Henry Murphy, who was both the superintendent and executive director, led to the September 1943 promotion of John W. Poe to the position of superintendent from that of assistant superintendent. In 1943, the charter was changed to aid any child in need. "Previous authorization of this phrase of charter change included the word 'delinquent.' This suggestion is to offer even broader scope to the work." The increase of delinquent children both black and white and a greater trepidation over the deficit led to a charter change to increase board membership from thirty to fifty, with a small executive board of fifteen to twenty persons, the latter having "full interim powers and the former to constitute the corporate membership." It was decided in June 1944 to have forty-eight trustees, with no more than thirty to be women. They also eliminated the "provision limiting liability of husbands of members of the corporation" as well as the "provision creating the relationship of guardian and ward between the trustees and those received into the home maintained by the corporation." A special board meeting on September 29 resulted in forty-three names being submitted for membership, including eleven white men and seven Jews. Among the suggested blacks were Hubert Delany, Dr. Arthur Logan, Marian Anderson, and Mrs. Richard Martin, who all became trustees within a few years. Other prominent individuals who were suggested but did not become members included the labor leader A. Philip Randolph, Dr. Channing Tobias, and Eslanda Robeson, the wife of Paul Robeson.[32]

The issue of child care and the ability of various agencies to properly provide became a problem that had to be solved. Murphy met during the spring of 1943 with the New York's Child Foster Home Service to seek greater cooperation between agencies that shared similar objectives and had mutual problems. He wanted this cooperation instead of having "the Federation of Protestant Welfare Agencies assume too great a degree of leadership." A lack of organization hampered the effectiveness of the child care agencies. Eleven of the seventeen agencies searching for foster homes were Protestant, even though "the largest numbers[s] of children to be served are in the Catholic and Jewish fields." Murphy questioned if the agencies were "spending [their] combined dollars on Protestant children as wisely" as were the Jewish and Catholic agencies. He also wondered if it was efficient for forty agencies to be competing for limited staff workers and foster homes as well as for well-behaved children. Murphy suggested the possibility of a merger between Riverdale Children's Association and the

New York Child's Foster Home Services because they had similar standards of service and similar financial situations and because they both had been in operation for about a century and had similar per capita costs and active boards. Although a merger meant the loss of an identity and public recognition, Murphy noted that it would lead to a better distribution of funds and an ability to attract the best civic-minded citizens as board members. For various reasons, however, the merger did not materialize.[33]

Funds and positive publicity was the agenda that occupied Murphy's energy and time during 1943. Duke Ellington aided the institution by reading daily a history and program of Riverdale Children's Association for a "spot notice prepared by the Greater New York Fund." This yielded eight hundred dollars by November 12, 1943. Earlier, Eleanor Roosevelt visited Riverdale on October 21 to be entertained by the joyful singing of 190 children. The following month, on November 14, Judge and Mrs. Hubert Delany entertained the First Lady with a tea in their home.[34]

Executive Director Murphy and the trustees faced a serious staff shortage, because they could not satisfy either the union or the workers with their low pay scale. Even though the donations for 1943 exceeded those of the previous year by $32,650, expenditures still exceeded income by $15,688. Nevertheless, Murphy, not wanting to risk losing more workers, recommended a $3,500 increase in the budget to retain workers. Equally distressing was the information that the value of their bonds, stocks, mortgages, and real estate amounted to $554,610.40, a decrease of $5,640 from their value in 1942.[35]

The first half of 1944 was hectic with various fundraisers. The publicity committee reported at the January trustees' meeting that forty thousand dollars had been raised since June 1943, with the aim of raising an additional thirty thousand. An April 28 dance sponsored by the Harlem Club, a division of Riverdale Children's Association, featuring the Duke Ellington and the Lucky Millinder orchestras; Lena Horne's appeal; the Bronx Campaign; a reception for Marian Anderson; an appeal for funds at twenty churches on May 7; and a party given for Lillian Smith, the author of *Strange Fruit,* at the home of Mr.

and Mrs. Heimerdinger all helped the publicity committee raise $43,300 from January 1, 1944, to June 1944.[36]

While the Riverdale Children's Association sought to survive amid a period of financial uncertainties, its longtime leader, Lillie Skiddy Parker, who had joined the organization in 1894, decided that she wanted to be relieved of responsibilities. Parker, who served as first directress from 1914 until 1944, was replaced in December by Mrs. Robert DeVecchi, who assumed the new title of president. The board, grateful for Parker's fifty years of devotion, initiated the Lillie Skiddy Parker Good Citizenship Award, from a thousand-dollar U.S. savings bond donated by her daughter and son-in-law Mr. and Mrs. Laurence Payson. The twenty-five dollars of interest from the bond provided annually for twelve years a five-dollar award to two children at Riverdale and three children in foster care who made their homes "a better and happier place in which to live." Besides her longtime support for the Colored Orphan Asylum, Parker was the founder and first president of the Protestant Big Sisters, a co-founder and first vice president of the Federation of Protestant Welfare Agencies, and a former president of the Katy Ferguson Home for Unwed Mothers in Harlem. Parker, who impressed others with her "flexibility and fairness, with which she would change her mind in the light of new situations and changed conditions," died at age seventy-nine on April 5, 1949.[37]

Shortly before Parker's resignation, the child welfare program in New York City was severely criticized by Mayor Fiorello LaGuardia, who threatened to "clean up the present confused and inadequate [system] even if it involves the abolition of the Society for the Prevention of Cruelty to Children, reformation of city courts and social agencies and enactment of new amendments in the state legislature." The mayor was angry about delays in foster home placements, "inadequate sheltering of neglected and dependent children, slow case-work procedures, and duplication of investigations by several agencies which [caused] suffering for helpless children." The war had compounded the problem with the separation of families by war service or migration to the North for jobs.[38]

The problem of placement had not escaped the notice of the Riverdale Children's Association. In early November 1944, the case committee reported that four hundred children awaited placement through the Department of Welfare and an additional one hundred awaited placement through the courts. Ironically, the board believed that they could be more efficient with four hundred to five hundred children than they were with their present number of 350 to four hundred children. Their problem was the thirty staff vacancies, which they were unable to fill because of low salaries and difficulty of competing with other agencies or businesses. Instead of foster homes, the directors (formerly known as trustees) advocated the establishment of group foster homes, which could be organized if foster parents earned eighty to one hundred dollars a month instead of the then-current twenty-five to thirty dollars. The extra income would be an incentive for foster parents to take in five to eight children. The problem of placement continued into 1945, when, early in the year, there were 370 children in the Department of Welfare and two hundred in the courts waiting to be placed. The problem was partly attributed to a lack of staff and de facto segregation. An additional "problem" from the perspective of Henry Murphy was that the Riverdale Children's Association was heavily financed by Jews. He urged the board to "use every effort to stimulate greater Protestant responsibility."[39] This was an interesting observation, because just a few years earlier the board had decided that more Negroes and Jews were needed as members, presumably to attract greater financial support from those two communities, especially from wealthier Jewish New Yorkers. However, perhaps Murphy feared that Jewish money meant unwelcome Jewish control over the institution's day-to-day affairs.

Riverdale Children's Association engaged in a vigorous fundraising effort in 1945. Receipts at the beginning of the year showed a net of $8,369 from a theater party; $3,500 came from the Brooklyn campaign, and the 1944 Christmas appeal added twenty thousand dollars to the treasury by early March. The leadership was especially pleased that the Christmas appeal had twenty-two hundred donors, compared to eight hundred donors who had contributed seven thousand dollars the previous year. The board was concerned that they did not have enough large donors who could contribute one hundred dollars or more to offset the expense of seeking funds. But the continued prospect of theater parties and the Christmas appeal did not please Secretary Charlotte Anderson, who noted that the members had to be aggressive if they wanted to increase their number of large contributors. It was reported in mid-June that Mrs. Wendell Willkie's summer appeal had netted four thousand dollars in four days and that the Harlem campaign had yielded thirty thousand dollars. Unfortunately, despite the promising fundraising, the institution did not meet its goal of raising $150,000 from voluntary sources by June 30, 1945.[40]

Internal and External Criticism

The important fundraising campaign was overshadowed by internal and external criticism of the institution. The executive committee noted in July 1945 that Walter Offutt, the religious instructor, had charged that the children lacked proper supervision and programs; sanitation was poor, and the administration was keeping the board in the dark about the true situation. An ally, Mrs. Malvin Proctor, the chair of the children's committee and one of the few African Americans on the board, agreed that Henry Murphy lacked a concern for the children's best interests. In defense, Murphy and Superintendent John Poe placed the blame on a staff that was only at 70 percent strength. They complained that low salaries had led to the unfortunate hiring of some incompetents who provided poor supervision of the children and that maintenance was behind schedule because of the high cost, but they denied that they were trying to conceal negative information from the board's knowledge. At the July 23 board meeting, the directors gave the administration a vote of confidence to give the board time to "work more closely with the staff in getting perspective and that the Board should give them help in solving the problem." A motion was adopted to form three committees to work with the staff on policy, program, and plants. The board demanded Offutt's resignation, citing his inability to work constructively with the administrative staff and his hostile attitude. The press began to air Offutt's grievances in August. The *Pittsburgh Courier*, a leading African American newspaper, quoted Offutt's complaint that the children had destroyed pianos in the cottages, that older boys beat and stole money from younger children, and that there were no activities for school-age children from 3:15 P.M. until bedtime, which was 9:30 P.M. for the older children. Offutt may have exaggerated on this latter point, because the children played baseball, basketball, and other sports after school hours and during the weekend. Perhaps he was criticizing the lack of supervised activities. Offutt also complained that the children wore one another's clothes and thus had no pride in keeping the clothes clean. He offered the shocking news that seventeen girls shared one toilet and shower.[41]

The *Pittsburgh Courier* printed even more damaging news. Leslie C. Summey, a former guidance worker, had resigned in protest. He stated that the children at Riverdale were "love starved." Summey indicated that he had often used his own funds to purchase soap, deodorant, and combs for the children's use. Like Offutt, he believed that the children had too much idle time. In September, the *Daily Worker*, the organ of the Communist Party USA, printed Mrs. Malvin Proctor's accusation that teenage girls were used to serve tuberculosis patients at the House of Rest in neighboring Yonkers, New York, despite a Board of Health prohibition.[42]

Having children working in a tuberculosis ward was a serious violation of the health code. (Despite the order to the children to stop working in the ward, some girls were still employed there. Superintendent Poe's lame excuse was that "he could not remove them bodily.") Henry Murphy was forced to resign on September 28, effective November 1, but the staff of the foster home and public relations department asked the board to reconsider his resignation. Five employees publicly defended the ousted executive director. David Harris, a janitor for seventeen years, stated that Murphy provided jobs for African Americans, who virtually controlled the institution's activities. Murphy declined to reconsider, and the board granted him three thousand dollars of severance pay, with the understanding that they were not establishing a precedent. The board decided at a September 28 special meeting to have a few outstanding New Yorkers form a temporary advisory committee to "study the agency's role in the community and assist in working out plans as to how the [institution] may best meet the community's needs." An advisory committee, formed in early October and chaired by Dr. Channing Tobias, consisted of Judge Justine Polier, Mrs. Marshall Field, Mrs. David Levy, Roy Wilkins, Mrs. Joseph Lash, and the board members Mrs. Robert DeVecchi, Mrs. Frederick Garnjost, and Charlotte Anderson.[43]

The temporary advisory committee recommended that Audre Delany, who had been associated with the institution for fourteen years, with the last six devoted to child placement, and who possessed an "excellent technical background in the field of social work," be appointed by the board to the interim executive director's position. The advisory committee commended Murphy for his leadership but noted that his failure was a result of the fact that "the Colored Orphan Asylum . . . and the Riverdale Children's Association seem like two quite different institutions." This was a valid point, as the Colored Orphan Asylum had for most of its history dealt with orphans or neglected children. The Riverdale Children's Association had the awesome task of dealing with those two groups plus delinquent children whose behavior had overwhelmed other child care agencies. It called for a type of management that was difficult to provide in times of low financial resources and when it was absolutely vital to have dedicated staff and support groups. The advisory committee recommended that all standing committees be dissolved and that appointments for those committees be done by a reorganization committee. The committee further called for a review of the board's financial situation, for changes in the children's living standards and activities, and for an integration of the school curriculum with the total program of the institution. They urged an aggressive fundraising program to hire staff, make repairs, and extend services. If these suggestions were not followed, the advisory committee warned that "it will be impossible to make changes that are a crying need in the institution today."[44]

A special board meeting was held on December 10, 1945, to plan for the future as well as to overturn the adverse publicity of recent months. Earlier in the fall, the institution had invested $518,000 but had to sell thirty thousand dollars' worth of capital funds in October. They held ten mortgages valued at $257,000, which yielded an annual income of $7,800. Another eight thousand dollars was earned annually from the $225,000 invested in stocks and bonds. Money was needed, but the prospects of selling all or some of the ten mortgages were not very high, and the trustees wanted to avoid selling under pressure, which would depress the value. The seriousness of the money situation was temporarily set aside in favor of responding to the damaging news of the State Board of Social Welfare, which found the institution "in violation of the rules and regulations . . . regarding the sanitary conditions of the building, provisions for the safety, reasonable comfort and well being of the children." The agency dictated that the Riverdale Children's Association adopt the following recommendations: (1) Provide proper supervision at all times for the children outside of school and organized recreational activity. (2) Replace antiquated toilet facilities with modern equipment. (3) Remove all hazardous items "such as broken iron grille over sewer drain on main roadway; broken wooden fence around the summer laundry drying gear; broken wooden planking on porch roof near exterior fire escape." (4) Fix or cover dormitory floors "to protect the feet of the children." (5) Prohibit the employment of children in places of potential health hazards. (6) "Conduct rapid fire dismissal drills regularly from cottages and administrative buildings." Failure to comply within a reasonable time to these demands would mean the possible loss of the institution's "certificate of compliance, thereby prohibiting expenditures of public money for care" at Riverdale. The trustees pondered the demands and discussed the following: (1) It would cost $400,000 to renovate Riverdale, but an extra $300,000 had to be raised yearly just to have an adequate program. (2) They could close the foster home department, with its 350 children, and keep Riverdale open, with its 167 children. (3) Sell Riverdale and relocate with the present number of children. (4) Close Riverdale and have "group homes in various localities," with "the possibility of developing a modern type of small institution to meet the needs of a specific group." They ultimately decided to close Riverdale, both because large-home grouping was no longer acceptable in child care circles and in order to maintain an interracial policy in future endeavors to best serve New York's various communities. There was a call also for increased fundraising efforts but not to inform the public until the publicity committee was ready, "in order that [trustees] interpret changes to the community alike." The last point was an oblique reference to a staff rumor that the white community wanted to rid Riverdale of black children because the valuable property was coveted by others.[45]

The Selling of Riverdale

In January 1946, it was decided to reorganize the institution. The case and children's committees became the children's services committee; the publicity committee became the community relations committee, with Charlotte Anderson, Susan Wortham, and Mrs. Melvin Proctor as the three African American members. Charlotte Anderson was the lone black woman on the executive committee. The interim executive director proposed a six-month budget of $259,246, an estimated income of $123,028, and a deficit of $120,418, which included the cost of closing Riverdale. The hope was to raise $6,500 in fundraising from those who had contributed in 1945, through theater parties, awards parties, and letters to individuals and foundations. The six-month budget was accepted with $6,500 deducted, which meant either a delay in opening six group homes or a reduction of the number of group homes to three. It was discussed at a special meeting on February 8 the possibility of merging with the Sevilla Home, a dormitory school for young girls aged five to sixteen established in the will of José Sevilla, who had died in 1897. They had high hopes that Theodore Dreiser's estate would provide them with a large grant, but that failed when his wife responded that his will called for her "to leave the bulk of his estate to a worthy negro [sic] orphanage" upon her death. She died in 1955, and there is no record of any large grant from her estate to Riverdale Children's Association.[46]

The March 19 special meeting offered little hope for a financial breakthrough. The mortgages held by the trustees were not readily marketable, nor was the Riverdale property. They lowered their asking price for Riverdale to $600,000 but did not expect to receive more than $400,000, given the depressed real estate market. There was only forty thousand dollars in restrictive funds, and the working cash balance was negative. The deficit for the past six months amounted to seventy thousand dollars, with an anticipated deficit of one hundred thousand dollars for the fiscal year. They would have to sell $67,000 worth of stocks and bonds to meet the deficit. The May trustees' meeting revealed that there was only $3,656.34 in capital funds and that the restricted funds amounted to $10,143.68. There was $16,490.54 in the general fund, along with stock and bonds worth $165,123.24. An appeal to the community netted $67,900, with the hopes that an additional forty thousand would be raised by July 1, 1946. A board member convinced friends to contribute five thousand dollars in gifts, with hopes to raise that figure to $110,000 by June 30. The frantic fundraising was not enough. Two group homes and one temporary home were ready for occupancy. The directors hoped to boost further community support by electing Roy Wilkins, the future executive secretary of the National Association for the Advancement of Colored People, as a member. These measures proved fruitless, and Riverdale was closed with fifty-five children sent to the homes of their relatives.[47]

The cost of closing Riverdale and providing terminal pay for workers produced a deficit of $15,108. The management had to sell capital stocks or bonds to meet the anticipated thirty thousand dollars in expenses for July, August, and September, a slow period for fundraising, to balance the budget by September 30. The various fundraising efforts, including the sale of shares in railroads and other companies, did not erase the budget deficit, because the purchase and renovation of two houses for offices at 221 and 223 East Thirtieth Street in Manhattan amounted to seventy-five thousand dollars. The staff's move in December prompted Audre Delany to note that "a new departure in child placement, the training of children to make them fit for foster homes," had been initiated. The institution established four group foster homes with six children each. This experiment was the first of its kind in New York City. Fundraising was undertaken with zeal, and Christmas appeals, the sale of stocks and bonds, and voluntary contributions were aggressively pursued in the hopes of garnering $250,000. The amount raised under trying times, however, did not solve the deficit problem, which remained at $120,000 at the end of October 1946. It was like putting icing on cardboard and pretending it was a luscious cake.[48]

Audre Delany's interim executive director's report in October noted that the institution, which had been established to aid colored orphans, now had sixteen white children. She stated that there was a need to "concern ourselves more and more with the causes for family break down and the 'whys' of child placement [because] no amount of service designed to treat children's problems, will suffice if we close our eyes to the condition that produced them."[49]

The adverse financial situation and the nation's growing disapproval of orphanages forced the inevitable: the property had to be sold; otherwise, the Riverdale Children's Association would be unable to serve children who needed foster care. Ironically, the trustees had declined an offer in 1920 to sell the Riverdale property. Perhaps tongue-in-cheek, they then "would not consider an offer of less than a million [dollars]." In August 1948, the Riverdale property, consisting of the main building, five large cottages, two smaller buildings, and a power house situated on 18.75 acres, was sold for $300,000, far less than the originally hoped for million, to the Hebrew Home for the Aged, which took title on December 1. The directors were unable to get their intended price because of poor sewage drainage, which made the area impractical for housing development.[50]

With the selling of the Riverdale property and the earlier removal of the children, an era had ended. Riverdale Children's Association and its predecessor, the Colored Orphan Asylum, had acted on behalf of African American children for just over a century. The changing times demanded that they use their energy and resources to place children into good homes that offered moral guidance and a sense of family stability. Through various mergers, this is exactly what they have continued to accomplish up to the present time.

Conclusion

The demise of the Riverdale orphanage was a sad event in the history of an institution that dated to 1836—nearly a mere decade after slavery was abolished in the Empire State. The founders and early managers were mainly women who sought to do God's will by caring for the uncared: the abused and forsaken black child. They took on this mammoth effort at a time when African Americans were shunned by society. Oppressive laws prohibited much of their daily contact with their fellow white residents unless they were in a subordinate position. The white women, many of whom personally abhorred the horrors of slavery and who wished to do God's will by feeding the hungry and clothing the naked, did so at the risk of "unsexing" themselves in the eyes of their less Christian contemporaries. These women achieved remarkable gains by forging a close alliance with some of New York City's finest families. Men and women of means such as John Jacob Astor, R. H. Macy, Theodore Roosevelt Sr., William Jay, Anna Jay, Caroline Stokes, and many others contributed generously to the betterment of the orphan black child.

The early managers eagerly sought the assistance of African Americans (even though they kept them at a distance) to advance the development of the asylum. Men and women of color were eager in return to assist the orphanage by donating their funds or the fruits of their labors, bringing to the institution foodstuffs or, lacking these, their muscle power to aid the ladies with physical work.

The destruction of their Fifth Avenue building in 1863 led to their migration to Harlem, which was not yet the Promised Land for thousands of African Americans. But with the demise of the building came slowly but continuously a decline in membership of the old type of manager who genuinely wanted to help the black race. Their replacements were certainly concerned with assisting children in need, but they had no real interest in developing or maintaining a relationship of equality with the leaders of black New York. Their perpetuation of the myth of white paternalism guided them well into the first third of the twentieth century, when finally forces beyond their control or comprehension forced them to realize that they could neither ignore Negroes nor wish them away. Harlem, only a few miles from the Riverdale, Bronx, property, was becoming not only the capital of black America but also a community beset with a multitude of problems that called for cooperation between the races. It was unfortunate and ironic that when Riverdale finally called upon Harlem for help, the institution was dying from a lack of funds. The wealthy philanthropists of the nineteenth century had died or found other causes more worthwhile than saving a few black children from the awful fates of the world. Criticized by social service agencies, the government, and the press, the Colored Orphan Asylum had no choice but to look to Harlem for salvation. Harlem, at first reluctantly but then more steadily, stretched her arms out to Riverdale. The gesture was genuine, but the effort was too little and far too late.

The selling of Riverdale in 1948 ended that period of the institution's service for orphans, but it did not terminate the existence of the Riverdale Children's Association. Over the past sixty years, the organization underwent a series of mergers, and now it is the Harlem Dowling–West Side Center for Children and Family Services. The mission of the Colored Orphan Asylum was to care for African American orphans and neglected or abused children. Today, Harlem Dowling's mission is to assist children and families in crisis, to provide foster care and adoption, and to help families live in an environment that is stable and nurturing. Young mothers who are at risk of having their children removed from the family home are provided with individual/ group counseling and mentoring to assist them with parenting and life management skills.

Whatever faults Riverdale had—and they were many—some of the children, now adults whom I befriended, who were there in the early

1940s recalled their time with fond memories. Harlem Dowling has organized several reunions, and I entertained on a warm June Sunday in 2003 five in my Harlem home. A seminar in 2005 at Lehman College in the Bronx brought together some of the alumni of Riverdale. All of them had nothing but fond memories of the place, and for them it was a lifesaver. Most were not orphans; few of the children housed at Riverdale in the 1940s were. Many were delinquents sent by the courts; others simply ran away from home far too often. Regardless of the situation that brought them to Riverdale, they all felt that their time there had given them a sense of family in a supportive environment. Louis Eaddy confided that Riverdale provided the environment for self-development. He entered the institution with two siblings and viewed his time at Riverdale (1933–1946) as "heaven," because to him "everything about it was perfect." He and others learned to ride horses at Riverdale and picked strawberries, apples, and cherries.[1] Fitz Harvey was sent to Riverdale by Family Court, which he declared "kept me off the streets."[2] Hearing their glowing words about an institution that was severely criticized for neglect made me better understand why it was common for former residents of the orphanage to send their own children there when financial reversals or the death of a spouse led to a family breakup. When I came across a child in the admission records whose mother or father had resided in the orphanage, I initially thought that perhaps there was a sense of profound shame that one who had left the orphanage had to face the humiliation of sending their own flesh and blood back to an institutional setting. Instead, my conversations with former residents convinced me that the orphanage was for them a place that they could look back on as being "home." That same sense of belonging was expressed in some of the letters indentured children sent to their teachers, the matron, or the superintendent. Orphanages had their faults, but for many it was a place that gave them a positive identity. Today, politicians, social workers, and child welfare reformers have expressed deep concerns and criticisms of the foster care system, which has generated headlines of abusive treatment of young children. Some have called for the return of orphanages as a solution to caring for children in need. This interest in orphanages as a possible solution to the child care crisis has received academic interest. The scholar Richard B. McKenzie, who wrote *The Home: A Memoir of Growing up in an Orphanage,* described his experience at the Barium Springs Home for Children in North Carolina in positive terms, despite the hardships he faced. McKenzie has aired his concerns that despite all the criticism of orphanages (which now are directed at foster care), living there did represent for many a family situation that allowed the children to develop self-confidence, gave them the ability to relate to others, and helped them to learn how to function in a group. Those who favor a return to the establishment of orphanages argue that children are better off there than they are in a home with abusive or neglectful parents or in a situation where they are shuttled between indifferent or predatory foster parents. It is his contention that while life in an orphanage was not idyllic, it provided stability, permanence, companionship, and a value system that taught hard work and self-reliance. Whether there will be a return to orphanages is a debate that must be worked out by politicians and child welfare workers. For Louis Eaddy, who spent thirteen years at Riverdale, there is no debate. Like others that I have spoken with, he was devastated when Riverdale had to close its doors in 1946. He bemoans the fact that for today's child, the courts send you to prison instead of to a home such as Riverdale, where a child can find himself without being influenced by hardened criminals.[3]

Harlem Dowling–West Side Center for Children and Family Services continues to care for children of all races and ethnicities, and the successor to the Colored Orphan Asylum looks forward to its two hundredth anniversary in 2036, as it daily reaches out in the spirit of Anna Shotwell and Mary Murray to assist families in need.

Appendixes

Appendix A: Founders of the Colored Orphan Asylum, 1836

Margaretta Cock
Abby Ann Cook
Jane U. Ferris
Sarah Hall
Sarah C. Hawxhurst
Elizabeth Little
Ernestine Lord
Eunice Mitchel
Phebe Mott
Hanna L. Murray
Mary Murray
Anna Shotwell
Eleanor Shotwell
Mary Shotwell
Sarah Shotwell
Stella Tracy
Sarah Underhill

Source: *Association for the Benefit of Colored Orphans Records,* New-York Historical Society, series 1: *Minutes* (26 November 1836).

Appendix B: Original Male Advisers to the COA, 1836–37

Robert C. Cornell
Charles King

Robert J. Murray
William F. Mott
Dr. James Proudfit

Source: *Association for the Benefit of Colored Orphans Records,* New-York Historical Society, series 1: *Minutes* (12 December 1836; 10 February 1837).

Appendix C: Early COA Major Financial Supporters in the 1830s

William Aspinwall
John Jacob Astor
A. Averill
George Douglas
William Douglas
Mary Few
Jonathan Goodhue
Mrs. N. D. Halstead
John Hancock
Samuel Howland
Ann Jay
John Johnson
Morris Ketchum
Rufus Lord
Robert B. Minturn
Samuel Parsons
Mrs. John Rogers
Gerrit Smith
Peter Stuyvesant
Benjamin L. Swan
Gulian C. Verplanck

Legacies

| 1830 | Mary Thompson | $300 |
| 1839 | William Turpin | $5,000 |

1847	Margaret Johnson	$290
	James M. Fletcher	$200
1849	John Horsburg	$5,000
1850	Elizabeth DeMilt	$5,000
	Sarah DeMilt	$2,000
1851	Mary Halsey	$200
1854	Samuel Howland	$1,500
	Anson G. Phelps	$1,000
	Henry Hallack	$200
1856	Jane Livesay	$200
	Mrs. C. Lyell	$500
	S. B. Morrison	$500
1857	Maria Banyer	$500 (John Jay's daughter)
	Ann Jay	$1,000 (John Jay's daughter)
1859	Robert I. Murray	$250
	John Clapp	$50
1860	Susan James	$195
1862	E. M. Verplank	$50
1864	John Rose	$20,000
	Madame Martelle	$4,275
1868	Abram B. Sands	$500
1869	Sarah Phelps	$500
1871	John and George Lowrie	$1,120
	Abby Hanson	$404
	Susan Ostrander	$100
1872	John Abraham	$2,000
	Silas Downing	$500
1874	George Merritt	$4,000
	Eliza Harper	$2,793
	William Mackey	$1,500
	Jane Hicks	$183.12

Additional legacies were received from January 1, 1869, to December 31, 1883.

Miss E. B. Stewart	$470
Lispenard Stewart	$1,135.14
Peter Van Dyke	$94
Abraham estate	$5,052.70
John Mayall	$1,000
Elizabeth McCullum	$500
Joseph Battell	$5,000
John C. Green	$10,000
Miss Kissam	$100
Miss Rosenkrans	$750
Joseph Seligman	$250
Caroline P. Stokes	$3,000
Mrs. Amos Eno	$5,000
James Stokes	$2,000
Daniel Marley	$1,739.50
Mahlon Day	$1,000
Estates of Eliza Mott and Maria M. Hobby	$3,940

Source: *From Cherry Street to Green Pastures: A History of the Colored Orphan Asylum* (New York, 1936), 10–11; *Association for the Benefit of Colored Orphans Records*, New-York Historical Society, series 1: *Thirty-fifth Annual Report* (1871), 18; *Thirty-seventh Annual Report* (1873), 13; *Thirty-eighth Annual Report* (1874), 16; *Forty-seventh Annual Report* (1883), 22.

Appendix D: COA Managers/Trustees,* 1837–1946

1836–37

Martha Codwise
Sarah C. Hawxhurst
Anna H. Shotwell
Mary Murray
Augusta Arcularius
Elizabeth Bowne (resigned 1902)
Fidelia Creagh
Margaretta Cock
Mary Day
Isabella Donaldson
Jane U. Ferris

Mary Few
Sarah Hall
Elizabeth Hydecker
Hetty King
Elizabeth Little
Ernestine Lord
Hannah S. Murray
Anicartha Miller
Eunice Mitchell
Elizabeth Parr
Mary Shotwell
Amy Sutton
Mary B. Trimble
Sarah F. Underhill
Mary Anna Wood
Elizabeth Woodward
Henrietta Wilcox

1838

Frances Chrystie
Hannah Eddy
Abby H. Gibbons
Martha C. Mason
Mary Pringle
Elinor K. Shotwell

1839

Elizabeth B. Collins
Mary A. Halstead
Anna Jay
Anna Mott
Mary Wheeler
Jane R. McLaughlin

Elizabeth Pringle
Mary Reynolds

1840

Sarah Munsell
Margaret Roosevelt
Mrs. John Heyer
Mary Jane Kelly

1841

Sarah Bunce
Emeline Cornell
Jane R. Day

1842

Mary J. Gelston
Charlotte Gardner
Elizabeth S. Kelly
M. Antoinette Varick

1843

Ruth Beatty
Martha C. Bliss
Jane Lawrence
Elizabeth Wigham

1844

Ann Franklin

1845

Margaret Tillotson
Sarah E. Weir

1846

Catherine Dunbar
Heloise Meyer
Harriet Skidmore
Matilda Titus
C. Van Renselaer
Caroline Wood

1847

Meta Brevoort
Mary Howland
Allison Johnson
Caroline Stokes
Anna H. Ferris

1848

Fanny P. Bartlett
Gertrude J. Cary
Cornelia Collins
Elizabeth North

1849

Emily Sampson

1850–51

Mrs. Jane Palen
Sarah B. Willets
Sarah Willets

1852–54

Mary Givan
M. H. Van Rensselaer

Rebecca Howland
Caroline Hasbrouck
Ruth S. Murray
Rachel Phelps
Eliza C. Jay
Elizabeth Stange
Eliza B. Stewart
Cornelia L. Westerlo
Mary S. Collins
Rachel Noyes
Mrs. J. L. Wilson
Mrs. William B. Thompson
Cornelia C. Hussey
Rebecca H. Roosevelt

1856

Anna Hall
Sarah S. Murray (honorary)
Mary F. Stoughton

1857

Sarah B. Brown
Sarah Camman
Catherine Mason
Catharine McVickar

1858

Joanna Bronson
Anna W. Dickinson
Lucy J. Eno
Pauline Sands
Ellen James

1859

Mrs J. M. Cockroft
Mrs. Disosway
Mrs. Dr. J. C. Hepburn
Mrs. James Hurd
Mrs. Sarah Langford
Mrs. Mead
Mrs. Jno. F. Park
Lydia G. Underhill
Mrs. E. P. Willets
Mrs. C. Schaffer
Anna F. Willis

1860

Ellen Burling
Hannah W. Collins
Mrs. S. N. Dodge
Mrs. Caroline C. Hull
Mrs. I. N. Phelps
Fanny Paxson
Anna C. Tatum
Rachel Whitehead

1861

Mrs. Robert Bowne
Rebecca S. Haviland
Mrs. P. Holt
Mrs. E. B. Sutton
Mrs. John Reid
Mrs. Lawrence

1862

Mrs. Hanson K. Corning
Mrs. Stacy B. Collins

Mary Jane Underhill
Mrs. Christopher Robert
Mrs. James B. Wright
Mrs. William Onderdonk
Lydia M. Probyn
Phebe M. Willis
Mrs. Elizabeth Leggett

1863

Mrs. Albert Spier
Mrs. Dr. Van Doren
Mrs Elizabeth Colgate
Maria Willets
Mrs. Charles G. Langdon
Mrs. Hobart Onderdonk

1864

Mrs. W. S. Haines
Mrs. Morris Ketchum
Mrs. Roeck
Elizabeth U. Wood
Mrs. E. L. Corning

1865

Mrs. Charles Strecker
Mrs. Augustus Taber, honorary
Helen Gilman
Mrs. Goodrich

1866

Mrs. S. B. Van Dusen
Mrs. Horace Webster

1867

Mrs. R. L. Kennedy
Mrs. Andrew Norwood
Mrs. Robert Stuyvesant
Isabella L. Jones
Mrs. Oswald Camman

1868

Mrs. William Green
Mrs. William H. Lee, honorary
Mrs. James Sanford
Mrs. Jeremiah Milbank
Mrs. Salem Wales
Miss A. A. Purdy
Julia F. Russell
Mary Sherwood

1869

Mrs. E. S. Jaffray
Mrs. D. S. Taber
Mrs. J. A. C. Gray, honorary
Mrs. T. R. Butler
Mrs. William A. Wheelock
Mrs. A. P. Wilcox

1870

Mrs. Francis Butler
Mrs. L. Murray Ferris Jr.

1871-73

Cornelia Underhill
Mrs. Benjamin B. Sherman

Mary Thurston
Sarah Sampson
Mrs. D. T. Hoag

1874

Mrs. E. S. West
Mary Taber

1875

Mrs. A. B. Darling
Mrs. Russell Sage

1876

Mrs. E. C. Marsh
Mrs. Henry Johnson
Mrs. Gilbert Congdon
Mrs. E. A. Packer

1877

Cornelia Taber (honorary)

1878

Mrs. Matthew Clarkson
Mrs. Dr. Frothingham
Ella F. Bunting

1879

Mrs. Isaac F. Wood

1880

Mrs. Henry E. Russell
Mrs. William S. Wyckoff

1881

Mrs. H. Clarkson
Mrs. J. L. Chapin

1882

Olivia E. P. Stokes
Annie Ferris

1883–84

Mrs. James W. Pinchot
Mrs. Charles Wood
Mrs. Jno. D. Wing

1885

Mrs. R. H. Ewart
Mrs. Edward S. Phillips
Mrs. R. Hall (honorary)
Elizabeth T. Wall

1886

Mrs. Leonard D. White
Mrs. E. P. Griffin
Mrs. Charles H. Wesson

1887–88

Mrs. William M. Jackson
Mrs. David S. Taber

1889-90

Mrs. R. I. Murray
Rachel H. Powell
Helen Willets

1891

Mrs. Willard Parker
C. T. Gilman

1892-93

Mrs. Henry C. Backus
B. L. Dodsworth
Alice H. Cock
Mrs. S. C. Van Dusen

1894

Mrs. Willard Parker Jr.
Mrs. George R. Bishop
Katharine Lambert
Mrs. Richard W. Underhill
Cecilia Herriman

1895

Mrs. Wilson M. Powell
Carolena M. Wood

1896

Sarah Collins

1897

Mary R. Haines
Mrs. Walter Edwards (resigned 1904)
Florence Taylor

1898

Helen Moore

1899

Mrs. William E. Bond
Mrs. Richard Burdsall
Ellen M. Wood
Mrs. Lemuel E. Quigg (resigned)
Edith Holden (resigned)

1900

Emily M. Smith
Mrs. Esther K. Alsop
Mrs. Knight D. Cheney Jr.
Marion Taylor, resigned

1901

Mrs. Malcolm Goodrich
Mrs. Joseph W. Tilton
Ella J. Truslow

1902

Mrs. Joseph Carson (resigned 1903)
Helena L. Knox
Florence Warner

1903

Mrs. Effingham Lawrence
Marion Marden
Elise Gignoux

1904

Mrs. E. D. Thurston
Mrs. John Hutton

1905

Elizabeth Walton

1906

Mrs. David R. Jacques

1907

Mrs. J. Tufton Mason

1908

Mrs. Abram S. Underhill

1909

Mrs. Henry Clinton Backus
Mrs. E. S. Phillips
Mrs. James Stokes
Mrs. F. H. Taylor

1910

Helena Emerson (resigned 1939)
Mrs. Charles E. Case
Mrs. J. L. Barton
Ruth S. Murray

1911

Mrs. Charles Bransom
Mrs. J. Elvin Courtney

1913

Eleanor Taber
Mrs. Morris Parker
Mrs. John Hutton

1914

Ruth Dickerson
Mrs. W. H. L. Edwards
Mrs. Royal J. Davis
Ethel Harper
Julia Coggill
Mrs. Robert N. MacLaran

1915

Helen W. Lambert

1916

Mrs. Harry H. Stout

1917

Mrs. S. E. Gardner Magill
Mrs. Wilson M. Powell

1920

Mrs. Laurence G. Payson

1922

Mrs. Boudinot Atterbury
Mrs. William J. Noonan

1923

Mrs. Amos J. Peasler
Mrs. Elliott Hughlee

1926

Dr. Mary Murray Lowden

1928

Mrs. C. Lemaire Zabriskie

1929

Mrs. Robert M. Field
Dr. Margaret Janeway

1930

Mrs. Paul D. Donchian
Mrs. Carl Shoup

1932

Constance Wright
Mrs. Herbert Barber Howe

1935

Mrs. George H. Bunker
Mrs. Moreau Yeomans

1937

Mrs. George F. Wagner (resigned 1939)
Mrs. Sidney D. Gamble (resigned 1939)
Mrs. Frederick Garnjost

1938

Mrs. Mary J. Willets

1939

Mrs. William H. Wortham
Mrs. William H. Rea

1940

Charlotte Anderson

1941

Mrs. Melvin Proctor
Mrs. Richard J. Bernhard

1942

Audre Delany

1944-46

Mrs. Robert DeVecchi
Mrs. Richard Martin

Dr. Ethel Wortis

Mrs. Leonard Scully

Marian Anderson

Mrs. Lawrence Orton

Hubert Delany

* Managers became known as trustees in the early 1900s.

Source: *Association for the Benefit of Colored Orphans Records, New-York Historical Society,* series 1: *Sixty-first Annual Report* (1897), *Minutes* (11 December 1939; 12 March, 17 September 1943; 21 June, 29 September 1944); "Elected Orphan Asylum Trustee," *New York Times* (August 11, 1941): 15.

Appendix E: First Directress/President*

Martha Codwise, 1837–March 1840

Anicartha Miller, 1840–47

Mary Few, 1848–55

Hetty King, 1856–58

Mrs. Mary W. Mason,1859–62

Rachel Phelps, 1863–65

Mrs. Augusta Taber, 1866–93

Mrs. Willard Parker, 1894–1908

Carolena M. Wood, 1909–13

Lillie Skiddy Parker (Mrs. Willard Parker Jr.), 1913–44

*Mrs. Robert DeVecchi, 1944–46

Appendix F: Superintendent/Executive Director*

Otho Shaw, 1844–47

William Davis, 1848–May 1869

Orville Hutchinson, June 1869–February 9, 1887

Martin K. Sherwin, 1887–March 1911

Frank W. Barber, 1911–13

Carolena M. Wood, acting superintendent, 1914

*Dr. Mason Pitman, 1914–38

John W. Poe, superintendent, 1943–46

*Henry R. Murphy, 1938–45 (he also served as superintendent during this period)

Audre Delany, interim executive director, 1945–46

Source: *Association for the Benefit of Colored Orphans Records*, New-York Historical Society, series 1: *Annual Reports* for the years 1837–46.

Appendix G: Locations of the COA's Homes

1. Twelfth Street near Sixth Avenue, Manhattan (1836–43)
2. Fifth Avenue, between Forty-third and Forty-fourth Streets, Manhattan (1843–July 1863)
3. Between 150th and 152nd Streets in the Carmansville section of Manhattan, facing Broadway (1863–68)
4. Amsterdam Avenue, between 143rd and 144th Streets, Manhattan (1868–1907)
5. Riverdale section of the Bronx, 261st Street and Palisade Avenue (1907–46)

Notes

Introduction

1. Linda K. Kerber, "Abolitionists and Amalgamators: The New York City Race Riots of 1834," *New York History* 48 (January 1967): 28–29. Herbert Aptheker, *A Documentary History of the Negro People in the United States* (New York: Citadel Press, 1951), 1:149–151. *Communications to Cornelius W. Lawrence, Mayor of New York City from Various Persons Including Lists of Volunteer Aids, Reports About Homes and Churches the Mob Threatened to Burn, Disposition of Militia, etc. 1834* (New-York Historical Society). *Philip Hone Diary* (1 January 1832 to 2 October 1834), microfilm reel, 2 (New-York Historical Society).

2. *Minutes of the Fifth Annual Convention for the Improvement of the Free People of Color in the United States* (Philadelphia: William P. Gibbons, 1835), 19. Peter M. Bergman, ed., *The Chronological History of the Negro People in America* (New York: Harper & Row, 1959), 68–69.

3. *Castigator and New-York Anti-Abolitionist* (August 1835): 1–2.

4. *First Annual Report of the New York Committee on Vigilance* (New York: Piercy & Reed, 1837), 3, 13–15. *North Star* (19 May 1848).

5. Timothy Hasci, *Second Home: Orphan Asylums and Poor Families in America* (Cambridge, Mass.: Harvard University Press, 1975), 2.

6. Ibid., 7, 56.

7. Ibid., 77.

8. Anne M. Boylan, *The Origins of Women's Activism: New York and Boston, 1795–1840* (Chapel Hill: University of North Carolina Press, 2002), 58–59, 229, 238, 244.

9. Hasci, *Second Home*, 78. Barbara Welter, "The Cult of True Womanhood, 1820–1860," in *The American Family in Social Historical Perspective*, 2nd ed., ed. Michael Gordon (New York: St. Martin's Press, 1978), 313.

10. Boylan, *Origins of Women's Activism*, 18, 21, 89. Lori D. Ginzberg, *Women and the Work of Benevolence: Morality, Politics, and Class in the Nineteenth-Century United States* (New Haven, Conn.: Yale University Press, 1990), 48.

1. The Early Years, 1836–42

1. The epigraph to this chapter is from "The Orphan Boy," *Colored American* (April 12, 1838): 48.

2. Leslie M. Harris, *In the Shadow of Slavery: African Americans in New York City, 1626–1863* (Chicago: University of Chicago Press, 2003), 50.

3. *From Cherry Street to Green Pastures: A History of the Colored Orphan Asylum at Riverdale-on-Hudson* (New York? 1936). Sarah S. Murray, *In the Olden Times: A Short History of the Descendants of John Murray the Good* (New York: Strettiner, Lambert & Co., 1894), 144. Mrs. [Augustus] Taber to my Dear Cousin [Carolyn M. Wood] (7 May 1910), in series xiii: *Miscellaneous Items*, folder 2, 1907–1972, *Assoc. for the Benefit of Colored Orphans Records*, New-York Historical Society (cited hereafter as *Colored Orphans Records*). Mary Braggrotti, "A Toiler in the Vineyard," *New York Evening Post* (5 June 1944), in *Riverdale Children's Association Records*, box 2, vol. 5, 1936–1946 scrapbook; Robert Sullivan, "The Two Quaker Ladies and the Golden Gloves," *Sunday News* (14 March 1938): 76–77, in *Riverdale Children's Association Records*, box 2, vol. 5, 1936–1946, scrapbook, Schomburg Center for Research in Black Culture.

4. Anne M. Boylan, *The Origins of Women's Activism: New York and Boston, 1795–1840* (Chapel Hill: University of North Carolina Press, 2002), 58–59. John Fox Jr., *Quakerism in the City of New York, 1857–1930* (New York: Quinn & Bolden Co., Inc., 1930), 42. *From Cherry Street*, 6–7. Kathleen D. McCarthy, "Women and Political Culture," in *Charity, Philanthropy, and Civility in American History*, ed. Lawrence J. Friedman and Mark McCarvie (Cambridge: Cambridge University Press, 2003), 182. *Association for the Benefit of Colored Orphans Records*, series 1: *Minutes of Board Meetings*, 1836–1965 (26 November, 3 December 1836). Cited hereafter as *Minutes* to distinguish them from the executive minutes.

5. *Minutes* (10 February, 9 June, 8 December 1837).

6. Harris, *In the Shadow of Slavery*, 162.

7. Mrs. [Augustus] Taber to my Dear Cousin [Carolyn M. Wood] (7 May 1910). Walter I. Trattner, *From Poor House to Welfare State*, 3rd ed. (New York: Free Press, 1984), 67–68.

8. *From Cherry Street*, 10.

9. *New-York Society for Promoting the Manumission of Slaves and Protecting Such of Them as Have Been, or May Have Been Liberated*, vol. 1, *Minutes of the Ways & Means Committee*, 1810–1838, p. 145, New-York Historical Society. Editorial, "Phoenix School," *Colored American* (30 December 1837): 2. *Minutes* (7 April 1837; 13 July, 14 September, 12 October 1838).

10. Editorial, "Orphan Asylum," *Colored American* (28 April 1837): 2. Editorial, "Colored Orphans," *Colored American* (28 April 1837): 2. Editorial, "Why We Should Have a Paper," *Colored American* (4 March 1837), 2.

11. "Colored Orphan Asylum," *Colored American* (28 October 1837): 3. Editorial, "Asylum for Colored Children," *Colored American* (22 December 1838), 2.

12. *Minutes* (12 May, 14 July, 8 September, 16, October 1837; 9 November, 14 December 1838). Boylan, *Origins of Women's Activism*, 58–59. Harris, *In the Shadow of Slavery*, 148. Timothy Hasci, *Second Home: Orphan Asylums and Poor Families in America* (Cambridge, Mass.: Harvard University Press, 1975), 113–114.

13. *New York Tribune* (25 September 1850): 1. *Anglo African* (16 June 1860): 1. Rhoda G. Freeman, *The Free Negro in New York City in the Era Before the Civil War* (New York: Garland Publishing, 1994), 180–181. *Minutes* (10 November 1837). Mary W. Thompson, *Broken Gloom: Sketches of the History, Character, and Dying Testimony of Beneficiaries of the Colored Home in the City of New York* (New York: John F. Trow, 1851), 75. *Minutes* (14 July 1837).

14. *Minutes* (13 October, 8 December 1837). *Association for the Benefit of Colored Orphans Records*, series 3: *Admissions (with Short Histories and Some Indentures)*, 1837–1866, Benjamin Matthews, 10–11; Jacob Beckett Lee, 12–13. Cited hereafter as *Admissions*, 1837–1866.

15. *Admissions*, 1837–1866, Jeremiah/Adeline Rawls, 12–13; Willy Rawls, 14–15. *Minutes* (24 November 1837).

16. *Admissions*, 1837–1866, John Tomota, 36–37; Henry Bushmen, 119; Harriet Beecher Stowe, 79. *Admissions*, 1849–1866, Harriet Beecher Stowe #384. *Admissions*, 1837–1866, Mary and Harriet Davis, 430–431.

17. *Admissions*, 1837–1866, Charles Barton, 12–13; James Anderson, 22–23; Mott Cornell, 20–21; *Minutes* (9 February, 9 March, 1838); *Admissions*, 1849–1866, Mary Ann Topsy (n.p., see index).

18. *Minutes* (14 March, 11 April, 13 June, 2 September 1851). *Admissions,* 1837–1866, Jane Guise, 164.

19. *Admissions,* 1849–1866, Benjamin Africanus (see index). *Admissions,* 1837–1866, Catharine Louise Smith, 439. *Association for the Benefit of Colored Orphans Records,* series 3: *Admissions and Short Histories,* 1867–1888, #2233, Charles Carter. Cited hereafter as *Admissions,* 1867–1888. David W. Blight, "America: Made and Unmade in Slavery," *The Chronicle Review* (February 2005): B15–16.

20. *First Annual Report* (1837), in *Minutes* (9 December 1837).

21. *Minutes* (9 March, 13 April, 11 May 1838). *Admissions,* 1837–1866, John Philip Bennet, 22–23.

22. *Minutes* (12 April 1839). *Admissions,* 1837–1866, Robert Atkinson, 26–27. "The Dying Boy," *Colored American* (17 November 1838): 4.

23. *Thirteenth Annual Report* (1849), 14.

24. *Minutes* (8 June, 9 November, 1838). *Admissions,* 1837–1866, Elizabeth Jackson, 20–21; Gustavus Thompson, 18.

25. *Minutes* (8 June, 13 July, 10 August, 1838).

26. *Minutes* (14 September, 14 December, 1838; 13 September, 22 November, 1839; 12 June 1840). *From Cherry Street,* 14.

27. John H. Grissom, *The Sanitary Conditions of the Laboring Population of New York* (New York: Harper & Brothers, 1845), 18, as quoted in Leonard P. Curry, *The Free Blacks in Urban America, 1800–1850: The Shadow of The Dream* (Chicago: University of Chicago Press, 1981), 53.

28. Laurence Lerner, *Angels and Absences* (Nashville, Tenn.: Vanderbilt University, 1997), 49–50. *Fifth Annual Report* (1841), 5, 11. *Sixth Annual Report* (1842), 3–6, 15–16.

29. *Admissions,* 1836–1866, William M. Jackson, 66. *Fifteenth Annual Report* (1852), 28 (see appendix, extract of superintendent's records from 1 December 1850 to 1 December 1851). *Thirteenth Annual Report* (1850), 2–3, 4–5 (see appendix, matron's recollections). *Twelfth Annual Report* (1849), 4, 5–7. *Admissions,* 1837–1866, David George Johnson, 117; Hannah Ann Franklin, 146; Henry Johnson, 83.

30. *Minutes* (12 May, 9 June, 1 July, 8 September, 16 October 1837; 1 January, 9 February, 13 April, 11 May, 10 August, 9 November, 14 December 1838).

31. *Minutes* (11 January, 8 February 1839).

32. William P. Letchworth, *Homes of Homeless Children: A Report on Orphan Asylums and Other Institutions for the Care of Children* (Albany, 1903),

198. *Third Annual Report* (in December 1839 minutes). *Executive Committee Minutes*, in 11 October 1839 minutes. *Minutes* (8 January 1839). *New York Society for Promoting the Manumission of Slaves and Protecting Such of Them as Have Been Liberated*, vol. 8. *Minutes* (29 January 1829–12 April 1849); see January 1829, 151, 155, 160–161, 166, 169. *Minutes* (10 January 1840). *Fifth Annual Report* (1841), 9. James McCune Smith, *A Sketch of the Haytien Revolution; with a Sketch of the Character of Toussaint L'ouverture* (New York: Daniel Fanshaw, 1841), 28.

33. See, for example, *The Colored American* (23 May 1840). *Minutes* (12 February 1847; 11 June, 8 October 1852). *Sixteenth Annual Report* (1852), 3. *Twenty-third Annual Report* (1859), 10. "A Hard Case," *New York Times* (25 September 1852): 2; "Card from Dr. Pennington," *New York Times* (26 May 1853): 3. "New York City," *New York Times* (26 September 1855). "Important and Interesting Trial: Can Colored People Ride in the City Cars," *New York Times* (18 December 1856): 2, and (20 December 1856): 2.

34. *Colored American* (19, 26 September; 7, 14, 21, 28 November 1840). *Fourth Annual Report* (1840), 6, 8, 12.

35. *Fifth Annual Report* (1841), 5, 11.

36. *Minutes* (April 14, 1848). Edward C. Smith, "Robert Barnwell Roosevelt," in Dumas Malone, ed., *Dictionary of American Biography* (New York: Charles Scribner's Sons, 1935), 16:134. Edward J. Renehan Jr., *The Lion's Pride: Theodore Roosevelt and His Family in Peace and War* (New York: Oxford University Press, 1918), 16–17.

37. *New-York Society for Promoting the Manumission of Slaves*, vol. 8, 173.

2. Fifth Avenue: Growth and Progress, 1843-54

1. *Seventh Annual Report* (1843), 6–10, 13, 15, 16. *Eighth Annual Report* (1844), 4–7, 9, 10, 12, 19, 20. *Twelfth Annual Report* (1848), 10. *Minutes* (24 April, June, n. d.; 27 September 1848).

2. John Jay, *An Address in Behalf of the Colored Orphan Asylum Delivered at Their Seventh Anniversary, 11 December 1843* (New York: Mahlon Day & Co., 1844), 3–5, 8, 11, 12–13.

3. *Ninth Annual Report* (1845), 4–11, 15, 19–23. To the editor, *New York Tribune* (29 January 1844), in *Journal of Negro History* 10 (July 1925): 454–464. Leslie M. Harris, *In the Shadow of Slavery: African Americans in New York City, 1626–1863* (Chicago: University of Chicago Press, 2003), 154.

4. Peter Ripley, ed., *The Black Abolitionist Papers* (Chapel Hill: University of North Carolina Press, 1985), 1:58–59, 2:191. "Return of Dr. Smith," *Colored American* (9 September 1837): 3, 14, and (March 1840): 3.

5. *From Cherry Street*, 16–17. *Minutes* (23 December 1846; 12 February, 9 April, 9 July 1847). *New York Times* (16 April 1858): 6. *Minutes* (8 January, 12 February, 9 April 1847; 22 January 1850). *Admissions*, 1837–1866, Henry Stephenson, 167.

6. *Minutes* (5, 14 May; 11 June, 12 November 1847). *Thirteenth Annual Report* (1849), 10. *Minutes* (12 October 1849; 11 October 1850).

8. *New-York Society for Promoting the Manumission of Slaves*, vol. 8, 182.

9. *Thirteenth Annual Report* (1849), 10, 14–16. *Minutes* (12 October 1849; 11 October 1850).

10. Henry W. Thurston, *The Dependent Child* (New York: Arno Press, 1974), 46.

11. Samuel Ringgold Ward to Frederick Douglass (March 1855), in Ripley, ed., *The Black Abolitionist Papers*, 1:418. *Fifteenth Annual Report* (1849), 9. *Minutes* (12 October 1849).

12. *Admissions*, 1837–1866, Henry Giles, 46–47; Thaddeus H. Freeman, 67; Henry Smith, 42–43.

13. *Twenty-fifth Annual Report* (1861), 75. *Admissions*, 1849–1866, George Coles, 434.

14. *Fifteenth Annual Report* (1851), 30. *Admissions*, 1837–1866, Aaron Lewis, 40.

15. *Twenty-third Annual Report* (1859), 26. *Admissions*, 1837–1866, James Gomes, 132. *Twenty-fourth Annual Report* (1860), 22.

16. *Twenty-fourth Annual Report* (1860), 19, 23–24. *Admissions*, 1837–1866, George Wesley Thompson, 153; George W. Potter, 144. *Twenty-fifth Annual Report* (1861), 23. *Admissions*, 1837–1866, Francis Potter, 143.

17. *Minutes* (11 January, 8 March, 1 July 1839).

18. *Admissions*, 1837–1866, Phebe Clark, 252. *Fifteenth Annual Report* (1851), 30. *Admissions*, 1837–1866, 124.

19. *Twenty-third Annual Report* (1859), 29. *Admissions*, 1837–1866, Elizabeth Thomas, 301; Charles Henry Cisco, 323.

20. *Admissions*, 1849–1866, Sophia Slossom, 528.

21. "Suicide of a Colored Girl at Seventeen," *New York Times* (19 September 1868): 8. *Minutes* (18 May 1868; 7 July 1871; 11 February 1881). *Admissions*, 1837–1866, Augustus Layton, 404. *Indentures*, 1860–1886, #118, Augustus Layton.

22. "Criminals And Their Deeds," *New York Times* (25 November 1879): 2. *Admissions*, 1867–1912, William Neal, *Indentures*, 1860–1886, #430. George W. Greene, *Admissions*, 1867–1912, #1012. George W. Greene, *Indentures*, 1860–1886, #435. William Beasley, *Admissions*, 1867–1912, #964. *Indentures*, 1860–1886, #377, Eugene Mitchell.

23. *Minutes* (13 May 1904). *Minutes of Indenturing Committee* (13 May 1904). "Girl Poisoned Family," *New York Times* (13 March 1904): 5. "Girl Prisoner Sentenced," *New York Times* (3 April 1904): 2. *Admissions*, 1867–1912, #1468. *Indentures*, #97, Alice Price.

24. Andrew Rankins to Sherwin [1902?], in *Sixty-eighth Annual Report* (1904), 22–23. *Admissions*, 1867–1888, #1498, Andrew Rankins.

25. *Admissions*, 1837–1866, John A. Dolan, 260. *Minutes* (7 August 1891). *Association for the Benefit of Colored Orphans Records*, series 2: *Executive Committee Minutes* (5 April 1891; 13 October 1922; 4 December 1925; 4 February 1927; 6 January, 3 February, 2 March 1928). *Association for the Benefit of Colored Orphans Records*, series 4: *After-Care Committee Minutes* (14 December 1928; 9 March 1928; 12 May 1933).

26. Twenty-third Annual Report (1859), 5. "The Monster of Paterson," *New York Sun* (4 October 1869), in *Admissions*, 1837–1866, Martha Washington, 358. *Minutes* (10 May 1867).

27. *Indentures*, 1878–1898; see #441 for an example of a contract.

28. *Minutes* (July, 7 September 1894). *Association for the Benefit of Colored Orphans Records*, series 5: *Records of Stipend Committee*, #1863, Patrick Hance.

29. Trattner, *From Poor House*, 116. Katz, *In the Shadow of the Poor House: A Social History of Welfare in America* (New York: Basic Books, 1986), 106. David M. Schneider and Albert Deutsch, *The History of Public Welfare in New York State* (Chicago: University of Chicago Press, 1941), 2:76.

30. As the Children's Aid Society Records do not allow the publication of names for reasons of confidentiality, I am permitted only to use initials and not to disclose the source of this information. Homer Folks, *The Care of Destitute, Neglected, and Delinquent Children* (Albany: N.Y.: J. B. Lyon Co., 1900), 43.

31. *Thirty-fourth Annual Report* (1870), 5, 9.

32. Ellen Simpson to Mr. Hutchinson (8 September 1878), in *Forty-third Annual Report* (1879), 17. *Indentures*, 1860–1886, #33, Ellen Simpson; #300, Samuel Simpson.

33. *Admissions, 1837–1866,* Ann Eliza Hinton, 80; Sarah Brown, 113; Benjamin and Joseph Bowen, 60. *Twenty-third Annual Report* (1859), 8–9. *Eighteenth Annual Report* (1854), 5–8. *Minutes* (10 March 1854).

34. *Seventeenth Annual Report* (1853), 9. Arnett G. Lindsay, "The Economic Condition of the Negroes of New York Prior to 1861," *Journal of Negro History* 6, no. 2 (April 1921): 190–199.

3. Disaster and Rebirth, 1855–63

1. *New-York Colonization Journal* 3, no. 12 (December 1853): 2. "Anson G. Phelps," *The National Cyclopedia of American Biography* (New York: James T. White & Co., 1949), 12:49.

2. *Minutes* (10 November 1854; 13 April 1855).

3. "Loss of the Arctic," *New York Times* (11 October 1854; 12 October 1854). "The Lost Citizens of New York," *New York Times* (12 October 1854): 12. "The Arctic," *New York Times* (13 October 1854): 1. "Phebe Hunt Crane," *New York Herald* (21 June 1857): 5. *Twentieth Annual Report* (1856), 8–9. *Minutes* (9 January 1857). Samuel Cooke, *The Funeral Sermons Preached in St. Bartholomew's New York on the 23rd and 24th Sundays After Trinity, Following the Deaths of Miss Jay and Her Sister Mrs. Banyer on the 21st of the Same Month* (New York: Thomas N. Stanford, 1857), 5, 11, 12, 43.

4. *Minutes* (13 January, 27 February 1855). *Nineteenth Annual Report* (1855), 5. "Colored Orphan Asylum Wants Aid," *New York Times* (3 March 1855): 5.

5. *Minutes* (13 April, 1 May, 1855; 9, 29 January 1856). *Nineteenth Annual Report* (1855), 23. Louis Auchincloss, ed. *The Horne and Strong Diaries* (New York: Abbeville Press, 1989) (George Templeton Strong's entry for 21 January 1855), 157.

6. *Minutes* (8 June 1855). *Nineteenth Annual Report* (1855), 7–8.

7. *Minutes* (11 November 1855).

8. *Minutes* (11 November 1855). *Nineteenth Annual Report* (1855), 5, 12.

9. *Minutes* (11 April, 14 November 1856; 13 February, 1 March 1857). "Communication from the New York Society for the Promotion of Education Among Colored Children," *The Anglo African Magazine* 1, no. 7 (July 1859): 222–224.

10. *Twentieth Annual Report* (1856), 5.

11. *Twenty-first Annual Report* (1857), 6.

12. *Twenty-first Annual Report* (1857), 10, 22. *Twenty-third Annual Report* (1859), 7, 22–24.

13. *Twenty-fourth Annual Report* (1860), 13. *Twenty-fifth Annual Report* (1861), 9, 13, 18, 21.

14. Frances Ellen Watkins, "Our Greatest Want," *Anglo African Magazine* 1, no. 5 (May 1859): 160. M. H. Freeman, "The Educational Wants of the Free Colored People," *Anglo African Magazine* 1, no. 4 (April 1859): 115–118. *Twenty-sixth Annual Report* (1862), 8, 20–21. Ella Forbes, *African Women During the Civil War* (New York: Garland Publishing Co., 1998), 74.

15. *Admissions*, 1849–1866 (for the Oviedo children, see #354, #355, #356, #502, #504), Mary Ella Williams, #346.

16. *Twenty-third Annual Report* (1859), 31. *Admissions*, 1837–1866, Anna Marie Piner, 212.

17. Communipaw (James McCune Smith) to editor, *Frederick Douglass Paper* (26 January 1855). James McCune Smith to Gerrit Smith (31 March 1855). James McCune Smith's speech in *New York Tribune* (9 May 1855), in Peter Ripley, ed., *The Black Abolitionist Papers* (Chapel Hill: University of North Carolina Press, 1991–1992), 4:259–262, 274–276, 290–293. James McCune Smith to Gerrit Smith (21 August 1861) in Ripley, ed., *The Black Abolitionist Papers* 5:113–114. John M. Stouffer, *The Black Hearts of Men: Radial Abolitionists and the Transformation of Race* (Cambridge, Mass.: Harvard University Press, 2002), 8, 155, 251–252.

18. *Twenty-second Annual Report* (1858), 5, 6, 8, 9. For Jay's obituary, see *Douglass' Monthly* (January 1859): 15; *Douglass' Monthly* (June 1859): 81–86.

19. *Twenty-fifth Annual Report* (1861), 5.

20. *Twenty-fifth Annual Report* (1861), 6.

21. *Twenty-sixth Annual Report* (1862), 5–6, 12–13.

22. William Seraile, *New York Black Regiments During the Civil War* (New York: Routledge, 2001), 17–29.

23. *Twenty-eighth Annual Report* (1864), 22. *Admissions*, 1837–1866, Lewis Henry White, 442.

24. *Admissions*, 1837–1866, Edward Daniel Hall, 427. *Thirtieth Annual Report* (1866), 24.

25. Virginia M. Adams, ed., *On the Altar of Freedom: A Black Soldier's Civil War Letters from the Front* (Amherst: University of Massachusetts Press, 1991), xxii, xxiv, xxvi–xxvii, xxxi–xxxiii; 118–120, 127–132. *Admissions*, 1837–1866, James Henry Gooding, 78.

26. Auchincloss, ed., *The Horne and Strong Diaries* (George Templeton Strong's diary entry for 19 July 1863), 222.

27. Editorial, "The Diabolic Riot in Brooklyn Yesterday," *New York Times* (5 August 1862): 4. Iver Bernstein, *The New York City Draft Riots: Their Significance for American Society and Politics in the Age of the Civil War* (New York: Oxford University Press, 1990), 5, 8, 10. Albon P. Mann, "Labor Competition and the New York Draft Riots of 1863," *Journal of Negro History* 36, no. 4. Adrian Cook, *The Army of the Streets: The New York City Draft Riots of 1863* (Lexington: University Press of Kentucky, 1974), 56–57, 194, 204–206.

28. *Minutes* (25 July 1863). Charles L. Chapin, *Personal Recollections of the Draft Riots of New York City, 1863* (unpublished, at the New-York Historical Society), 2:110. Mrs. [Augustus] Taber to "my dear cousin" [Carolena M. Wood] (7 May 1910), *Association for the Benefit of Colored Orphans Records*, series 13: *Miscellaneous Items*, folder 2, 1907–1972. *Sixtieth Annual Report* (1896), 7.

29. *Sixtieth Annual Report* (1896), 8. T. H. Barnes, *My Experience as an Inmate of the Colored Orphan Asylum, New York City* (unpublished copy at the New-York Historical Society and the Schomburg Center for Research in Black Culture, New York Public Library), 20–21. *Twenty-seventh Annual Report* (1863), 14.

30. *Report of the Committee on Merchants for the Relief of Colored People Suffering From the Late Riots in the City* (New York: George A. Whitehorne, 1863), 15, 18–19, 30.

31. Allan Nevins and Milton H. Thomas, eds., *The Diary of George Templeton Strong* (New York: Macmillan Co., 1952), 4:340, 342 (entries for 10, 19 July 1863).

32. Walter M. Merritt et al., eds., *The Letters of William Lloyd Garrison* (Cambridge, Mass.: Harvard University Press, 1971–1981), 5:165–166 (see letter of 14 July 1863).

33. *Minutes* (14 December 1863; annual report included), 26. Forbes, *African American Women During the Civil War*, 157.

34. *From Cherry Street*, 22. Henry Highland Garnet, *A Memorial Discourse Delivered in the Hall of the House of Representatives, February 12, 1865* (Philadelphia: Joseph M. Wilson, 1865), 59–62.

35. *Twenty-seventh Annual Report* (1863), 25. *Minutes* (14 December 1863; annual report included), 26.

36. *Minutes* (14 December 1863). *Report of the Committee of Merchants for the Relief of Colored People*, 31.

37. *Association for the Benefit of Colored Orphans Records*, series 13: *Miscellaneous Items*, folder 1, 1853–1865.

38. *Admissions*, 1849–1866 (see index). *Admissions*, 1867–1888, #2261 Elizabeth Robinson, #2276 Lewis Yates or Gates.

39. *Twenty-ninth Annual Report* (1865), 24–25. *Thirtieth Annual Report* (1866), 24–25. *Thirty-first Annual Report* (1867), 24–25. *Thirty-third Annual Report* (1869), 5. *Admissions*, 1837–1866, Jane Guise, 164. *Indentures*, #34, John Henry Hicks.

40. *Minutes* (25 July, 11 September, 9 October 1863; see annual report in December 14 minutes). Barnes, *My Experience as an Inmate of the Colored Orphan Asylum*, 27–28.

4. Harlem, 1864–83

1. *To the Commissioners of the Almshouse*, n.d. [1863]. *Association for the Benefit of Colored Orphans Records*, series 13: *Miscellaneous Items*, folder 1, 1853–1865. *Twenty-seventh Annual Report* (1863), 18. *Minutes* (8 January 1864).

2. *Minutes* (12 January, 11 March, 10 June, 14 October 1864). Theodore Roosevelt et al. to Mrs. John J. Phelps (6 October 1864), *Association for the Benefit of Colored Orphans Records*, series 13: *Miscellaneous Items*, folder 1, 1853–1865. "Riot Claims—Statement of the Comptroller," *New York Times* (30 November 1864): 8.

3. *Minutes* (14 October 1864). "The Site of the Colored Orphan Asylum to Be Disposed of," *New York Times* (10 January 1865): 2; *New York Times* (7 April 1889). *Twenty-eighth Annual Report* (1864), 6. *Twenty-ninth Annual Report* (1865), 7.

4. *Twenty-eighth Annual Report* (1864), 5, 7, 8, 13, 14. *Minutes* (13 November 1863). "Ladies Union Bazaar for the Benefit of Colored Orphans," *The Liberator* (22 April 1864): 67. *Twenty-ninth Annual Report* (1865), 20–21.

5. *Minutes* (12 February, 11 March, 14 October, 9 December 1864). *Minutes* (annual meeting; 12 December 1864). *Minutes* (10 March 1865). T. H. Barnes, *My Experience as an Inmate of the Colored Orphan Asylum, New York City* (unpublished copy at the New-York Historical Society and the Schomburg Center for Research in Black Culture, New York Public Library), 29. *Minutes* (12 June 1875).

6. *Twenty-eighth Annual Report* (1864), 6, 10–11.

7. *Twenty-ninth Annual Report* (1865), 5. *Minutes* (13 January 1865).

8. *Minutes* (9 June, 13 October, 10 November 1865). *Twenty-ninth Annual Report* (1865), 5.

9. Editorial, "Black Cars," *Office Holder's Journal* (August 1865): 2. *Nigger-head and Blue Law Advocate* 1 (September 1868): 1.

10. *Twenty-ninth Annual Report* (1865), 5, 8, 9, 10, 11, 13, 20, 21.

11. *Minutes* (12 January, 21, 28 February, 13 April, 9 November, 10 December 1866). *Minutes* (11 January, 8 February, 12 April, 10 May 1867).

12. *Minutes* (11 January, 8 February, 12 April, 10 May 1867).

13. "The Colored Orphan Asylum," *New York Times* (15 May 1868). *Thirty-first Annual Report* (1867), 5–12. *Thirty-second Annual Report* (1868), 5. William P. Letchworth, *Homes of Homeless Children: A Report on Orphan Asylums and Other Institutions for the Care of Children* (Albany, 1903), 199. J. F. Richmond, *New York and Its Institutions, 1609–1872* (New York: E. B. Treat, 1872), 304.

14. Michael B. Katz, *In the Shadow of the Poorhouse: A Social History of Welfare in America* (New York: Basic Books, 1986), 66.

15. *Thirty-second Annual Report* (1868), 12–13. *Forty-second Annual Report* (1878), 5.

16. *Thirty-second Annual Report* (1868), 15–16. *Fortieth Annual Report* (1876), 5, 10, 55.

17. *Minutes* (7 December 1868; 8 January, 12 March, 8 October, 12 November 1869; 29 January 1870; 13 May, July, August, September 1876; 6 July 1877).

18. *Thirty-fifth Annual Report* (1871), 10, 18. *Thirty-sixth Annual Report* (1872), 11. *Thirty-eighth Annual Report* (1874), 5. "The Colored Orphan Asylum," *New York Times* (24 May 1878): 2.

19. *Thirty-fourth Annual Report* (1870), 18. *Thirty-fifth Annual Report* (1871), 5, 10. *Thirty-sixth Annual Report* (1872), 11. *Thirty-seventh Annual Report* (1873), 11. *Minutes* (12 December 1870; 14 April 1871; 8 March, 12 April, 5 July 1872; 9 January, 9 October 1874).

20. *Association for the Benefit of Colored Orphans Records*, series 3: *Admission and Short Histories*, 1867–1888, #2304, Mattole Bronson. *Association for the Benefit of Colored Orphans Records*, series 3: *Admission and Short Histories*, 1867–1912, #885, Mattole Bronson, #2493, Sherman Collidge; #990, Minnie Green. Hereafter cited as *Admissions, 1867–1888*; and *Admissions, 1867–1912*.

Admissions, 1867–1888, #2515, Charles Jenkins; #2516, Joshua Jenkins, #2455, Sarah Hinton; *Admissions,* 1837–1866, Keziah Hinton, 76; Anna Stewart, 383. *Admissions,* 1867–1888, #2544, John Andrew Lewis.

21. *Minutes* (9 April, 8 October 1869; 14 March, 11 April, 8 May 1879). *Thirty-eighth Annual Report* (1879): 5, 6, 8, 11. *Forty-third Annual Report* (1879), 7, 9. Katz, *In the Shadow of the Poor House,* 104. *Minutes* (14 March, 11 April, 9 May 1879).

22. *Minutes* (8 January, 11, 12, February, 12 March, 8, 9 April 1870; 13 May 1870; 11 October, 8 November 1872; 13 November, 5 December 1874; 12 March, 9 April 1875).

23. *Minutes* (8 February, 7 June 1878; 14 March, 11 April, 9 May 1879; 1 July, 12 December 1881). "A Good Woman," *Harper's Weekly* (6 July 1878): 527. "A Colored Woman's Career," *New York Times* (15 June 1878): 8. *Forty-second Annual Report* (1878), 7.

24. *Thirty-third Annual Report* (1869), 5. *Minutes* (12 November 1869). George W. Potter to A. H. Shotwell (12 December 1870), in *Thirty-fourth Annual Report* (1870), 23. *Admissions,* 1837–1866, George W. Potter, 144. *Admissions,* 1867–1888, #2661, George W. Potter. Sarah A. Guilder to Mrs. [Frances] Butler (31 July 1875), in *Thirty-ninth Annual Report* (1875), 19. *Admissions,* 1837–1866, Sarah A. Guilder, 512. Mary Keenan to Miss M. [?] (9 May 1875), in *Thirty-ninth Annual Report* (1875), 20. *Admissions,* 1837–1866, Mary Keenan, 520. *Admissions,* 1867–1888, #2384, Edwin Maynard. Edward Maynard to Miss Jane Pearson (12 April 1876), in *Fortieth Annual Report* (1876), 21. *Indentures,* 1860–1886, #209, Edwin Maynard. *Indentures,* 1860–1886, #291.

25. *Admissions,* 1867–1888, #2523, John D. Johnson; #2651, Louise Taylor; #2652, Annie Taylor. *Indentures,* #328, Alexander Campbell.

26. *Minutes* (9 April, 12 June, 8 October, 12 November 1875; 14 January 1876). *Thirty-ninth Annual Report* (1875), 10. *Fortieth Annual Report* (1876), 5, 11. Editorial, "How Children Die," *New York Times* (28 July 1875): 4. Editorial, "Sick Children," *New York Times* (27 July 1875): 4.

27. *Minutes* (10 November, 11 December 1876). J. M. Heffron, "Samuel Chapman Armstrong," in *American National Biography,* ed. John A. Garraty and Mark C. Carnes (New York: Oxford University Press, 1999), 1:624–625. Josephine Brown to Jane Pearson (3 January 1876), in *Fortieth Annual Report* (1876), 19–20. Josephine Brown to Mrs. J. A. C. Gray (26 February 1877), in *Forty-first Annual Report* (1877), 18. Ezra Wright to Mr. Hutchinson (8 October 1877), in *Forty-first Annual Report* (1877), 19. *Admissions,* 1867–1912, #987

Ezra Wright. Charles Minnie to Mrs. James Stokes (19 October 1879), in *Forty-third Annual Report* (1879), 16. *Minutes* (8 April 1880).

28. *Minutes* (13 December 1875). "Margaret Olivia Slocum Sage," in *American National Biography*, 19:199–200. *North American Review* 181 (November 1905): 712–721. *The Survey* 40 (1918): 151. "Mrs. Russell Sage Dies at Her Home," *New York Times* (4 November 1918): 13.

29. *Minutes* (11 March, 13 October, 1 December 1881; 11 December 1882; 9 February 1883). "Death of Mrs. James Stokes," *New York Times* (10 March 1881): 8. Anna B. Warner, *Some Memories of James Stokes and Caroline Phelps Stokes* (Cambridge, Mass.: Riverside Press, 1892), 2, 181, 207, 212–213, 219. Harold W. Faulkner, "Anson Greene Phelps," in *Dictionary of American Biography*, ed. Dumas Malone (New York: Charles Scribner's Sons, 1934), 14:525–526. "Amos Eno's Life Ended," *New York Times* (22 February 1898): 1. "A. R. Eno's Will Probated," *New York Times* (12 March 1898): 12. "William F. Mott," *New York Times* (26 May 1882): 4. For Onderdonk, see *New York Times* (13 December 1882): 5. "Samuel Willets," *New York Times* (7 February 1883): 5. "Samuel Willets," in *National Cyclopedia of American Biography* (New York: James T. White & Co., 1900), 8:358–359.

30. *Forty-fourth Annual Report* (1880), 9. *Forty-sixth Annual Report* (1882), 7, 14. *Forty-seventh Annual Report* (1883), 6, 15. *Minutes* (10 February, 10 March, 12 May, 10 November 1882; 12 January, 9 February 1883).

5. Harlem, 1884–1906

1. *Minutes* (8 February, 1 March, 11 April, 9 May, 1 October, 14 November 1884). *Forty-eighth Annual Report* (1884), 11.

2. *Forty-ninth Annual Report* (1885), 13.

3. "Dr. Frothingham's Death," *New York Times* (20 November 1885): 1. "Funeral of Dr. Frothingham," *New York Times* (23 November 1885): 8. "Dr. Frothingham's Will," *New York Times* (24 November 1885): 8.

4. *Forty-ninth Annual Report* (1885), 5–7, 10.

5. *Fiftieth Annual Report* (1886), 5–6. "A Brooklyn Firm's Policy," *New York Age* (1 February 1890): 2.

6. Wm. H. Gardner to Mr. H[utchinson] (19 October 1886), in *Fiftieth Annual Report* (1886), 33–34. *Admissions, 1867–1888*, #1334, William H. Gardner. *Minutes* (7 August 1886; 5 August 1887; 3 August 1888).

7. *Minutes* (2 September, 14 October, 11 November 1887; 6 February, 5 July 1889; 14 February 1890; 13 October, 10 November 1893; 12 January, 9 February, 13 April 1894). *Fifty-first Annual Report* (1887), 5, 13. *Fifty-third Annual Report* (1889), 6–7. *Fifty-seventh Annual Report* (1893), 13–14. *Fifty-ninth Annual Report* (1895), 11.

8. *Minutes* (1, 8 April, 13 May, 5 August 1892).

9. For poetry, see the inside back cover of the *Forty-ninth Annual Report* (1885). *Minutes* (8 January, 7 October 1886; 10 February 1888).

10. *Forty-first Annual Report* (1887), 5. *Minutes* (11 February, 11 March 1887). Ruth Williams to Dear Sir, in *Fifty-first Annual Report* (1887), 30.

11. *Fifty-first Annual Report* (1887), 5, 8. *Minutes* (11 March 1887; 22 May 1887).

12. William B. Shaw, "Robert Leighton Stuart," in *Dictionary of American Biography* (New York: Charles Scribner's Sons, 1936), 18:176–177. *Minutes* (10 November 1899).

13. *Minutes* (9 February, 9 March 1894). *Fifty-eighth Annual Report* (1894), 6, 7, 9. *Admission Registers*, box 1, vol. 1, 1889–June 1907, #1811, Eugene Blaines. See unidentified newspaper, "Beats Daughter with Strap," n.d., in *Admission Registers*, box 1, vol. 1, 1889–June 1907 (Thomas Greenwood).

14. *Fifty-eighth Annual Report* (1894), 34. *Admissions*, 1867–1912, #967, George Douglass. *Minutes* (10 May 1895; 10 January, 8 May, 14 December 1896). Richard R. Wright Jr., "The Negro in Pennsylvania: A Study in Economic History" (Ph. D dissertation, University of Pennsylvania, 1912), 77, 80.

15. *Executive Committee Minutes* (6 October, 3 November, 1 December 1893; 5 January 1894). "Children Not Collateral," *New York Times* (14 September 1907): 4.

16. *Minutes* (January, n.d.; 8 February 1895). *Executive Committee Minutes* (4 January, 3 May 1895). *Fiftieth-ninth Annual Report* (1895), 6. "Many Small Fires but Small Damage," *New York Times* (2 January 1895): 1. "Fire in an Orphan Asylum," *New York Times* (2 January 1895): 10.

17. *Minutes* (11 June, 2 August, 6 September, 8 November 1895; 10 January, 12 June, 2 July, 7 August, 14 September, 9 October, 11 November 1896; 8 January, 6 August, 13 December 1897; 11 February 1898; 14 February 1902). *Executive Committee Minutes* (1 June, 7 December 1894; 7 June 1895; 3 January 1896; 7 May, 4 October 1907). *Sixty-first Annual Report* (1897), 5–6. Kenneth Cmeil, *A Home of Another Kind: One Chicago Orphanage and the Tangle of Child Welfare* (Chicago: University of Chicago Press, 1995), 27. Matthew A.

Crenson, *Building the Invisible Orphanage* (Cambridge, Mass.: Harvard University Press, 1998), 135.

18. *Minutes* (8 November, 9 December 1895; 10 April 1896). *Fiftieth-ninth Annual Report* (1895), 10.

19. Marcelino Sanchez to Martin K. Sherwin (26 October 1895); Sarah E. Thompson to Sherwin (24 January 1895), both in *Fiftieth-ninth Annual Report* (1895), 27-28. *Admissions, 1867-1888*, #1801, Marcelino Sanchez. Howard Price to Sherwin (1 December 1896), in *Sixtieth Annual Report* (1896), 29. *Association for the Benefit of Colored Orphans Records*, series 3: *Admissions and Discharges*, #1876, Howard Price, 132. Henry Wentworth to Miss B. [Ellen Bunting?] (16 July 1896), in *Sixtieth Annual Report* (1896), 32. *Admissions, 1867-1912*, #1001, Henry Wentworth. *Indentures*, #414, Henry Wentworth.

20. *Minutes* (10 January, 13 February 1885; 8 January, 9 April, 14 May, 11 June, 13 December 1897; 14 January 1898; 13 May 1904; 6 July, 7 September, 10 December 1906). *Seventieth Annual Report* (1906), 10. *Executive Committee Minutes* (4 March, 1 April, 3 June 1898; 1 December 1905). Robert S. Steel, "Teachers College," in *The Encyclopedia of New York City*, ed. Kenneth T. Jackson (New Haven, Conn.: Yale University Press, 1995), 116.

21. *Executive Committee Minutes* (3 February 1899). *Minutes* (13 January, 10 March 1899; 8 December, 12 December [annual meeting] 1902). Louis R. Harlan, ed., *The Booker T. Washington Papers* (Urbana: University of Illinois Press, 1972), 1:308. *Sixty-sixth Annual Report* (1902), 10.

22. *Sixty-third Annual Report* (1899), 5. *Executive Committee Minutes* (3 March, 6 October 1899). *Association for the Benefit of Colored Orphans Records*, series 7: *Visitors Register*, 1908-1935 (inside cover).

23. Mabel Ballard to Mrs. [Adelia] Duval? (1902) in *Sixty-sixth Annual Report* (1902), 21. Martin K. Sherwin to Miss Emmett (7 April 1911), in *Admission Records*, box 1, vol. 2. *Indentures, 1898-1911*, #1356, Mabel Ballard. *After-Care Committee Minutes* (9 November 1917; 14 January 1918).

24. Rachel Hardy to Sherwin (26 November 1902), in *Sixty-sixth Annual Report* (1902), 22. *Admissions, 1867-1912*, #1327, Rachel Hardy. *Admissions and Discharges*, #1327, Rachel Hardy, 241. *Indentures, 1878-1898*, 3764, Rachel Hardy. *Minutes of Indenturing Committee* (3 December 1897). Rachel Hardy to Sherwin (5 May 1903), in *Sixty-seventh Annual Report* (1903), 22. Rachel Hardy to Sherwin (31 March 1904), in *Sixty-eighth Annual Report* (1904), 22.

25. *Minutes* (8 March, 14 June, 2 August, 6 September 1889; 9 October, 13 November 1903; 2 May, 6 May [special meeting], 4 October, 9 December 1904;

12 January 1905). "Colored Orphan Asylum Buys Johnson Estate," *New York Times* (28 December 1904): 7. "In the Real Estate Field," *New York Times* (9 May 1905): 13.

26. *Minutes* (3 September 1888; 13 January, 10 February, 17 March, 20 March, 12 May, 31 October, 6 November 1905). *Sixty-ninth Annual Report* (1905), 7, 8, 10.

27. *Executive Committee Minutes* (4 May 1906), 2–9. *Minutes* (11 January 1907). "For Colored Orphans," *New York Times* (13 May 1906): 6. "Mary C. Thompson Dead," *New York Times* (29 July 1907): part 2, 6. "Will Gives Charity Nearly $5,000,000," *New York Times* (17 August 1923): 16. *Sixty-ninth Annual Report* (1905), 10, 14. S *Association for the Benefit of Colored Orphans Records*, series 8: *Building Committee Report*, 1905–1907 (see undated letter 1907 to the Board of Trustees). *Report of the Building Committee Relating to the Proposed Plan of Construction of New Building* (14 March 1905), 1–9. Payson Merrill to Mrs. Joseph W. Tilton (9 July 1907), in folder 2, 1907–1972, *Association for the Benefit of Colored Orphans Records*, series 13, *Miscellaneous Items*. Timothy Hasci, *Second Home: Orphan Asylums and Poor Families in America* (Cambridge, Mass.: Harvard University Press, 1975), 169.

28. *Minutes* (9 November 1906; 11 January 1907).

29. John D. Weaver, *The Brownsville Raid* (New York: Norton, 1970). Lewis N. Wynee, "Brownsville: The Reaction of the Negro Press," *Phylon* 33 (Summer 1972): 153–160. "Reprieve Granted Black Soldiers After 66 Years," *Jet* 43 (19 October 1972): 20–21.

30. *Seventieth Annual Report* (1906), 13.

31. Thomas H. Barnes to Superintendent (6 December 1906), in *Seventieth Annual Report* (1906), 22. *Admission of Children*, 1849–1866 (see index for Thomas H. Barnes).

6. New Start in Riverdale, 1907–22

1. Matthew A. Crenson, *Building the Invisible Orphanage* (Cambridge, Mass.: Harvard University Press, 1998), 138, 142, 212. David M. Schneider and Albert Deutsch, *The History of Public Welfare in New York State* (Chicago: University of Chicago Press, 1941), 158. *Care and Training of Orphans and Fatherless Girls: Proceedings of a Conference on the Prospective Work of Carson College for Girls and Charles E. College, Held at Philadelphia, October 13–14, 1915* (Philadelphia, 1916), 3, 4, 144.

2. *Minutes* (12 April, 14 June, 6 September 1907; 14 January 1910; 13 January 1911).

3. *Seventy-first Annual Report* (1907), 7, 9, 10.

4. *Minutes* (13 December 1907). *Executive Committee Minutes* (1 November 1907). *Seventy-first Annual Report* (1907), 15.

5. *Executive Committee Minutes* (2 October, 4 December 1908; 8 January, 7 May 1909; 3 April 1914; 15 January 1917). *Minutes* (8 January, 19 February, 13 August 1909; 9 April, 10 July, 14 August 1914). *Seventy-third Annual Report* (1909), 11, 21. *Seventy-seventh Annual Report* (1913), 12. Crenson, *Building the Invisible Orphanage*, 113, 116.

6. *Seventy-seventh Annual Report* (1908), 7–8.

7. *Admission Records*, #1763, #2517, box 1, vol. 1, series 3, *Admissions and Discharges*, 1904–1942, #1105, #2517, p. 6. *Indentures*, 225, 258. For Marion Cumbo, see Ellen Southern, *Biographical Dictionary of Afro-American and African Musicians* (Westport, Conn.: Greenwood Press, 1998), 89.

8. *Minutes* (10 December 1909). *Executive Committee Minutes* (5 November 1909).

9. *Executive Committee Minutes* (2 April 1909). *Seventy-third Annual Report* (1909), 10.

10. *Minutes* (13 March, 12 June, 11 December 1908). *Minutes of Indenturing Committee* (January ?, 21 February, 8 May, 13 November, 11 December 1908; 11 March 1910; 13 January, 13 April 1911; 11 June, 9 July 1915). *After-Care Committee Minutes* (13 October, 10 November 1916; 4 May, 13 August 1920).

11. "Roosevelt Speaks on Care of Children," *New York Times* (26 January 1909):10. Andrew Billingsley and Jeanne M. Giovannoni, *Children of the Storm: Black Children and American Child Welfare* (New York: HBJ, 1972), 68, 72. "An Address Before the White House Conference on the Care of Dependent Children" (25 January 1909), in *The Booker T. Washington Papers*, ed. Louis R. Harlan (Urbana: University of Illinois Press, 1972), 1:17–23. Timothy Hasci, *Second Home: Orphan Asylums and Poor Families in America* (Cambridge, Mass.: Harvard University Press, 1975), 38, 39, 47. Crenson, *Building the Invisible Orphanage*, 17. Walter I. Trattner, *From Poor House to Welfare State*, 3rd ed. (New York: Free Press, 1984), 202.

12. *Minutes* (11 March, 10 June, 11 November 1910; 7 July 1911). "Smith Ely Dies, 86 Years Old," *New York Times* (2 July 1911): 9. *Executive Committee Minutes* (4 February, 6 May, 1910). William B. Shaw, "Daniel Willis James,"

in *Dictionary of American Biography,* ed. Dumas Malone (New York: Charles Scribner's Sons, 1932), 9:573–574. "D. Willis James Dies in New Hampshire," *New York Times* (14 September 1907): 9.

13. *Indenturing (After-Care) Committee Minutes* (8 February, 8 March, 12 April, 10 May, 8 November 1912).

14. *Minutes* (8 August, 12 September, 8 December [annual meeting] 1913).

15. *Seventy-eighth Annual Report* (1914), 7–9. *Minutes* (14 August, 11 September, 13 November 1914; 15 January, 12 March 1915; 14 January 1916; 4 May 1917; 12 September, 12 December 1919; 13 February, 9 April 1920). *Executive Committee Minutes* (5 June 1914). *Indenturing (After-Care) Committee Minutes* (9, 19 October, 13 November 1914). *Seventy-ninth Annual Report* (1915), 11, 12, 23–25. *Eightieth Annual Report* (1916), 13. *Eighty-first Annual Report* (1917), 12–15.

16. *Minutes* (9 October, 13 November 1903). *Executive Committee Minutes* (7 April 1911). *Minutes* (3 March, 7 April, 4 August, 8 September 1911). *Indenturing Committee Minutes* (13 January, 10 March 1911). *Seventy-second Annual Report* (1908), 13, 21.

17. *Executive Committee Minutes* (4 March 1910). *Minutes* (14 January 1910; 14 March 1919; 13 May, 8 July, 14 October, 11 November, 9 December 1921). *Seventy-fourth Annual Report* (1911), 14; *Eighty-second Annual Report* (1918), 12, 19–20; *Eighty-third Annual Report* (1919), 17–18, 20; *Eighty-fifth Annual Report* (1921), 14. *Indenturing Committee Minutes* (2 November 1910).

18. *Executive Committee Minutes* (2 March, 16 April, 4 May 1900). *Minutes* (12 January, 9 February, 16 March, 12 April, 1900; 12 June 1908; 10 March, 13 April, 12 May, 9 June 1911). *Executive Committee Minutes* (6 March, 3 April, 1 May, 1908; 3 March 1911).

19. *Seventy-fifth Annual Report* (1911). *Executive Committee Minutes* (3 November 1911).

20. *Executive Committee Minutes* (5 January 1912). *Minutes* (12 January, 12 February, 8 March 1912).

21. *Minutes* (11 October 1912; 9 May, 13 June 1913). *Executive Committee Minutes* (2 February, 1 March, 7 June, 6 December 1912). *Seventy-sixth Annual Report* (1912), 10.

22. *Indenturing Committee Minutes* (2 November 1910).

23. *Indenturing Committee Minutes* (8 December 1911; 12, 22 January, 8 February 1912). *Minutes* (2 August 1912). *Executive Committee Minutes* (3 May 1912). *Minutes* (10 May 1912).

24. *Indenturing Committee Minutes* (18 November, 9 December 1912; 10 October 1913; 9 January, 13 February 1914). *Executive Committee Minutes* (3 May 1912). *Minutes* (10 May 1912).

25. *Executive Committee Minutes* (5 November 1915). *Indenturing (After-Care) Committee Minutes* (12 November 1915). *Minutes* (12 November 1915); see *Executive Committee Minutes* for December 1915. *Seventy-ninth Annual Report* (1915), 13–15. *Eightieth Annual Report* (1916), 10. *Minutes* (14 July, 3 October 1916; 10 May 1918).

26. *Eighty-third Annual Report* (1919), 13, 15, 22.

27. *Eighty-fourth Annual Report* (1920), 12–13, 17–19. *Eighty-fifth Annual Report* (1921), 19–20. *Executive Committee Minutes* (3 March 1920). *After-Care Committee Minutes* (10 December 1920, 13 October, 8 December 1922).

28. *Minutes* (10 March, 13 April, 13 October 1911). *Seventy-fifth Annual Report* (1911, 13).

29. *Seventy-sixth Annual Report* (1912), 9, 12.

30. *Seventy-sixth Annual Report* (1912), 12, 14.

31. *Executive Committee Minutes* (5 April 1913; 16 March 1914). *Minutes* (14 November 1913; 8 May 1914; 8 April, 11 September 1936). "Carolena M. Wood Dies of Pneumonia," *New York Times* (13 March 1936): 23. Carolena M. Wood to the Committee on Superintendent (7 October 1913); Carolena M. Wood to Mrs. Willard Parker Jr., in *Association for the Benefit of Colored Orphans Records*, series 13, *Miscellaneous Items*, folder 2, 1907–1972. *Seventy-eighth Annual Report* (1914), 7. *One Hundredth Annual Report* (1936), 2.

32. Editorial, "Orphans," *The Crisis: A Record of the Darker Races* 6 (August 1913): 184–186. *Minutes* (18 September 1913). *Association for the Benefit of Colored Orphans Records*, series 7, *Visitors Registers*, 1908–1935 (for Du Bois's visit).

33. *Executive Committee Minutes* (7 November 1913). *Minutes* (13 June, 18 September, 14 November 1913; 14 May 1915; 14 June 1918; 17 January 1919; 11 May, 13 July, 11 October, 9, 19 November 1923).

34. *Seventy-seventh Annual Report* (1913), 7, 9, 10. *Minutes* (8 May, 11 September 1914).

35. *Seventy-seventh Annual Report* (1913), 12.

36. *Minutes* (9 April, 10 July, 14 August 1914). *Executive Committee Minutes* (3 April 1914; 5 January 1917). "Girls the Drudges in Children's Home," *New York Times* (3 February 1916): 20. "Admits 'Strapping' His Orphan Charges," *New York Times* (16 February 1916): 22.

37. *Minutes* (14 August 1914; 12 January 1917). *Executive Committee Minutes* (16 March 1914).

38. *Seventy-eighth Annual Report* (1914), 9. "Negroes in Mass Meeting," *New York Times* (29 August 1913), 3. *After-Care Committee Minutes* (23 March 1917).

39. *Executive Committee Minutes* (5 February 1915). *Minutes* (6 August, 8 October, 10 December 1915; 14 January, 10 March, 14 April, 12 May, 9 June 1916; 11 July 1924). *Eighty-first Annual Report* (1917), 15.

40. *Minutes* (14 September 1917).

41. *Minutes* (14 June 1918; 17 January, 14 March 1919).

42. *Seventy-eighth Annual Report* (1914), 12, 17–18.

43. *Seventy-ninth Annual Report* (1915), 22–23. *Minutes* (14 January 1916).

44. *Eightieth Annual Report* (1916), 18–19.

45. *Minutes* (13 April, 11 May, 8 June 1917).

46. *After-Care Committee Minutes* (23 March 1917). *Minutes* (10 September 1920).

47. "Colored Orphans Want a Piano," *New York Times* (14 November 1922): 13. "Negroes in Mass Meeting," *New York Times* (29 August 1913): 3. "Music in Review," *New York Times* (17 March 1935): section 2, 8. "Tibbets to Give Prize," *New York Times* (13 March 1935): 17. *Minutes* (8, 19 March 1935).

48. "Negro Guardsmen in San Juan Riot," *New York Times* (4 July 1917): 9. "Hayward Defends His Men," *New York Times* (6 July 1917): 9.

49. *After-Care Committee Minutes* (8 June, 10 August 1917). Peter M. Bergman, ed., *The Chronological History of the Negro in America* (New York: Harper & Row, 1969), 381, 385. "Fear Negro Troops in Spartanburg," *New York Times* (31 August 1917): 4. "Pro Germans Busy at Spartanburg," *New York Times* (17 September 1917): 4.

50. *After-Care Committee Minutes* (12 April, 11 October 1918). *Minutes* (11 January 1918; 11 February 1921). *Eighty-second Annual Report* (1919), 17, 19. *Executive Committee Minutes* (21 January 1921).

51. "Townsmen Protest on Rector's Behalf," *New York Times* (6 October 1917), 12.

52. *Minutes* (12 April, 14 June, 12 July, 13 September, 11 October, 13 December 1918; 10 January, 14 March, 11 April, 9 May, 10 October, 12 December 1919; 13 May, 10 June, 19 December 1921). Schneider and Deutsch, *The History of Public Welfare in New York State*, 248.

53. *Eighty-second Annual Report* (1918), 10.

54. *Minutes* (21 January, 8 February, 8 March, 13 March, 12 July 1918). *Eighty-second Annual Report* (1918), 9, 17, 21.

55. *Minutes* (12 May 1922). *Eighty-seventh Annual Report* (1923), 7–8.

56. *Eighty-second Annual Report* (1918), 11–12. *Eighty-fourth Annual Report* (1920), 10–11. *Executive Committee Minutes* (1 March 1921).

57. *Minutes* (11 February, 11 March 1921; 10 February, 12 April, 12 May 1922; 12 January 1923). *Executive Committee Minutes* (17 January, 21 March, 10 November 1922; 5 January 1923). *Eighty-fifth Annual Report* (1921), 12; *Eighty-sixth Annual Report* (1922), 9; *Eighty-seventh Annual Report* (1923), 8. *Educational Committee Minutes* (April 1922). Series 13, *Miscellaneous Items*, folder 2, 1907–1922.

58. *Eighty-sixth Annual Report* (1922), 18–19, 22. *Executive Committee Minutes* (21 December 1921; 3 January 1922). *Minutes* (10 March, 10 April 1922).

7. Riverdale: Trials and Tribulations, 1923–36

1. *Minutes* (9 February, 1 September, 1923; 14 November 1924; 11 February 1927). *New York Times* (23 May 1923): 43; *New York Times* (12 August 1923): 61; *New York Times* (25 November 1923): E1; *New York Times* (15 February 1924): 30; *New York Times* (28 May 1924): 46. *Executive Committee Minutes* (7 January 1927).

2. *Eighty-seventh Annual Report* (1923), 11–12; *Eighty-eighth Annual Report* (1924), 14; *Ninetieth Annual Report* (1926), 18; *Ninety-first Annual Report* (1927), 7. Anna Kendrick Walker, "Unique Commencement," *New York Times* (7 July 1926): 4. Anne K. Walker, "Graduation at the Orphan Asylum, Riverdale, N.Y.," *The Riverdale News* (August 1928), in *Ninety-second Annual Report* (1928), 14–15. *Minutes* (9 November 1928).

3. *Eighty-seventh Annual Report* (1923), 13; *Eighty-eighth Annual Report* (1924), 17. *After-Care Committee Minutes* (2 December 1924; 13 November 1925).

4. *Minutes* (13 November 1925).

5. *Minutes* (8 February, 14 November, 12 December 1924). *Eighty-eighth Annual Report* (1924), 8.

6. *Eighty-seventh Annual Report* (1924), 14; *Ninetieth Annual Report* (1926), 11; *Ninety-third Annual Report* (1929), 9–10; *Ninety-ninth Annual Report* (1935), 8–10. *Executive Committee Minutes* (7 May 1926). "An Appeal for Orphans," *New York Times* (17 March 1939): 22.

7. *Eighty-ninth Annual Report* (1925), 7, 10–11. *Executive Committee Minutes* (1 May 1925). *Minutes* (13 April, 8 May 1925; 11 February, 10 December 1926). *A Study of Delinquent and Neglected Negro Children Before the New York City Children's Court,* 6, 22, 24–26.

8. *Eighty-ninth Annual Report* (1925), 16–17; *Ninetieth Annual Report* (1926), 19–20. *Executive Committee Minutes* (6 January, 5 February 1926).

9. *Minutes* (14 May, 13 August 1926; 12 August 1927). *Ninety-first Annual Report* (1927), 6, 8; *Ninety-second Annual Report* (1928), 9.

10. *Minutes* (11 March, 8 April, 13 May, 12 August, 14 October, 11 November, 9 December 1927). "Miss Stokes Left Wealth to Charity," *New York Times* (25 December 1927): 14. *Ninety-first Annual Report* (1928), 28.

11. "25 Child agencies to Their Ideas," *New York Times* (29 November 1927): 2.

12. *Ninety-first Annual Report* (1927), 2, 18, 19; *Ninety-second Annual Report* (1928), 4–5.

13. *Ninety-first Annual Report* (1927), 4–7; *Ninety-Fifth Annual Report* (1931), 9.

14. *Ninety-first Annual Report* (1927), 11. *Minutes* (11 April 1929).

15. *Ninety-second Annual Report* (1928), 8.

16. *Ninety-third Annual Report* (1929), 11, 13.

17. *Ninety-fourth Annual Report* (1930), 15.

18. *Ninety-fourth Annual Report* (1930), 5, 10, 14; *Ninety-fifth Annual Report* (1931), 8, 21; *Ninety-sixth Annual Report* (1932), 9; *Ninety-ninth Annual Report* (1935), 6. *Minutes* (9 October 1931; 12 August 1932; 15 March, 10 April, 8 May, 10 July, 11 December, 18 December 1931).

19. *Ninety-fifth Annual Report* (1931), 14–16.

20. *Minutes* (11 March 1932; 10 March 1933).

21. *Minutes* (9 September 1932; 9 June, 2 September, 8 December 1933; 12 January, 9 February 1934). *Ninety-sixth Annual Report* (1932), 3, 11–12. *Ninety-seventh Annual Report* (1933), 4, 7, 9; *Ninety-eighth Annual Report* (1934), 7.

22. *Executive Committee Minutes* (3 March, 7 April 1933). *Minutes* (10 March 1933). *Ninety-seventh Annual Report* (1933), 10.

23. *Minutes* (14 December 1934; 14 June 1935). *Ninety-eighth Annual Report* (1935), 7.

24. *Ninety-eighth Annual Report* (1935), 14.

25. *Ninety-ninth Annual Report* (1939), 15. *Minutes* (13 November, 1936). *One Hundredth Annual Report* (1936), 16.

26. *Minutes* (27 May, 14 June 1935). Lillie Skiddy Parker to editor, "Aid For Negro Children," *New York Times* (27 May 1935): 16. *Ninety-ninth Annual Report* (1935), 6; *One Hundred and First Annual Report* (1937), 14.

27. Gwendolyn Bennett, "Rounding the Century," *The Crisis: A Record of the Darker Races* 42 (June 1935): 180, 181, 188. *Ninety-ninth Annual Report* (1935), 9–10.

28. "Rift in Home Laid to Father Divine," *New York Times* (18 July 1935): 2. *Executive Committee Minutes* (11 December 1936; February 1937). Henry R. Murphy to Father Divine (6 December 1943); Father Divine to Henry R. Murphy (9 December 1943), in *The New Day* (16 December 1943), *Riverdale Children's Association Records*, box 2, vol. 6, 1940–1944 scrapbook, Schomburg Center for Research in Black Culture, New York Public Library.

29. *Ninety-fifth Annual Report* (1931), 9; *Ninety-sixth Annual Report* (1932), 8.

30. *Minutes* (30 December 1930; 10 July 1931; 14 December 1934; 11 December 1936). *After-Care Committee Minutes* (13 June 1930). "Orphan Asylum Marks Century of Existence," *Yonkers Herald Statesman* (7 December 1936), in *Riverdale Children's Association Records*, box 2, vol. 5, scrapbook. *Negro Organizations in New York City Research Studies, Compiled by Workers of the Writer's Program of the Works Projects Administration in New York City for "Negroes of New York"* (New York, 1940), 1–6 (microfilm, Schomburg Center for Research in Black Culture, New York Public Library). "Prejudice 1836: Pride 1936," *The Survey* 72 (November 1936): 329. "Colored Asylum Is 100 Years Old," *New York Times* (6 December 1936): 54. *Ninety-fifth Annual Report* (1931), 9; *Ninety-sixth Annual Report* (1932), 8. "Stern Will Gives $580,000 to Public," *New York Times* (6 February 1930): 26; "Benjamin Stern, Merchant, Dead," *New York Times* (9 March 1933): 13. "Benjamin Stern's Will Filed," *New York Times* (18 March 1933): 15. "$2,344,382.00 Is Left by Benjamin Stern," *New York Times* (15 December 1934): 10.

31. *One Hundred and First Annual Report* (1937), 8.

8. From the Colored Orphan Asylum to the Riverdale Children's Association, 1937–46

1. *One Hundredth Annual Report* (1936), 5, 13.

2. *One Hundred and Second Annual Report* (1938), 17–19.

3. *Executive Committee Minutes* (5 November 1937). *One Hundred and First Annual Report* (1938), 9, 26.

4. *One Hundred and First Annual Report* (1937), 16. "Negro Child Care Listed," *New York Times* (13 February 1938): 47.

5. *One Hundred and First Annual Report* (1937), 5–6, 8; *One Hundred and Third Annual Report* (1939), 14. Peter M. Bergman, *The Chronological History of the Negro People in America* (New York: Harper & Row, 1969), 471.

6. *One Hundred and Second Annual Report* (1938), 11–12.

7. *One Hundred and Third Annual Report* (1939), 6–8. "Progress Is Noted in Negro Charity Aid," *New York Times* (16 April 1939): G5.

8. "Project Will Aid Negro Children," *New York Times* (8 February 1939): 9. "Foster Homes Sought," *New York Times* (2 November 1939): 19.

9. *One Hundred and Third Annual Report* (1939): 5, 10–15, 18.

10. *One Hundred and Third Annual Report* (1939), inside cover, 13. *Minutes* (annual meeting, 11 December 1939).

11. *One Hundred and Third Annual Report* (1939), 9. *Minutes* (9 February, 8 March, 9 December 1940). "Dr. Peyton Anderson, Harlem Civic Leader," *New York Times* (12 October 1945): 19.

12. *Minutes* (12 January, 8 March, 9 February, 12 April, 10 May, 12 July 1940). "Public Gets Most of Morse Estate," *New York Times* (13 January 1939): 20.

13. *Minutes* (14 June, 12 July, 13 September, 11 October 1940). *Executive Committee Minutes* (26 July 1940).

14. *Minutes* (8 November, 9 December [annual meeting] 1940). "Varieties of Hobbies to Be Shown today," *New York Times* (13 March 1940): 24.

15. *Minutes* (10, 17 January 1941). "New Case Load Is Too Great, Riverdale Orphan Asylum Says," *Yonkers Statesman* (5 April 1941), in *Riverdale Children's Association Records*, box 2, vol. 6, 1940–1944 scrapbook, Schomburg Center for Research in Black Culture, New York Public Library.

16. *Minutes* (14 February, 9 April, 9 May, 13 June, 14 November, 8 December [annual meeting], 12 December 1941). "Showing of 'Native Son' Will Aid Colored Asylum," *Bronx Home News* (18 May 1941), in *Riverdale Children's Association Records*, box 2, vol. 6, 1940–1944 scrapbook, Schomburg Center for Research in Black Culture, New York Public Library.

17. *Minutes* (23 July [special meeting], 14 November, 8 December [annual meeting] 1941).

18. *Minutes* (14 November 1941). "New York Orphanage Adds 2 to Staff," *Baltimore Afro-American* (1 March 1941). "Staff Promotions and Additions Announced at Colored Orphanage," *New York Age* (1 March 1941). "Orphan Asylum Promotes Poe," *Yonkers Herald Statesman* (22 September 1941), in *Riverdale Children's Association Records*, box 2, vol. 6, 1940–1944, Schomburg Center for Research in Black Culture, New York Public Library. "Elected Orphan Asylum Trustee," *New York Times* (11 August 1941): 15. "Support Is Urged for Negro Youth," *New York Times* (4 May 1941): 48.

19. "Joe Louis to Entertain at Colored Orphanage," *Bronx Home News* (1 February 1941). "Star of 'Wind' to Adopt Child," *Baltimore Afro-American* (19 April 1941). "Child Composer Plays at Orphanage Benefit," *Yonkers Herald Statesman* (29 April 1941). "Leader Visits Riverdale," *New York Amsterdam News* (29 November 1941), in *Riverdale Children's Association Records*, box 2, vol. 6, 1940–1944 scrapbook, Schomburg Center for Research in Black Culture, New York Public Library.

20. *Minutes* (15 March, 10 April 1931; 14 March 1941). *Ninety-fifth Annual Report* (1941), 19. *Executive Committee Minutes* (9 March 1934; 11 December 1936).

21. *Minutes* (9 April, 12 September 1941). Lillie Skiddy Parker to editor, "Enterprising Youngsters Need Help," *New York Times* (1 August 1940): 20. "Orphans Get Their Own Pool," *New York Times* (4 August 1941): 8.

22. *Minutes* (9 January, 5 March, 10 April, 8 May, 12 June, 9 October, 6 November, 14 December 1942; 8 January, 19 February, 12 March, 11 June, 17 September, 12 November 1943).

23. *Minutes* (13 February, 13 March 1942).

24. "Want 'Parents' For Home," *New York Amsterdam News* (14 November 1942), in *Riverdale Children's Association Records*, box 2, vol. 6, 1940–1944 scrapbook, Schomburg Center for Research in Black Culture, New York Public Library.

25. *Minutes* (10 August 1928; 12 July, 11 October, 8 November, 13 December 1940; 11 February 1941; 8 May, 11 September 1942; 12 March, 26 May 1943).

26. *Minutes* (11 February [special meeting] 1944; 11 December 1944). William Seraile in phone conversation with Fitz Harvey (11 August 2005). "War Bond for a Name," *New York World Telegram* (7 April 1944), in *Riverdale Children's Association Records*, box 2, vol. 6, 1940–1944 scrapbook, Schomburg Center for Research in Black Culture, New York Public Library.

27. *Minutes* (12 March, 8 May, 26 May 1943; 14 April, 3 July 1944). *Executive Committee Minutes* (12 January, 9 March, 13 April 1945).

28. *Executive Committee Minutes* (5 February 1937). Robert Sullivan, "The Two Quaker Ladies and the Golden Gloves," *Sunday News* (4 March 1948): 76–77, in *Riverdale Children's Association Records*, box 2, vol. 5, 1936–1946 scrapbook, Schomburg Center for Research in Black Culture, New York Public Library.

29. "Children's Aid Bond Drive," *New York Times* (11 February 1943), in *Riverdale Children's Association Records*, box 2, vol. 6, 1940–1944 scrapbook, Schomburg Center for Research in Black Culture, New York Public Library.

30. *Minutes* (8 January, 9 April, 11 June, 15 October 1943). "Elvin Bell Naval Hero Due Honors," *Amsterdam Star News* (20 March 1943), in *Riverdale Children's Association Records*, box 2, vol. 6, 1940–1944 scrapbook, Schomburg Center for Research in Black Culture, New York Public Library.

31. "Prayers for Safety of 180 Former Inmates of Riverdale Orphanage Asked by Children," *New York Age* (8 January 1944), in *Riverdale Children's Association Records*, box 2, vol. 5, 1936–1946 scrapbook, Schomburg Center for Research in Black Culture, New York Public Library. *Minutes* (13 April, 9 May 1945).

32. *Minutes* (12 March, 17 September 1943; 21 June, 29 September 1944).

33. *Minutes* (14 May, 26 May, 15 October 1943).

34. *Minutes* (12 November 1943). "First Lady Sees Orphanage," *New York Times* (22 October 1943): 6.

35. *Minutes* (12 November, 13 December 1943).

36. *Minutes* (14 January, 11 February, 14 April, 12 May, 9 June 1944). "Duke and Lucky to Play for Riverdale's Ball," *New York Amsterdam News* (8 April 1944), in *Riverdale Children's Association Records*, box 12, vol. 5, 1936–1946 scrapbook, Schomburg Center for Research in Black Culture, New York Public Library.

37. *Minutes* (8 September 1944; 13 April 1949). Mary Braggioti, "A Toiler in the Vineyard," *New York Evening Post* (5 June 1944), in *Riverdale Children's Association Records*, box 2, vol. 5, 1936–1946 scrapbook, Schomburg Center for Research in Black Culture, New York Public Library.

38. "Mayor Is Aroused by Child Neglect," *New York Times* (28 October 1944): 18.

39. *Minutes* (23 November 1944; 12 January 1945).

40. *Minutes* (12 January, 9 March, 3 April, 15 June 1945).

41. *Executive Committee Minutes* (23 July 1945). "Scores Discipline Lack at Riverdale," *Pittsburgh Courier* (18 August 1945), in *Riverdale Children's Association Records*, box 2, vol. 5, 1936–1946 scrapbook, Schomburg Center for Research in Black Culture, New York Public Library.

42. "Ex Worker Calls Home a Failure," *Pittsburgh Courier* (11 August 1945), in *Riverdale Children's Association Records*, box 2, vol. 5, 1936–1946 scrapbook, Schomburg Center for Research in Black Culture, New York Public Library. "Admit Evils at Riverdale Orphanage, Plan Relief," *Daily Worker* (12 September 1945), in *Riverdale Children's Association Records*, box 2, vol. 5, 1936–1946 scrapbook, Schomburg Center for Research in Black Culture, New York Public Library.

43. *Minutes* (28 September, 10 October 1945). *Executive Committee Minutes* (9 November 1945). "Riverdale Committee Adds Three," *Pittsburgh Courier* (13 October 1945), in *Riverdale Children's Association Records*, box 2, vol. 5, 1936–1946 scrapbook, Schomburg Center for Research in Black Culture, New York Public Library. "Five Riverdale Employees Defend Executive Director," *Pittsburgh Courier* (6 October 1945), box 2, vol. 5, 1936–1946 scrapbook, Schomburg Center for Research in Black Culture, New York Public Library.

44. *Minutes* (10 October, 9 November 1945).

45. *Minutes* (10 December 1945). "Home to Be Closed," *New York Times* (14 December 1945): 34. "State's Report May Cause Riverdale to Close," *New York Age* (15 December 1945), in *Riverdale Children's Association Records*, box 2, vol. 5, 1936–1946 scrapbook, Schomburg Center for Research in Black Culture, New York Public Library.

46. *Minutes* (11 January, 8 February 1946). Mrs. Robert De Vecchi to Mrs. Theodore Dreiser (4 March 1946); Mrs. Theodore Dreiser to Mrs. Robert De Vecchi (13 March 1946), Theodore Dreiser Papers, Rare Book and Manuscript Library, University of Pennsylvania.

47. *Minutes* (19 March, 2 May 1946).

48. *Minutes* (11 June, 8 October, 12 December 1946). "Riverdale Home in New Quarters," *New York Times* (8 December 1946): 64.

49. *Minutes* (8 October 1946).

50. *Minutes* (10 September 1929; 31 August 1948). "Home Buys in Riverdale," *New York Times* (31 October 1948): 75. "Hebrew Home Buys Riverdale Property," *New York Times* (11 November 1948): 4.

Conclusion

1. Comments of Louis Eddy, Lehman College (14 April 2005).

2. "Recalling a Place of Sanctuary for Black Orphans," *New York Times* (7 April 2003): F3.

3. Comments of Louis Eddy, Lehman College (14 April 2005).

Bibliography

Books

Adams, Virginia M., ed. *On the Altar of Freedom*: *A Black Soldier's Civil War Letters from the Front*. Amherst: University of Massachusetts Press, 1991.

Aptheker, Herbert, ed. *A Documentary History of the Negro People in the United States*. Vol. 1. New York: Citadel Press, 1951.

Auchincloss, Louis, ed. *The Horne and Strong Diaries of Old Manhattan*. New York: Abbeville Press, 1989.

Bergman, Peter M., ed. *The Chronological History of the Negro People in America*. New York: Harper & Row, 1959.

Bernstein, Iver. *The New York City Draft Riots: Their Significance for American Society and Politics in the Age of the Civil War*. New York: Oxford University Press, 1990.

Billingsley, Andrew, and Jeanne M. Giovannoni. *Children of the Storm: Black Children and American Child Welfare*. New York: HBJ, 1972.

Boylan, Anne M. *The Origins of Women's Activism*: *New York and Boston, 1797–1840*. Chapel Hill: University of North Carolina Press, 2002.

Cmiel, Kenneth. *A Home of Another Kind: One Chicago Orphanage and the Tangle of Child Welfare*. Chicago: University of Chicago Press, 1995.

Cook, Adrian. *The Armies of the Streets: The New York City Draft Riots of 1863*. Lexington: University Press of Kentucky, 1974.

Cooke, Samuel. *The Funeral Sermons Preached in St. Bartholomew's, New-York on the 23rd and 24th Sundays After Trinity Following the Death of Miss Jay on 13th of November and of Her Sister Mrs. Banyer on the 21st of the Same Month*. New York: Thomas N. Stanford, 1857.

Crenson, Matthew A. *Building the Invisible Orphanage*. Cambridge, Mass.: Harvard University Press, 1998.

Curry, Leonard P. *The Free Blacks in Urban America, 1800–1850: The Shadow of the Dream.* Chicago: University of Chicago Press, 1981.

Dulberger, Judith A. *"Mother Donit fore the Best": Correspondence of a Nineteenth-Century Orphan Asylum.* Syracuse, N.Y.: Syracuse University Press, 1996.

Folks, Homer. *The Care of Destitute, Neglected, and Delinquent Children.* Albany, N.Y.: J. B. Lyon Co., 1900.

Forbes, Ella. *African American Women During the Civil War.* New York: Garland Publishing, 1998.

Fox, John, Jr. *Quakerism in the City of New York, 1857–1930.* New York: Quinn & Bolden, 1930.

Freeman, Rhoda G. *The Free Negro in New York City in the Era Before the Civil War.* New York: Garland Publishing, 1994.

Friedman, Laurence J., and Mark McCarvie, eds. *Charity, Philanthropy, and Civility in American History.* Cambridge: Cambridge University Press, 2003.

From Cherry Street to Green Pastures: A History of the Colored Orphan Asylum at Riverdale-on-Hudson. New York, 1936.

Gellman, David N., and David Quigley, eds. *A Documentary History of Race and Citizenship, 1777–1887.* New York: New York University Press, 2003.

Ginzberg, Lori D. *Women and the Work of Benevolence, Morality, Politics, and Class in the Nineteenth-Century United States.* New Haven, Conn.: Yale University Press, 1990.

Gordon, Michael, ed., *The American Family in Social-Historical Perspective.* New York: St. Martin's Press, 1973.

Grissom, John H. *The Sanitary Condition of the Laboring Population of New York.* New York: Harper & Brothers, 1845.

Hacsi, Timothy. *Second Home: Orphan Asylums and Poor Families in America.* Cambridge, Mass.: Harvard University Press, 1997.

Harris, Leslie M. *In the Shadow of Slavery: African Americans in New York City, 1626–1863.* Chicago: University of Chicago Press, 2003.

Katz, Michael B. *In the Shadow of the Poorhouse: A Social History of Welfare in America.* New York: Basic Books, 1986.

Lerner, Laurence. *Angels and Absences.* Nashville, Tenn.: Vanderbilt University Press, 1997.

Letchworth, William P. *Homes of Homeless Children: A Report on Orphan Asylums and Other Institutions for the Care of Children.* Albany, N.Y., 1903.

McKenzie, Richard B. *Rethinking Orphanages for the Twenty-first Century.* London: Sage Publications, 1999.

Merritt, Walter M., et al. *The Letters of William Lloyd Garrison.* Vol. 5. Cambridge, Mass.: Harvard University Press, 1971–1981.

Murray, Sarah S. *In the Olden Times: A Short History of the Descendants of John Murray the Good.* New York: Strettiner Lambert & Co., 1894.

Nevins, Allan, and Milton H. Thomas, eds. *The Diary of George Templeton Strong.* New York: Macmillan, 1952.

Renshan, Edward J. *The Lion's Pride: Theodore Roosevelt and His Family in Peace and War.* New York: Oxford University Press, 1918.

Richmond, J. F. *New York and Its Institutions, 1609–1872.* New York: E. B. Treat, 1872.

Ripley, Peter, ed. *The Black Abolitionist Papers.* Vols. 3–5. Chapel Hill: University of North Carolina Press, 1991–1992.

Schneider, David M., and Albert Deutsch. *The History of Public Welfare in New York State.* Vol. 2. Chicago: University of Chicago Press, 1941.

Seraile, William. *New York's Black Regiments During the Civil War.* New York: Routledge, 2001.

Smith, James McCune. *A Sketch of the Haytian Revolution.* New York: Daniel Fanshaw, 1841.

Southern, Ellen. *Biographical Dictionary of Afro-American and African Musicians.* Westport, Conn.: Greenwood Press, 1998.

Stauffer, John M. *The Black Hearts of Men: Radical Abolitionists and the Transformation of Race.* Cambridge, Mass.: Harvard University Press, 2002.

Thompson, Mary W. *Broken Gloom: Sketches of the History, Character and Dying Testimony of Beneficiaries of the Colored Home in the City of New York.* New York: John F. Trow, 1851.

Thurston, Henry. *The Dependent Child.* New York: Arno Press, 1974.

Trattner, Walter I. *From Poor Law to Welfare State.* 3rd ed. New York: The Free Press, 1984.

Warner, Anna B. *Some Memories of James Stokes and Caroline Phelps Stokes.* Cambridge, Mass.: The Riverside Press, 1892.

Weaver, John D. *The Brownsville Raid.* New York: Norton, 1970.

Articles

Bennett, Gwendolyn. "Rounding the Century." *The Crisis: A Record of the Darker Races* 42 (June 1935): 180–188.

"Communications from the New York Society for the Promotion of Education Among Colored Children." *Anglo African Magazine* 1 (July 1859): 222–224.

Freeman, M. H. "The Educational Wants of the Free Colored People." *Anglo African Magazine* 1 (April 1859): 115–118.

Gilje, Paul A. "Infant Abandonment in Early Nineteenth-Century New York City: Three Cases." In *Growing up in America: Children in Historical Perspective*, ed. J. M. Hawes. Urbana: University of Illinois Press, 1985.

Kerber, Linda K. "Abolitionists and Amalgamators: The New York City Race Riots of 1834." *New York History* 48 (January 1967): 28–39.

Lindsay, Arnett G. "The Economic Condition of the Negroes Prior to 1861." *Journal of Negro History* 6 (April 1921): 190–199.

Mann, Albon P. "Labor Competition and the New York Draft Riots of 1863." *Journal of Negro History* 36 (October 1951): 375–405.

"On the Fourth Query of Thomas Jefferson's Notes on Virginia." *Anglo African Magazine* 1 (August 1859): 225–238.

"Orphans." *The Crisis: A Record of the Darker Races* 6 (August 1913): 184–186.

Porter, Dorothy B. "The Organized Educational Activities of Negro Literary Societies, 1828–1846." *Journal of Negro Education* 5 (October 1936): 56–57.

"Prejudice 1836: Pride 1936." *The Survey* 72 (November 1936): 309.

"Reprieve Granted Black Soldiers After 66 Years." *Jet* 43 (October 19, 1972): 20–21.

Romanofsky, Peter. "Saving the Lives of the City's Foundlings." *New-York Historical Society Quarterly* 61 (January/April 1977): 49–68.

Rury, John L. "The New York African Free School, 1827–1836: Conflict Over Community Control of Black Education." *Phylon* 44 (September 1983): 187–198.

Watkins, Francis Ellen. "Our Greatest Want." *Anglo African Magazine* 1 (May 1859): 160.

Welter, Barbara. "The Cult of True Womanhood: 1820–1860." In *The American Family in Social-Historical Perspective*, 2nd ed., ed. Michael Gordon. New York: St. Martin's Press, 1978.

Wynee, Lewis N. "Brownsville: The Reaction of the Negro Press." *Phylon* 33 (Summer 1972): 153–160.

Unpublished Materials

Association for the Benefit of Colored Orphans Records, New-York Historical Society

Series 1. *Minutes of Board Meetings*, 1836–1840; 1846–1857; 1863–July 1930. Includes the *Annual Reports*.

Series 2. *Minutes of the Executive Committee*, 1891–1929.

Series 3. *Admission Records*, 1837–1912.

Series 4. *Indentures*, 1878–1916.

Series 5. *Book of Records of Stipend Committee*, 1881–1905.

Series 6. *After-Care Committee Minutes*, 1916–1930.

Series 7. *Visitors' Registers*, 1908–1935 (see October 9, 1910, for W. E. B. Du Bois's visit).

Series 8. *Building Committee*, 1905–1907.

Series 9. *Bequests* [1883]–1893.

Series 13. *Miscellaneous Items*, folders 4 and 5.

Barnes, Thomas H. *My Experience as an Inmate of the Colored Orphan Asylum* (New York: n.p., 1924). Schomburg Center for Research in Black Culture and New-York Historical Society.

Chapin, Charles L. *Personal Recollection of the Draft Riots of New York City, 1863.* Vol. 2. New-York Historical Society Children's Aid Society Records, New-York Historical Society

Dreiser, Theodore. Theodore Dreiser Papers, Rare Book and Manuscript Library, University of Pennsylvania.

New-York Society for Promoting the Manumission of Slaves and Protecting Such of Them as Have Been Liberated. Vols. 1, 8. New-York Historical Society.

Hone, Philip. *Diary*, January 1, 1832, to October 2, 1834. Microfilm. New-York Historical Society.

Lawrence, Cornelius W. *Fifty-five Communications to Cornelius W. Lawrence, Mayor of New York City, from Various Persons, Including Lists of Volunteer Aids, Report About Homes and Character of the Mob Threatened to Burn, Disposition of Militia, etc.* 1834. Microfilm. New-York Historical Society.

Riverdale Children's Association Records. Box 2, vol. 5, 1936–1946 scrapbook; box 2, vol. 6, 1940–1944 scrapbook. Schomburg Center for Research in Black Culture, New York Public Library.

Proceedings and Reports

Annual Reports of the Association for the Benefit of Colored Orphans, 1837–1946. Schomburg Center for Research in Black Culture, New York Public Library

Care and Training of Orphans and Fatherless Girls; Proceedings of a Conference on the Prospective Work of Carson College for Girls and Charles E. Ellis College, Held at Philadelphia, October 13–14, 1915. Philadelphia, [1916].

Report of the Committee on Merchants for the Relief of Colored People Suffering from the Late Riots in the City of New York. New York: George A. Whitehorne, 1863.

Second Annual Report of the Governors of the Almshouse New York for the Year 1850. New York: William C. Bryant & Co., 1851.

Addresses, Constitutions, Discourses, Minutes, Orations, and Speeches

An Address to the Citizens of New-York in Regards to the Abuses and Reforms in the Almshouse and Prison Department of the County [of New York], *1849.* New-York Historical Society.

Constitution of the African Marine Fund for the Relief of the Distressed Orphans and Poor Members of the Fund. New York: John C. Totten, 1910.

Garnet, Henry Highland. *A Memorial Discourse Delivered in the Hall of the House of Representatives, Washington D.C., February 12, 1865.* Philadelphia: Joseph M. Wilson, 1865.

Hamilton, William. *Oration Delivered in the African Zion Church on the Fourth of July 1827: Commemoration of the Abolition of Domestic Slavery in the State.* New York: Gray & Bunce, 1827.

Jay, John. *An Address in Behalf of the Colored Orphan Asylum Delivered at Their Seventh Anniversary, December 11, 1843.* New York: Mahlon Day & Co., 1844.

Minutes and Proceedings of the Third Annual Convention for the Improvement of People of Color. New York: n.p., 1833.

Minutes of the Fifth Annual Convention of the Free People of Color in the United States. Philadelphia: William P. Gibbons, 1835.

Speech of the Hon. James E. Talmadge, Jr., of Dutchess County, New York in the House of Representatives of the United States on Slavery to Which Is Added, the Proceedings of the Manumission Society of the City of New-York and the Correspondence of Their Committee with Messrs. Tallmadge and Taylor. New York: E. Conrad, 1819.

A Study of Delinquent and Neglected Negro Children Before the New York City Children's Court: New York: Joint Committee on Negro Child Study in New

York. 1927. In cooperation with the Department of Research of the National Urban League and the Women's City Club of New York).

Wright, Theodore S. *An Address to the Three Thousand Colored Citizens of New York Who Are Owners of One Hundred and Twenty Thousand Acres of Land in the State of New York, Given to Them by Gerrit Smith . . . September 1, 1846.* New York, 1846.

Theses and Dissertations

Sappol, Mike. "The Uses of Philanthropy: The Colored Orphan Asylum and Its Clients, 1837 to 1863." New York: Columbia University, 1990.

Wright, Richard R., Jr. "The Negro in Pennsylvania: A Study in Economic History." Philadelphia: University of Pennsylvania, 1912.

Newspapers

Afro-American (Baltimore)
Bronx Home News (New York)
Castigator and New-York Anti-Abolitionist (New York)
Colored American (New York)
Daily Worker (New York)
Frederick Douglass' Paper
Douglass' Monthly
Freedom's Journal (New York)
Harper's Weekly
Herald Statesman (Yonkers, New York)
The Liberator (Boston)
New York Age
New York Amsterdam News
New York Evening Post
New York Herald
New York Sun
New York Times
New York Tribune
New York World Telegram

Niggerhead and Blue Law Advocate (New York)
Office Holder's Journal (New York)
Pittsburgh Courier
Ram's Horn (New York)
Rights of All (New York)
Riverdale News (New York)
Weekly Advocate (New York)
Weekly Anglo African (New York)
Yonkers Herald Statesman (Yonkers, New York)

Index

Race Discrimination bill (New York),
195
race mixing, 1, 3, 80, 152
race prejudice, 1, 6, 9, 13, 28, 33, 35,
38, 39, 69, 80, 119, 152, 209
Raddick, Wilbur, 128, 129
Randolph, A. Philip, 198
Rankins, Andrew, 47
Rawle, Adeline, 15
Rawle, Jeremiah, 15
Rawle, Willy, 15
Ray, Ann, 26
Reason, Charles L., 33, 61
Reed, Joseph, 71
Reid, Dr., 111
Reid, Miss, 111
resignations: of Frank W. Barber,
142; of Mary Murray, 54; of
Henry Murphy, 202; of Mason
Pitman, 143, 181; of Lillie
Skiddy Parker, 200; of Mrs.
Willard Parker Sr., 137; of
Martin K. Sherwin, 134; of Anna
Shotwell, 78
Richards, Ann, 74
Richards, Margaret, 74
Richards, Sarah, 74
Richmond, J. F., 83
riots: of 1834, 1–2; of 1863, 69–72; of
1917, 152; of 1935, 182
Riverdale Children's Association:
admission of white children,
195–96; appeal for funds, 199,
201–2; cooperation with child
care agencies, 198; and decision
to close orphanage, 207; internal
criticism, 202–3; on mergers,
195; negative press of, 202–3;

origin of name change, 195;
outside criticism, 205; reorgani-
zation of, 198–206; selling of,
208–9; and World War II
servicemen, 197
Robbins, Henry Parker, 176
Roberts, Charles H., 111
Roberts, Christopher, 76
Roberts, Mrs. E. P., 148
Robeson, Paul, 198
Robeson, Eslanda (Mrs. Paul), 195
Robinson, Bill "Bojangles," 6, 176,
181, 192, 193
Robinson, Elizabeth, 74
Robinson, Jeremiah, 74
Rodman, Miss, 132
Roman Catholic Orphanage, 15, 116
Roosevelt, Cornelius V. S., 29
Roosevelt, Eleanor, 6, 199
Roosevelt, James, 75
Roosevelt, Margaret, 29, 78
Roosevelt, Theodore, 29, 119
Roosevelt, Theodore Sr., 6, 73, 76, 78,
209
Rose, Chauncey, 78
Rose, Emma, 126
Rose, James, 126
Rose, John, 78, 215
Roundtree, Henry, 40
Rue, Martha M., 49
Ruggles, David, 3
Rural New Yorker, 167
Russell, Julia F., 223
Russell Sage Foundation, 126. See
also Sage Foundation

Sage, Margaret Olivia Slocum (Mrs.
Russell), 94